DESIGNING TECHNOLOGY, WORK, ORGANIZATIONS AND VICE VERSA

Edited by

Attila Bruni

Department of Sociology and Social Research of the Faculty of Sociology of the Trento University

Laura Lucia Parolin

Faculty of Design and Art, Free University of Bozen-Bolzano

Cornelius Schubert

DFG Research Training Group "Locating Media", University of Siegen

Vernon Series in Sociology

VERNON PRESS

www.vernonpress.com

In the Americas:
Vernon Press
1000 N West Street,
Suite 1200, Wilmington,
Delaware 19801
United States

In the rest of the world
Vernon Press
C/Sancti Espiritu 17,
Malaga, 29006
Spain

Vernon Series in Sociology

Library of Congress Control Number: 2015934751

ISBN: 978-1-62273-145-9

Table of Contents

INTRODUCTION: DESIGNING TECHNOLOGY, WORK,
ORGANIZATION AND VICE VERSA   1
    Attila Bruni
    Laura Lucia Parolin
    Cornelius Schubert

SECTION 1 Designing Technology, Work and Organization
in Institutionalized   Organizational Settings
    BUSTER AT WORK: INTERTWINING TECHNOLOGY WITH
    ORGANIZATIONAL AND WORKING PRACTICES   21
        Attila Bruni

    DESIGNING ADMINISTRATIVE PRACTICES THROUGH ARTIFACTS:
    PAPER-BASED REMEMBERING IN BACK-OFFICE WORK   43
        Sari Yli-Kauhaluoma
        Mika Pantzar

    STUDYING PRACTICES TO INFORM DESIGN: ORGANIZATIONAL
    ISSUES AND LOCAL ARTIFACTS   71
        Alessandra Talamo
        Barbara Mellini
        Stefano Ventura
        Annamaria Recupero

SECTION 2 Designing Technology, Work   and
Organization in Emerging   Organizational Settings
    DESIGNING A NEW CHAIR, TRANSGRESSING ORGANIZATIONAL
    BOUNDARIES   117
        Laura Lucia Parolin

DESIGN EXHIBITION THROUGH TECHNOLOGICAL
INFRASTRUCTURING   137
   Teresa Macchia

CONTINUOUS RE-CONFIGURING OF INVISIBLE SOCIAL
STRUCTURES   163
   Yoko Akama

SECTION 3 Issues of Technology, Work and   Organization in Design Settings

DISTRIBUTED DESIGN TRAJECTORIES THE GLOBAL
MANUFACTURE OF TECHNOLOGIES AND ORGANIZATIONS   191
   Cornelius Schubert

THE MEANS OF DESIGN WORK MODELS, SKETCHES, AND RELATED
OBJECTS IN THE CREATION OF NEW TECHNOLOGIES   217
   Valentin Janda

HOW THINGS ARE DESIGNED AND HOW THEY DESIGN   247
   Sandra Plontke

INDEX   275

INTRODUCTION:
DESIGNING TECHNOLOGY, WORK, ORGANIZATION AND VICE VERSA

Attila Bruni
Laura Lucia Parolin
Cornelius Schubert

Technology, work, and organizations (TWO) are three main pillars of contemporary societies. Much has been written about each of them separately as well as about their interrelations. This volume collects empirical cases and conceptual discussions which explicitly look for the close interweaving of work, technology, and organizations by questioning their design. Although largely used, in mainstream organization and management studies, the concept of design has been "black-boxed" and easily implied as an updated (and more fashionable) version of the traditional idea of structuring organizational processes. A quick and telling example can be found in the work by Galbraith (1973, 2002; Galbraith, Downey and Kates, 2001), where the aim of organizational design is defined as the alignment between people, strategy, structure, rewards and processes. Even most recent books on organization design (Bøllingtoft, 2009), despite addressing contemporary organizational issues (such as networking and virtuality), continue to frame it in terms of contingency, resource-based processes and strategic choice.

Notwithstanding this literature, we want to take a different approach, using the idea of *design* as a sensitizing concept (Blumer, 1954) in order to unpack and highlight at the same time the relations that hold together technology, work, and organization. From this point of view, we can borrow from Latour (2009) at least three "good reasons" for adopting it as a conceptual (more than theoretical) lens.

First, compared to "manage", "plan", and/or "build", design is a humble concept, in that it makes explicit that an intervention has been made on something that was already there and that already had a function. Things are "designed" in order to face specific problems, issues and/or interests, and in relation to existing infrastructures and social practices. In this sense, more than with "creation" and "innovation", design has to do with "remedy" and "taken for grantedness". Moreover, design is usually related to future scenarios, so that the relationship between the activity and its result can always be a matter of debate.

Second, the idea of design brings attention to details and to the skillfulness of details. Things are not simply "made" or "fabricated", but rather the result of "art" and "craft". As an artistic and crafting activity, the idea of design calls into action also symbolic and interpretative processes, shedding light on how the meaning of objects is grounded in the material and semiotic relations that we establish with them.

Third, design introduces ethical and aesthetical issues for it raises questions about good and bad design, whether something is "nice" or not. The morality and the aesthetics objects bring with them are inscribed in their materiality, which, in turn, becomes questionable. In this way, things stop being "matters of fact" and become "matters of concern" (Latour, 2005), thus allowing for debating and critiquing them.

Using design as a sensitizing concept, we can frame TWO not as pre-constituted entities, but as processes in search of alignment. This alignment is not simply the result of strategic choices and/or contingencies, but it depends on the ways in which TWO are translated into actual practices and infrastructures. What interests us is not the singular beings of technology, work, and organization, but the practices through which they become mutually entangled. We want to emphasize the processes that inextricably link work and organization to the use of artifacts and technological systems (and vice versa); explore in detail the socio-material articulations and disarticulations of daily work; the doings of objects and technologies in everyday organizational life; the reconstruction of organizational processes through technological practices; the relation between innovations and technologies in organizational settings. We want to understand how technologies, work, and organizations are designed – or more specifically – how work and organizations are designed through technologies, how organizations design work and technology, and how technologies and organizations are designed through work.

We see design in itself as an activity, so that we prefer to adopt it as a verb (designing), in order to further emphasize its processual dimension. And given that design is a practical activity as well, we are also willing to unpack it as socially organised, technically mediated and sensually embodied work: which technologies are used in design and in which way is design organised?

In addition to the focus on design – both empirically and conceptually – the contributions largely draw on two related, but not always congruent fields: organization studies (OS) and science and technology studies (STS). TWO are central to both fields, but their relative importance varies depending on the case and question under study. From one side, working and organizing today seem to be embedded in increasingly complex and situated technologies and practices. The spreading of information and communication technologies (ICTs) has changed workplaces (and even the very meaning of "workplace" as an area marked by the physical presence of different human actors), so that working and organizing mobilize the joint action of humans, technologies and situated knowledge (Bruni, 2005; Bruni and Gherardi, 2007). Complex socio-material practices support collective work, blurring the distinction between the design of technology, work and organizational processes: organizational routines and structures are inscribed in ICTs, embodied in roles, rules and habits, incorporated into technical arrangements and built into architectures. Objects and technologies are increasingly "social", in that they presume the active engagement of users and acquire meaning and relevance in relation to social practices. Several of the contributions of this book thus make a close connection between the socio-materiality of design and the notion of "heterogeneous engineering" (Law, 1987). Furthermore, contemporary objects and technologies often imply a constant activity of maintenance and repair (Denis and Pontille, 2015; Denis, Mongili and Pontille, 2015), as well as some kind of expert knowledge in order to work properly and a community of users taking care of them. This highlights the contingencies of everyday action and the manifold instances of maintenance and repair required to keep technology, work and organizational practices (well) aligned.

It is worth noticing that if OS have adopted and incorporated theoretical concepts and suggestions coming from STS (Suchman, 2000; Bruni, 2005; Czarniawska and Hernes, 2004; Law and Singleton, 2005; Leonardi and Barley, 2008; Orlikowski, 2010; Carlile et al., 2013), the same cannot be said in regards of STS. In fact, although one of the distinctive features of STS since their beginning has been to look for science at technology as socially organized working activities (Latour and Woolgar, 1979; Garfinkel, Lynch and Livingston, 1981), in contemporary STS we do not find explicit reference to OS, or to issues of work and organization (with remarkable exceptions – see for example the work by Lucy Suchman, Karin Knorr Cetina, or Susan Leigh Star). From this point of view, we hope this book will strengthen the links between OS and STS by repositioning work and organization at the core of the study of technologies and material artifacts, and by making explicit how STS could benefit from concepts and analysis coming from OS.

We do not aim to separate all these complex relations and put design, technology, work, and organizations into different boxes, but rather see the contributions of this book as proof of their inherent entanglement. This way, we want to shed light on design, technology, work, and organizations alike – mainly through a better understanding how all are linked through concrete practices.

On the flipside of OS and STS interests in design as a concept, design researchers have themselves developed a focus on social practices and use situations. There is a notable increase of studies in the past years that conceive design as a distinct social practice, if not as a new kind of social and political "regime" (Wilkie, 2011). Recent publications on "design anthropology" (Clarke, 2010; Gunn Otto and Smith, 2013), for instance, focus on situations of design and use by employing detailed ethnographic fieldwork. Ethnography offers a close look at how people make and use artifacts, how they construct technical systems and organizational realities at the same time. Not by chance, interdisciplinary approaches such as "workplace studies" (Suchman, 1987; Heath, Hindmarsh and Luff, 2000), "computer supported cooperative work" (Bowers and Benford, 1991) and/or "participatory design" (Schuler and Namioka, 1993; Bødker, Kensing and Simonsen, 2004) seek to combine theoretical reflections with concrete design based on in-depth observations of working and organising with modern ICTs. Design is not thought of as an ephemeral or abstract cognitive task, but one that fundamentally engages with problematic situations and concrete artifacts.

This perspective has effectively challenged mainstream distinctions between use and design (Orlikowski, 1992). Even though design and use often constitute distinct social worlds, designers now acknowledge the creative practices of users in their appropriation of new technologies (Mareis, Joost and Kimpel, 2010; Bredies, 2014). Users are not seen as preconfigured by technical systems (Woolgar, 1991), but as active and knowledgeable agents engaged in domesticating or co-constructing technologies (Silverstone and Hirsch, 1992; Oudshoorn and Pinch, 2003) and (technologically dense) environments (Bruni, Pinch and Schubert, 2013). The increased attention towards users sensitises design research towards the intricate connections between design and use and not to see them as separate, but as complementary social worlds. Local creations and appropriations of new objects are two sides of the same coin, of a continually transformative process that shapes the relations of technology, work, and organizations in everyday practice.

This perspective also highlights the role of material artifacts in design and use. Design is design of things. Use is use of things. STS has a long tradition in arguing that the fabric of everyday practice consists of heterogeneous socio-material relations (Law and Mol, 1995). By focussing on the socio-material relations of design and use, we gain a better understanding how social orders are created, transformed, and maintained through objects (Bruni, 2005). Putting artifacts front and center of design research would seem to be an obvious move, but we must be careful not to reduce design to the application of abstract, cognitive or semiotic principles. We should rather look for the ways in which the materiality of objects facilitates the transition from design to contexts of use. As research on technology transfer from industrial countries to developing countries has shown, it is the materiality of the objects that transports the links between designers and users (Akrich, 1992; de Laet and Mol, 2000). At the time, we could benefit from further investigation on the role of materiality for situated knowledge, or sensible knowing (Parolin and Mattozzi, 2013).

Situating design and use as social practice bears importance to a third issue, namely that design is not finished once it leaves the lab, studio, or production site. We should not conflate design with "new" and use with "old", i.e. conceiving of the relation of design and use as a simple difference between change and continuity. Design, even though it is most commonly (and sometimes not very modestly) associated with novelty and creation, follows certain rules, techniques or established practices at the same time. On the flipside of this, users more often than not are ingenious improvisers when it comes to adapting artifacts to their local needs. Artifacts are thus seen to be re-invented in diffusion processes (Bijker, 1992; Kline and Pinch, 1996). This perspective converges with a practice-based approach in OS (Gherardi, 2000, 2006; Orlikowski, 2007; Nicolini, 2012) in underlining the provisional nature of work, technology and organization, by driving our attention to the continuous accomplishments of everyday actions.

All these lines of research have implicitly or explicitly worked at the conjunctions of OS, STS, and design issues. The multiplicity of the empirical cases and conceptual approaches forbids a uniform convergence into a simple formula. What is more, the aim of the book is to allow this heterogeneity to be maintained and to associate the contributions not as a co-

herent picture, but as a collection that emphasizes their differences as well
as their similarities. Whereas the differences are often easy to spot, some
of the similarities are less obvious. We would like to bring attention to
three themes that run through the contributions of this book and which
we hope will further our understanding of the relations of OS, STS, and
design issues.

The first theme concerns *situated action and knowledge*. In all the
studies presented in this volume, knowledge is not envisaged as a body of
knowledge, rather as a process emerging from working practices where
human and non-human actors are constructing each other (Suchman,
1987). Knowledge and agency are distributed in socio-material ensembles
and must be realised through situated practices. As Blackler (1995) points
out, the shift form knowledge to knowing allows us to analyze it as a phenomenon that is: (a) mediated (in that it is manifest in systems of language, technology, collaboration and control); (b) situated (in that it is
located in time and space and specific to particular contexts); (c) provisional (in that it is constructed and constantly developing); (d) pragmatic
(in that it is purposive and object-oriented); (e) contested (in that, for the
previous reasons, it cannot be taken for granted).

A second reoccurring theme throughout the book will be that of *invisible work*. Originally coined by Star and Strauss (1999) in order to refer to
situations where work is taken for granted to the point of "disappearing"
(such as for domestic work), we follow Nardi (1999) in identifying four
main reasons for the invisibility of work at the organizational level: (1)
work is done in hidden places; (2) work is purely manual, although it requires considerable problem solving and knowledge; (3) work is done by
invisible organizational actors (such as cleaners); (4) work is linked to informal work processes that are not part of anybody's job description (such
as informal conversations and storytelling). In reference to TWO, thus, we
will see how there is an invisible work required to users in order to make a
new technology or design "usable" (and useful) within an ecology of organizational and working practices, as well as an invisible work made by
technologies in order to incorporate users' needs and requirements.

The third theme that links all the chapters has only been addressed in
passing so far. By emphasizing the *processual dimension of design* in terms
of designing, we conclude that design should be analyzed as a temporal
phenomenon. Designing TWO does not merely happen, but it carries a
past, unfolds in the present and engages the future. Thinking of design as
a temporal extension, a "trajectory", to use another concept coined by

Strauss (1993: pp. 52), takes into account that distributed design processes are shaped by the interactions of the actors and artifacts involved and that they are always subject to unanticipated contingencies. From this point of view, designing technology, work, and organization, and design tout court, should be considered open-ended and in-the-making processes.

In sum, our brief recapitulation of design and TWO has brought some common themes to the fore: heterogeneous engineering, sociomateriality, performativity, situated action and knowledge, invisible work and design trajectories. All these themes, it must be noted, rely heavily on ethnographic fieldwork and/or qualitative research. If "designing" is our conceptual lens for addressing the relations between technology, work, and organization, ethnographic observations and qualitative interviews are our empirical gateways for making this possible. The reader should thus take the individual chapters as an effort of creating a collage rather than fixing a triangulation (Kalthoff, 2010). We are not trying to determine what design, technology, work and organization actually are, but to enlarge the boundaries and the meanings of each of them by investigating and questioning their relations.

Structure of the book

All chapters share a similar structure: they begin with theoretical references and continue focusing on a case study for showing the practical relevance of the concepts adopted in order to improve analysis, interpretation and action. In addition, each chapter devotes a section on the methodological aspects of studying technology, work, and organizations, so to offer practical insights on doing research in organizational settings characterized by complex technological dynamics.

We have set the chapters in three different sections, so to present a "structured discourse" to the reader. The first section focuses particularly on *institutionalized organizational settings* (such as hospitals or administrative offices), where relations between the design of work and technology are usually intended to follow purely functional and instrumental paths, but where in fact objects and technologies take an active role in producing everyday work. The second concentrates more on *emerging organizational settings* (such as museums, design industries and disaster preparedness practices), where relations between the design of work and technology are usually intended to follow more "free" and innovative paths, but where, again, objects and technologies are often intended as a means to stabilize a socio-material assemblage of organizational practices and knowledge. The third section partially reverses the perspective and looks towards the *tools, work and organizational processes of design practices*. In many design settings, there is only a vague understanding of how novel artifacts might be used in future work settings as designers actively seek to keep their design open for different uses. Yet, the designers themselves follow routine design practices and employ standard design artifacts.

In presenting pieces of empirical research investigating different organizational fields, we aim at showing the ways in which the reciprocal design of TWO takes place through situated practices and, at the same time, translates from one setting to another. We hope to provide scholars interested in this kind of issues with the ability to move between different theoretical perspectives and methodological techniques, so to be able to produce interpretations and suggestions that are meaningful for the phenomenon at stake, its actors and practices.

The first section begins with a study taking into account the introduction in a hospital of a technology for the automatic delivery of pharmacological therapy. Then it moves to a university back office, and finally gets back to hospitals. In all the three cases, at the center of the analysis we find the ways in which technology, work and organization chase each other, together with a practice oriented approach, albeit with different nuances.

The chapter by Attila Bruni shows how the adoption and stabilization in use of a new technology can be seen as the result of heterogeneous organizational processes, involving a plurality of actors and requiring a reconfiguration of collective work and of the technology itself. Adopting a performative approach, the chapter underlines how technology, work and organization come into being (and disappear) with the practices in which they are manipulated. Taking into account the introduction of the "Busterspeed" (a pharmaceutical automatized closet using a mechanical arm for the handling of medicines) in a hospital, Bruni highlights how (new) technologies become concrete only through their daily use, thus requiring the active involvement of a community of practice. Furthermore, given that a performative approach fosters a symmetrical stance, the author shows also how a community of practice can coagulate exactly around the practices that accompany a (new) technology. This is why, from an organizational point of view, it is crucial for technologies to be acknowledged to users and (for managers and designers) to consider the situated practices and working infrastructures they will encounter.

Working infrastructures are central also to the study presented by Sari Yli-Kauhaluoma and Mika Pantzar. Here, the issue regards organizational remembering practices. The study rests on an empirical examination of administrative work in a university back office to examine how people in organizations perform retention and retrieval work, particularly through the use of material artifacts. The analysis shows how administrators engage in three kinds of remembering practices ("memoing", "verifying", and "backing-up" practices) and how these differ in terms of the duration of memory retention ("memoing" practices use short term devices, whereas the "backing up" imply more long term artifacts). In so doing, the study shows that working and organizing practices in administration are closely connected to material artifacts: post-it notes, print-outs, paper piles, paper copies to be shared with others, and original documents differ because of the affordances they present, the skills they imply, and the aims they are intended to serve. This has implications for the designing of future remembering practices based on digitalization and the internet, given that these memory devices design administrators' office space, and that administrators rely on them in the design of their everyday working and organizational life. Furthermore, the authors emphasize how a socio-material approach to remembering practices in work and organization reframes the idea of remembering tout court, given that retrieving a document is something that has to do with the future maybe more than with the past.

The chapter by Alessandra Talamo, Barbara Mellini, Stefano Ventura and Annamaria Recupero concludes the first section, offering an interesting example of how a closer look at the relationships between organizational artifacts and working practices can inform the design of technological tools. Drawing on Halverson's categorization of artifacts in professional contexts (and thus distinguishing between received artifacts, inherited artifacts and locally designed artifacts – Halverson, 2003), and referring to a research project explicitly aimed at providing guidelines for the design of digital tools to support nurses' everyday work, the authors highlight a sort of loop process. Hospitals arrange over time institutional tools for documenting nursing, but nurses include in their own practice locally designed artifacts in order to fulfil specific needs. In order to stop this organizational loop, the researcher agreed with nurses to focus on the use of the local artifacts, so to produce insights for the design of future (and more effective) tools. In other words, the observation of nurses' work unveils taken

for granted tools necessary to smooth everyday organizational and working practices. In this way, the "discovery" by the researchers of locally designed organizational artifacts highlights areas of design that are still uncovered, helping at the same time the professionals involved as well as
tool developers.

Altogether, thus, the chapters presented in the first section frame the
design of technology, work and organization as a recursive activity, made
of heterogeneous elements, and performed through situated socio-
material practices.

Section two starts with two studies carried out in Italy: one in an industrial setting, and the other at a science museum. The third contribution is
an investigation on a participatory approach for disaster preparedness
with the population in Australia. All three share a relational emphasis on
the relationships between environment, artifacts, bodies, and situated
knowledge. The chapter by Laura Lucia Parolin focuses on the design
practices of a new artifact (a chair) as it comes out of the studio and all the
way along the production chain at the manufactory industry. In the chapter by Teresa Macchia, the designing of users (museum staff and visitors)
underline the provisional nature of an exhibition as the product of the
fruition experience of museum spaces. Finally, the chapter by Yoko Akama
describes and analyzes a visual design participatory approach directed to
scaffolding the implicit knowledge on social relationships for disaster preparedness.

In her chapter, Parolin proceeds with an in-depth exploration of the
process of the stabilization of a new model of a chair inside production
sites. By applying an ANT approach, this chapter shows how the stabilization of a new artifact can be seen as the result of heterogeneous processes
that involve a plurality of (human and non-human) actors in a process of
reciprocal definition. By tracing the articulation chain that takes place
across boundaries we are able to see the emergence of a new network of
actors, including new relationships between materials, bodies, knowledge,
skills, production modalities, etc. By the use of the concept of "network
within" (Parolin and Mattozzi, 2014), she wants to shed light on the process that involves a (continuous) articulation of a network to make of an
object a part of a broader system formed by (human and non-human)
actors that enter a relationship with it. In so doing she conceives design
practices not only as the process of stabilization of a new object, but also
as the reconfiguration of the entire network implied (included scripts and
sensitive knowledge). This way of conceptualizing design practices allows

us to read in a symmetrical way both the process of the emergence of a new artifact and the knowledge of production, be they within and/or out of organizational boundaries.

In the second chapter of the session Macchia explores the interconnections of design activities, technologies, and organizational environments by focusing her attention on experiencing and on knowledge production at a science museum. With reference to the concept of cultural infrastructure, Macchia describes an exhibition as an ongoing activity that occurs between visitors, museum professional staff, and its context. By touching and experimenting scientific objects or natural phenomenal representations, visitors combine and enrich their previous knowledge with new information. Macchia stresses the role of the museum in stimulating the interaction of the visitors with tools and technology, but also with the experts who inhabit the museum environment. The way in which visitors experience the museum space and interact with the objects, activates a set of practices that influence the museum staff actions as well as other visitors, and vice versa. In so doing Macchia underlines the continuous, collective, and situated activity of (re)designing an exhibition, of shedding light on practices of users in "technology enriched environments" like a science museum.

The chapter of Akama re-claims the interest of designing as a continuous and distributed activity by focusing on designing performed by non-design experts that can bring local knowledge and specific competences in disaster preparedness. The theoretical ground is set on the contemporary evolution of participatory design discourse. Designing is conceived as a way to support innovation between people, among personal, professional, and community relationships, that draws upon the latent creativity and the social capital that lies in-between such networks. Akama's chapter details a visual participatory approach used to make social relations for fire preparedness visible in a research program carried out with regional communities and an emergency agency in Australia. The work of Akama investigates how design can assist in making hidden relational structures detectable in order to improve population fire preparedness. By the use of excerpts from three participants, the chapter gives account of how, through the engagement in participatory visual methodology, they are able to reveal and make sense of their social relationships in encouraging their ongoing re-configurations to build and strengthen resilience for disasters. In so doing Akama illustrates how designing, in the absence of a professional designer or a researcher, continues through people's participation thus providing the reconfiguration of new social structures for preparedness in disasters.

All together, the chapters presented in the second section provide an interpretation of the process of knowing conceived as situated activities embedded in socio-material practices.

Section three starts with a longitudinal analysis of techno-organizational innovation in the global semiconductor industry. It is followed by two ethnographic studies of design practice, one in a university design laboratory, the other in the context of internet game design. All three focus on how design is mediated through technological artifacts and information infrastructures. Design is considered a "messy" and situated process that assembles heterogeneous components in an orderly fashion, yet without being determined by them.

The chapter on the semiconductor industry by Cornelius Schubert gives an account of innovating semiconductor manufacturing technology since the 1980s. The design of an increasingly sophisticated systems technology is related to the design of inter-organizational networks. The paper uses concepts from interactionist sociology and pragmatism in order to analyze the long-term processes of simultaneously creating new technologies and new organizational arrangements. Based on the concept of "trajectory" developed by Anselm Strauss and his colleagues, a notion of a "distributed design trajectory" is spelled out. It seeks to extend the interactionist understanding of trajectory from the medical and hospital contexts, in which it was mainly used, towards long term creative processes that simultaneously shape technologies and organizations over several decades. It thus integrates the temporal and material dimensions of design into a processual understanding of socio-technical emergence.

Valentin Janda conceives design as a coordinated work process that is mediated through distinct means of design (e.g. pictures, use scenarios, models, and prototypes). He draws on pragmatism and interactionist sociology in order to analyze the practices of turning ideas into objects in case of a university design laboratory. Janda uses close ethnographic observations and descriptions of instructional sequences in which specific means and methods of design are practiced with students so as to develop new navigational tools for tourists. The paper shows how uncertainties are mindfully created and dissolved during the design process and how the different stages are organised in a sequence from rough ideas to first prototypes. This sequence is conceived as a collectively organised "arc of design" in which teachers, students, models, sketches and prototypes are assembled and mobilised and in which design and (projected) use systematically intersect.

In the last chapter of this book, Sandra Plontke argues that authorship in graphic design is fundamentally distributed between humans and non-humans. Drawing on STS and ANT, she reconstructs the design of a digital trading card motive in terms of John Law's "heterogeneous engineering" and Karin Knorr Cetina's notion of "viscourses". Plontke draws on detailed ethnographic fieldwork and video recordings in order to analyze the fine grained situated activities in which the graphic designers create a realistic style for their digital motives. Designing the motive combines artistic competencies with technical, organizational and economic considerations. They compose the environment in which the design must prove itself in a trial of strength. Plontke thus challenges the idea that design is process in which humans impose themselves on objects, but shows how humans are themselves reconfigured through non-humans in the process of design.

The reader will find each chapter to take an individual and distinctive approach to our overarching concerns. This way, similarities and differences between cases and concepts should provide a useful resource for scholars and professionals interested in broadening their understanding of the places and practices involved in designing technology, work and organization.

References

Akrich, M. (1992), "The de-scription of technical objects", in Bijker, W.E., Law, J. (eds.), *Shaping technology - building society. Studies in sociotechnical change*. Cambridge: MIT Press, pp. 205-224.

Bijker, W. E. (1992), "The social construction of fluorescent lighting, or how an artifact was invented in its diffusion stage", in Bijker, Wiebe E., Law, J. (eds.), *Shaping technology - building society. Studies in sociotechnical change*. Cambridge: MIT Press, pp. 75-102.

Blackler, F. (1995), "Knowledge, Knowledge Work and Organizations: An Overview and Interpretation", *Organization Studies*, 16, pp. 1021-1046.

Blumer, H. (1954), "What's wrong with social theory?", *American Sociological Review*, 19 (1), pp. 3-10.

Bødker, K., Kensing, F., Simonsen, J. (2004), *Participatory IT design: Designing for business and workplace realities*. Cambridge: MIT Press.

Bowers, J. M., Benford, S.D. (eds.) (1991), *Studies in computer supported cooperative work. Theory, practice and design*. Amsterdam, North-Holland.

Bredies, K. (2014), *Gebrauch als Design. Über eine unterschätzte Form der Gestaltung*. Bielefeld: Transcript.

Bruni, A. (2005), "Shadowing software and clinical records. On the ethnography of non-humans and heterogeneous contexts", *Organization*, 12 (3), pp. 357-378.

Bruni, A., Gherardi, S. (2007), *Studiare le pratiche lavorative*. Bologna: Il Mulino.

Bruni, A., Trevor T.J., Schubert, C. (2014), "Technologically Dense Environments: What For? What Next?", *Tecnoscienza: Italian Journal of Science & Technology Studies*, 4 (2), pp. 51–72.

Carlile, P.R., Nicolini, D., Langley, A., Tsoukas, H. (eds.) (2013), *How Matter Matters. Objects, Artifacts, and Materiality in Organization Studies*. Oxford: Oxford University Press.

Clarke, A. J. (ed.) (2010), *Design Anthropology. Object Culture in the 21st Century*. Wien: Springer.

de Laet, M., Mol, A. (2000), "The Zimbabwe bush pump. Mechanics of a fluid technology", *Social Studies of Science*, 30 (2), pp. 225-63.

Denis, J., Pontille, D. (2015), "Material Ordering and the Care of Things", *Science, Technology & Human Values*, 40 (3), pp. 338-367.

Denis, J., Mongili, A., Pontille, D. (2015), "Maintenance and Repair In Science and Technology Studies", 6 (2), *Tecnoscienza – Italian Journal of Science & Technology Studies*, pp. 5-16

Garfinkel, H., Lynch, M., Livingston, E. (1981), "The work of a discovering science construed with materials from the optically discovered pulsar", *Philosophy of the Social Sciences*, 11 (2), pp. 131-158.

Gunn, W., Otto, T., Smith, R.C. (eds.) (2013), *Design Anthropology. Theory and Practice*. London: Bloomsbury.

Halverson, R. (2003), "Systems of practice: How leaders use artifacts to create professional community in schools", *Education Policy Analysis Archives*, 11 (37), London: Sage.

Harper, D. (1987), *Working Knowledge. Skill and Community in a Small Shop*. Chicago: University of Chicago Press.

Gherardi, S. (2000), "Practice-Based Theorizing on Learning and Knowing in Organizations", *Organization*, 7 (2), pp. 211–224.

Gherardi, S. (2006), *Organizational Knowledge: The Texture of Workplace Learning*. Oxford: Blackwell.

Kalthoff, H. (2010), "Beobachtung und Komplexität. Überlegungen zum Problem der Triangulation", *Sozialer Sinn*, 11 (2), pp. 353-365.

Kline, R., Pinch, T.J. (1996), "Users as agents of technological change. The social construction of the automobile in the rural United States", *Technology and Culture*, 37 (4), pp. 763-795.

Latour, B. (2005), *Reassembling the social. An introduction to Actor-Network-Theory*. Oxford: Oxford University Press.

Latour, B. (2009), "A Cautious Prometheus? A Few Steps Toward a Philosophy of Design (With Special Attention to Peter Sloterdijk)" in Hackney, F., Glynne, J., Minton, V. (eds.), *Networks of Design. Proceedings of the 2008 Annual International Conference of the Design History Society (UK) University College Falmouth*, 3-6 September. Boca Raton, Universal Publishers, pp. 2-10.

Latour, B., Woolgar, S. (1979), *Laboratory life. The social construction of scientific facts*. London: Sage.

Law, J. (1987), "Technology and heterogeneous engineering. The case of portuguese expansion", in Bijker, W.E.; Hughes, T.P.; Pinch, T.J. (eds.), *The social construction of technological systems*. Cambridge: MIT Press, pp. 111-135.

Law, J., Mol, A. (1995), "Notes on materiality and sociality", *The Sociological Review*, 43 (2), pp. 274-294.

Law, J., Singleton, V. (2005), "Object Lessons", *Organization*, 12 (3), pp. 331-355.

Leonardi, P.M., Barley, S.R. (2008), "Materiality and change. Challenges to building better theory about technology and organizing", *Information and Organization*, 18 (3), pp. 159-176.

Luff, P., Hindmarsh, J., Heath, C. (2000), *Workplace Studies: Recovering Work Practice and Informing System Design*. Cambridge: Cambridge University Press.

Mareis, C., Joost, G., Kimpel, K. (eds.) (2010), *Entwerfen – Wissen – Produzieren. Designforschung im Anwendungskontext*. Bielefeld, Transcript.

Nardi, B. (1996), *Context and Consciousness: Activity Theory and Human-Computer Interaction*. Cambridge: MIT Press.

Nicolini, D. (2012), *Practice Theory, Work, and Organization: An Introduction*. Oxford: Oxford University Press.

Orlikowski, W.J. (1992), "The duality of technology. Rethinking the concept of technology in organizations", *Organization Science*, 3 (3), pp. 398-427.

Orlikowski, W.J. (2007), "Sociomaterial Practices: Exploring Technology at Work", *Organization Studies*, 28 (9), pp. 1435–1448.

Orlikowski, W.J. (2010), "The sociomateriality of organisational life. Considering technology in management research", *Cambridge Journal of Economics*, 34 (1), pp. 125-141.

Oudshoorn, N., Pinch, T.J. (ed.) (2003), *How users matter. The co-construction of users and technology*. Cambridge: MIT Press.

Parolin, L.L., Mattozzi A. (2013), "Sensitive Translations: Sensitive Dimension and Knowledge within Two Craftsmen's Workplaces", *Scandinavian Journal of Management*, 29 (4), pp. 353–366.

Schuler, D. and Namioka, A. (eds.) (1993), *Participatory Design: Principles and Practices*. Hillsdale: Lawrence Earlbaum Associates.

Silverstone, R., Hirsch, E. (eds.) (1992), *Consuming technologies. Media and information in domestic spaces*. London: Routledge.

Star, S.L., Strauss, A.L. (1999), "Layers of silence, arenas of voice. The ecology of visible and invisible work", *Computer-Supported Cooperative Work: The Journal of Collaborative Computing*, 8 (1-2), pp. 9-30.

Strauss, A.L. (1993), *Continual Permutations of Action*. New York: de Gruyter.

Suchman, L.A. (1987), *Plans and situated actions. The problem of human-machine communication*. Cambridge: Cambridge University Press.

Suchman, L.A. (2000), "Organizing Alignment. A Case of Bridge-Building", *Organization*, 7 (2), pp. 311-327.

Wilkie, A. (2011), "Regimes of Design, Logics of Users", *Athenea Digital*, 11 (1), pp. 317-334.

Woolgar, S. (1991), "Configuring the user. The case of usability trials" in Law, J. (ed.), *A sociology of monsters. Essays on power, technology and domination*. London: Routledge, pp. 58-99.

SECTION 1

Designing Technology, Work and Organization in Institutionalized Organizational Settings

BUSTER AT WORK:
INTERTWINING TECHNOLOGY WITH ORGANIZATIONAL AND WORKING PRACTICES

Attila Bruni

Introduction

What is the role performed today by technologies in organizational and working practices? And what about the ways in which working practices perform technologies in organizational settings?

These two questions, and this way of framing the relationship between technology, work and organization, already presupposes some theoretical assumptions.

First, considering technologies not only for their technical features, but for the practices and the situated knowledge their use entails, together with the affordances, the meanings and the representations they enact. In a few words, this means considering technology as technology-in-use (Suchman et al., 1999).

Secondly, the assumption that organizations are verbs (Cooper and Law, 1995), meaning that organizations are made of processes and practices of organizing (Czarniawska, 2008). As such, they are the result of the heterogeneous engineering (Law, 1987) of different elements: people, materials of various kind and situated knowledge. Around these same elements, can usually take place a community of practice (Lave and Wenger, 1991), which could be considered the *locus* of organizational and working practices (Gherardi, 2006). This is also why, to quote the title of a well-known paper by Barley and Kunda (2004), to look at organizations in processual and practical terms, requires to 'bring work back in'.

Thirdly, in the mentioned questions, technology, work and organization are a matter of performance. This is not to neglect the role structures, roles, norms, and hierarchies have in organizational life, but to look for their (continuous) accomplishment, transgression and innovation in everyday action (Cooper and Law, 1995). In this way, a performative approach allows to take into account not just human action, but also the material world action implies.

Referring to the introduction in an Italian hospital of a new technology for the automatic delivery of pharmacological therapy (the "Buster-speed"), this chapter shows how the introduction, adoption and stabilization in use of a new technology can be seen as the result of heterogeneous organizational processes, involving a plurality of actors and requiring a reconfiguration of collective work. Coherently with a framework that looks at organizations as open-ended processes (Law, 1994) and at technology as social practice (Suchman et al., 1999), the paper will underline the multiple and recursive relationships that tie organizational and working practices to technology and vice versa.

The chapter proceeds as follows. The first paragraph will present in more detailed terms the theoretical framework just sketched. Then, after a brief illustration of the research context and methodology, the analyses will concentrate on a case study, in order to account for the intertwining of technology, work and organization.

Finally, a few answers to the questions formulated at the beginning of this paragraph will be given, together with a reflection on the implications of a performative approach for the designing of technology, work and organization.

1. A performative approach to technology, work and organization

In organization studies, technology has typically been defined in terms of:

- objects or artifacts (including products, tools and equipment used to produce them);

- activities or processes (and, therefore, methods of production);

- knowledge necessary to develop and enable systems (ie, the know-how on how to design, build and operate a particular technological tool).

This leads to consider technology for its more evident aspect, as an instrument, as something that once designed takes the form of the prototype, and which, once tested in its technical reliability, can be introduced in the workplace. As noted by MacKenzie and Wajcman (1999) and other organizational scholars, the taken-for-granted behind this interpretation is that technologies are somehow independent from the system of activity in which they are inserted and to which they participate. In this assumption is enclosed the idea of technology-per-se, as something that works and is effective regardless of its users and environment of use.

By the way, as from the studies that look at technology "in action" (Heath and Luff, 2000), "in-practice" (Timmermans and Berg, 2003), or "in-use" (Suchmann et al., 1999), technologies become "operational" only under the practical use of a community of users. In this regard, it can be useful to recall the famous study by Julian Orr (1996) on Xerox technicians. Sometimes, technicians could not understand the reason of the failure. In these cases, technicians were used to "interview" the users of the photocopier, because they knew from experience that technical failures could depend from different events. It may be that someone placed a cup of tea or coffee on the copier and that, inadvertently, a few drops dropped over it; the copier was not working properly and someone tried to repair it (causing further problems); users did not observe the procedures of switching on and off, or made the machine run too long, and so forth. In some cases, therefore, technicians had to repair the machine, but in some cases they had to repair the user or, better, the relationship between the user and the photocopier. In other words, much of technicians' work was directed in trying to align the way the photocopier was used in practice with what was prescribed by its instruction manual. And when, just after the work conducted by Orr and other researchers working at the Xerox Park (Suchman et al., 1999), Xerox tried to condense technicians' experiential knowledge in a repository technicians could access remotely, this turned out to be of little use. In case of doubts or ambiguities, technicians were used to rely on the knowledge embedded in the "war stories" they shared in moments of spare time (typically, at lunch), and/or to call each other on the phone and to find a solution collaboratively (Whalen and Bobrow, 2011).

Considering technology as technology-in-use, therefore, means to adopt a relational approach, which does not analyze separately technologies, users and contexts of use, but sees them in their mutual interactions. This is one of the main differences between technology-per-se and technology-in-use: the first approach looks at the object and its potential in a de-contextualized way, while the second identifies the technology and its potential in respect to a community of users, as well as in relation to other instruments, techniques and practices accompanying it (Bruni and Gherardi, 2007).

From a conceptual and methodological point of view, to shift from the study of technology-per-se (and the effects it produces) to the study of technology-in-use makes it possible to uncover the invisible work (Star and Strauss, 1999) required to users in order to make a technology "usable" (and useful) within an ecology of working practices and relations, as well as the invisible work made by technologies in order to incorporate users' needs and requirements. In fact, as shown intuitively by the example given so far, technologies are not "usable" and "reliable" regardless of their users, but they become so when their practical use construct them as such. Particularly in technologically dense organizational environments (Bruni, Pinch and Schubert, 2013) – such as centers of coordination, online services, hospitals and transports – humans and technologies work "together" and their alignment is constitutive of the activity (Heath and Luff, 2000). This means that organizational processes are not simply mediated by technological artifacts, but they are inextricably bound up with them.

This way of framing technology inevitably implies also a different framing of the very idea of organization. Instead of looking at organizations from a "distal" point of view, as discrete and bounded entities, we should adopt a "proximal" perspective. This means to look at organizations as fuzzy processes (Cooper, 1992; Cooper and Law, 1995), effects of continuous network relations and situated interactions (Star, 1992). In other words, in proximal terms organizations are the result of what John Law (1987) has labelled "heterogeneous engineering", to denote the process which gives (relative) temporal and spatial stability to persons, texts and objects. As nicely written by Lucy Suchman (2000: p. 313): "The focus is on organizations as ongoing performances involving heterogeneous modes of action and materialization, both of which must be actively affiliated and aligned across a range of often unruly contingencies".

As for technology, looking at organizations as preconstituted entities poses some problems in that it leads to ignore processes by which they are formed. As Hernes (2007: xxiii) writes: "the challenge lies in analyzing organizations as relational phenomena rather than as correlation between entities". Not by chance, one of the leading concepts in contemporary organization studies is that of practice (Gherardi, 2000, 2006; Orlikowski, 2007; Jarzabkowski, Balogun and Seidl, 2007; Nicolini, 2012), so that the study of organization often resolves in that of organizational and working practices (Barley and Kunda, 2004). This is probably due partly to the "rediscovery" of ethnomethodology (with its focus on the practical accomplishment of social order) by organizational scholars (Rawls, 2007), and partly to the success of the concept of community of practice (Lave and Wenger, 1991). As for Xerox technicians, communities of practice arise from the collective debating and shared understanding of the practical problems actors experience in everyday work. Communities of practice imply a certain way of doing and of being as well (Wenger, 1998), and, most importantly, are able to preserve and generate organizational knowledge.

Although originally intended to focus attention on the close relationship between knowing and doing, depending on the strand of inquiry (and on the theoretical interests of the scholars involved), the concept has been used to manage community and identity processes, as well as to open up a reflection on the role of practice and situated knowledge in organization (Gherardi, 2006). In this latter case, the concept can be seen also as an attempt to relocate working practices at the core of organizational analysis and to attract attention on the situatedness of organizational activity.

The common ground of all these discourses is to look at technology, work and organization from a performative point of view (Carlile, et al., 2013), as practical accomplishments. This means to follow the action (more than actors – Latour, 2005) and to look for the associations that tie heterogeneous elements and processes together. A performative approach, thus, encourages in looking at technology, work and organization from a symmetrical perspective, without assuming pre-ordered relations of cause and effect: they are performed and performative of each other (Law, 2002). A performative approach forces to understand technology, work and organization as emergent in practice, and thus interrelated with the sociomaterial conditions of their enactment. To paraphrase Annemarie Mol (2002: 5), technology, work and organization come into being (and disappear) with the practices in which they are manipulated.

Given this framework, I will describe the process that led a sanitary organization to improve organizational and working processes through the introduction of a new technological machinery, underlying the heterogeneous engineering of actors, technologies, and practices that contributed to its adoption and stabilization.

2. The research setting and a methodological note

The data presented are part of a broader research conducted between 2006 and 2007 in the department of a hospital (in the north of Italy), in order to examine the introduction of a new technology, namely a pharmaceutical automatized closet using a mechanical arm for the handling of the medicines[1]. It is worth noticing that at that time automatized technol-technologies were not that common in Italian hospitals, so that the occasion was almost unique.

Data were collected basically through two different kinds of interview: a semi-structured one and the interview with the double. The semi-structured interview was explicitly oriented to the description of the introduction of the new technology and its principal aim was to focus on how actors related about it, how did they perceive its introduction into their everyday work, and on how did they solve initial problems and ambiguities related to its use. Aim of the so-called "interview with the double" (a projective technique in which a person is asked to imagine that s/he has a double and sends him/her into the office in his/her place after providing instructions on what to do/not to do so that nobody notices the switch - Gherardi, 1990; Nicolini, 2009), was to collect information and accounts about the everyday work, so to understand also the organizing and working practices that characterized the activity.

The "theoretical sampling" (Glaser and Strauss, 1967) led to identify 8 nurses (out of a total of 16, all women) and the head of the department. They were all interviewed twice through the techniques just sketched. For reconstructing the whole process of introduction (that, as the reader will see, is the result of an articulated process), other information was collected through informal conversations with significant witnesses of the whole process and various documents and reports produced by the organization at stake.

3. Working with the Busterspeed: intertwining organizational practices and technology

This story begins in the summer of 2003, when the Head Office of a public hospital in the north-east of Italy applied a policy for improving safety, aimed at acquiring the level of excellence according to the Joint Commission International model. The rationale of the policy implied in such a model is, on the one hand, the application of proactive actions targeting the improvement of the safety of the patient (i.e. minimizing any

---

[1] The study was conducted together with three students of mine, Paolo Barelli, Eleonora Di Furia and Lia Tomasini. I thank them for letting me use part of the data collected, whose interpretation is all my responsibility.

risk through the development of corrective actions into the more critique processes) and, on the other hand, the development of monitoring sys-systems that allow keeping under observation the very same processes. Among the processes the Joint Commission International identifies as particularly critique, there is the management of the therapy.

In the hospital, up to 2003, the management of the therapy followed a traditional practice: the doctor used to record the prescription (usually during the medical examination) in the case file and afterwards the nurse used to transcribe the prescriptions on a special working sheet included in the nursing file. Although there was no tracing error system available, as it has been stressed by medical literature, it is likely that the practice just mentioned displayed a high probability of error.

3.1. The Busterspeed: a new technology in search of a community of users

Given that the main risk was located into the prescription and administering phases, a unified sheet for the prescription and the recording of the therapies (to be used jointly by doctors and nurses) was introduced, with the intent to avoid transcriptions. After a few months, a new system of therapy management is introduced, substituting the paper instrument with a computerized one and automatizing parts of the process.

The system is the Busterspeed®, a pharmaceutical automatized closet using a mechanical arm for the handling of the medicines (inside of it). This closet is also equipped with a touch-screen monitor that allows the user to do both drawing and loading operations. The identification of the pharmaceutical packages comes out through the automatic reading of the bar codes (by a camera) and it is run on a software which records all the patients' pharmaceutical prescriptions. The software generates automatically the periodical and urgent requests of replenishment of the medicines to the pharmacy of the hospital and distributes them according to the daily therapeutic needs.

This experiment started in the spring of 2005, when the system was installed in a 45 beds department of medicine. The rationale of the choice of such a department was the presence in it of a doctor already part of the interdisciplinary group for the improvement of the quality (and well acknowledged within the medical group), as well as the presence of a charge nurse particularly able in integrating the nursing staff. For a certain period, the medical and nursing personnel were trained on the field (by the technicians of the company that provided the system), while it was agreed the immediate availability in the ward of the same technicians (so to intervene in case of technical problems).

At this stage, the system provided the use of a computer, connected on line to the closet and a printer. Doctors had to use the terminal one by one in order to insert the prescriptions after the daily examinations of the patients. As soon as the prescriptions were inserted, a therapy schedule of the day was printed out and the doctor signed the prescription. Only afterwards, the charge nurse could start running the medical supplies and the nursing staff had access to the preparation and administering of the therapies only after receiving the therapeutic program printed and signed by the doctor.

Practically speaking, the system required a substantial change to the organization of doctors and nurses daily work, giving birth to unexpected troubles. First of all, the new system resulted in a time consuming activity, partly due to doctors' (in)ability in using it, partly because of the limited usability of the system (given the only computer position available). Secondly, nurses received the prescriptions usually late, and there were other delays, often caused by printed prescriptions which were not signed (forcing nurses to run after the doctors as to get their confirmation signs). A further problem was linked to the (huge) quantity of prints produced for every patient (a new one each time there was a change in the therapy).

Last but not least, the main and most apparent result of the introduction of the Busterspeed was the forming of two groups of doctors, one opposing and the other favouring this new system. The "opponents" simply disregarded it. Paradoxically, their behaviour was balanced by the group of doctors who believed in the new system and who spent time to insert the prescriptions of the opposing colleagues.

Despite the constant presence of technicians in the department (assisting the medical personnel and modifying the system according to the feedback received), the relevant discomforts produced by the Busterspeed soon led to interrupt the experiment, and forced the sponsoring group to reconsider the whole project. The machinery continued to be in the Unit, though its use was limited to the storage and order of medicines to the Pharmacy of the hospital.

3.2. Adopting a new technology: the Busterspeed finds a community of users

On the fall of 2005, in another hospital department (neurology, 29 beds), a group of doctors manifested interest in introducing the computerized system for therapy prescription. On the basis of the previous experience, the system was reviewed, both at the technical and organizational level, so that this time the Busterspeed was connected to a wireless network and made accessible by many tablet PCs at the same time. Now the doctor could prescribe the therapy directly at the bedside, likewise for the nurse it was possible to receive the doctor's prescription in real time on his/her tablet PC (fig. 1). This way, time consuming problems as well as those linked to the great increase of prints were overcome.

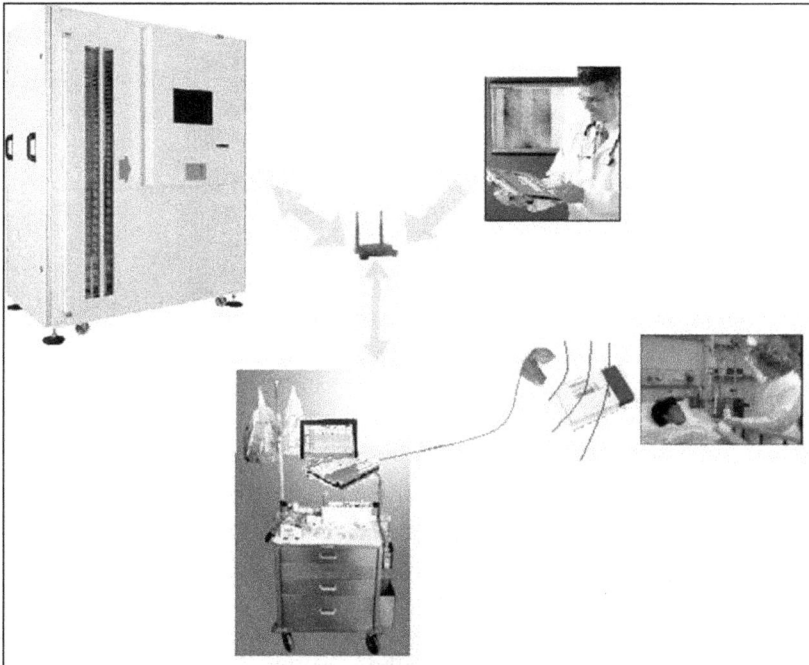

Fig. 1 - The Busterspeed® system

Moreover, the system provided the possibility to do checks just by reading barcodes. Thereafter, the nurse could record the administering of the therapy with a barcode scanner at the bedside, after verifying that the medicine to administer corresponded to the medicine prescribed. Finally, the system was equipped with numerous alarm devices, in order to signal eventual missing correspondences between the medicine prescribed and the administered one, and to set the time of the therapies.

While this updated version of the Busterspeed gathered the interest (and the active involvement) of doctors, nurses (who in the first experience demonstrated a good attitude) showed uneasiness toward its use. To some extent, the reasons were ideological ("we don't need it"), but they were also the result of the unexpected arrival of the new machinery (in parallel with another organizational innovation, the opening of a Stroke Unit), and of the need to "get used to it":

> *"Especially at the beginning we have had some problems, just because we didn't have enough personnel, we had to get used..." (N5)*

> *"At the beginning, the Busterspeed was not acknowledged by anyone, perhaps because the personnel have not been warned about this change. There were rumours, and all of a sudden we found it in the ward. At the beginning we were somehow ill-disposed..." (N3)*

> *"Up to the day before, we were working in a certain way and then, unexpectedly, we found ourselves working in a totally different way, completely computerized...in fact, I don't know anything about computers and I found myself working with a tablet PC..." (N7)*

Moreover, there were concrete difficulties in integrating the system in daily working practices. The possibility/necessity to check the matching of the prescribed medicine with the medicine to be administered (through the reading of the barcode on the package), for example, required an extreme precision in the prescription and supply of the medicines from the central Pharmacy of the hospital. In fact, there were often inconsistencies between the medicine prescribed and the available one (although equivalent), as the alternative medicine provided by the pharmacy was not always recorded in the database of the Busterspeed. This resulted in a visual alert on the nurses' tablet PC, a situation to be solved manually, therefore creating delays and interruptions in everyday work.

After a while, because of the hard tensions with the nursing group, the system was further modified. Doctors kept using the PC tablet for the prescription of the therapy at the bedside. Nurses did not, as they continued using the traditional paper sheet, graphically more user friendly and compatible with the existent organizational practices.

However, there is a further reason why nurses partly opposed to the new technology: the Busterspeed not only required a reconfiguration of daily practices, it was also activating a reconfiguration of the roles of "expert" and "novice" within the same nursing group. The latter realized how through the introduction of the new technology their status could have changed from 'novices' (of the traditional community) to "experts" (of the new machinery). Supporting the functioning of the new system, they slowly marginalized the former group, so that after some time expert (and older) nurses asked to be transferred to other units, while the younger ones were giving form to a new community of practices.

3.3. Aligning technology with working practices and vice versa

After an initial period, working processes started getting a new organizational settlement. Now, the community of practice coagulates around the new technology, interpreting it as a new s-object (Bruni, 2005), a "colleague" in charge of part of the daily activities and to whom it is possible to entrust part of the daily job. "It gives you", "It sees", "It does its own calculations" and similar expressions are easy to be found in the interviews[2], as in the following excerpts:

> "...all of us, at night, do the daily supply, in the sense
> that...the computer does it...It looks and counts, in the sense

---

[2] English grammar defines things as neuter. Italian, by contrast, does not have a neuter form and therefore gives gender definition even to things. Because the Busterspeed is a 'machine' and a 'technology' (nouns which are feminine in Italian), it could have been given feminine gender, but this did not happen (and perhaps not by accident), so that in the Italian transcripts of the conversations the Busterspeed is "he".

that if for instance three pills per day are administered...and
in the package there are 20 pills...so it does count how many
days that package can last and as soon as those days are gone
it automatically replaces it with a new package..." (N7)

"We just click, as it tells you: "Do you want to supply the
medicines for tomorrow?" You respond positively and it takes
out all the medicines that are needed the day after, except in
the case there are already some in the drawer..." (N5)

As from the excerpts, the Busterspeed keeps under control the stocks, therefore avoiding the risk to run out of medicines and suggesting to check the expiry date of the medicines that have been in stock for six months already. The agency the interviewees ascribe to the machinery is a clear trace of the intimate relationship that the new technology has established with organizational and working practices, to the point of black-boxing (to paraphrase Latour) other organizational practices and actors. In fact, the refilling of the Busterspeed involves another group of actors, the supporting staff, which experienced the introduction of the Buster-speed as a further difficulty affecting the daily work ("It is more difficult, because all the medicines coming from the Pharmacy in the big box have to be put in, it takes time...", reported to us one person from the support-ing staff during an informal conversation).

In accordance with other studies (Suchman et al., 1999; Star, 1999), it is therefore important to point out how technologies can "save" or "waste" time according to the activity and the actors involved. In fact, even though the Busterspeed is now considered "useful", "comfortable" and "simple", it has not always been this way. As accounted in the previous paragraph, at the beginning the Busterspeed "was not acknowledged by anyone" and its arrival was anticipated just in form of "rumours". Suddenly working practices shifted from "analogic" (pen and paper) to "computerized", but nurses in some cases did not have the background knowledge necessary to face such a situation (as said by one nurse in one of the previous excerpts: "I don't know anything about computers and I found myself working with a tablet PC"). To "get used" to the Busterspeed, thus, required some extra work, precisely in a moment in which nurses were already overload, given that in the department "there was not enough personnel". Moreover, the functioning of the machinery was somehow detached from the organiza-tional reality inhabited by actors:

"The company had conceived it somehow away from our working reality. They thought their closet was the core of the matter, the core of the management. It is not. The core of the matter is the software regarding the prescriptions, the closet just executes what the software requests...They came and said: "Here it is the system!", but the system wasn't good, it was hardly readable, it required a more continuous printing activity than what it is now...the writing on the therapy sheet was different, for every change we needed to print a new sheet...it was a bit muddled. We simplified it and we polished it, seeing that it could work in the daily practice, but only if the system adapted to our practices, not vice versa..." (N4)

"At the beginning we had a scan of the medicine's barcode by the optical scanner, and it was perfect as it scanned the barcode and it was impossible to take the wrong medicine...and moreover the computer would record the medicine administered, so that even the checking off was done just by clicking on the computer the administering of the medicine. Yet this resulted in longer periods of administering as referred to the schedule, thus the computer gave us also flexible schedules, a time within which to administer the medicines, but then again nothing more. Indeed, schedules cannot always be respected inside a Hospital department...there are emergencies, there is always some hitch, so that it was not possible to strictly follow the schedule, therefore the manual checking off of the administering is more practical..." (N5)

These excerpts highlight how not only the Busterspeed changed some of the organizational and working practices, but also how the Busterspeed as well had to go through a series of changes and modifications in order to meet the practices of the community it was about to encounter and not interfere too much. A striking example of the invisible work made by humans and technologies in order to incorporate each other's basic needs and requirements.

The need to align the new technology with working practices depends also on the fact that the linear structure of the Busterspeed sometimes clashes with organizational processes, causing unexpected situations:

> *"Then it also happens, for instance, that you discharge a patient on Friday and...on Saturday and Sunday the doctor in charge is not available so that you are forced to give the therapy also for the week end. This also affects the situation, but the Busterspeed doesn't consider it...when you discharge a patient, the patient is discharged, and that's it. Therefore the system doesn't count those four pills we give back to the patient. That's a limit..." (N6)*

Anyhow, in nurses' accounts the Busterspeed seems to have the merit of having obliged doctors to respect prescriptions' formal completeness, while 'liberating' the nurses from the task of interpreting doctors' handwriting. A further point regards the traceability of the accesses to the machine, stressing personal responsibilities and the grown accountability of organizational processes:

> *"...there's a major control even over its use, as we have the password...so that if I get a medicine with my password, the event will be recorded. On the contrary, everybody formerly used to go grabbing their medicines on their own..." (N5)*

> *"Medicines are checked, because everybody access with a password, so that it is possible to know who gets the medicine..." (N1)*

Yet, like any other colleague, the Busterspeed has its negative sides, as for instance the (disturbing) noise it produces when it is working:

> *"The machine is noisy, but the noise gets less loud as the door is closed or...since it works on its own...we try not to be in there while it is working..." (N5)*

This short excerpt points out how technologies can be evaluated not only in relation to their technical features, but also with regard of more aesthetic aspects (such as the sound they produce). This highlights the relevance of aesthetic judgement and understanding in (and of) organizational activities (Strati, 1999): as in this case, nurses try to organize their work so to be somewhere else when the Busterspeed is "working".

To this extent, it is also possible to notice how the same process of administering the medicines by the Busterspeed has interfered with some consolidated practices exactly from an aesthetic point of view:

> *"Once I used to open my closet and I had all the packages in front of me, with their names, I knew already the color of a specific medicine, I had a picture in my mind...In the buster instead you can't see the medicines, but in a moment you know whether the medicine is inside or not." (N3)*

The interviewee stresses the aesthetic, sensitive and material dimensions of daily working practices, that is, the body as the very first element of contact and relation with the organizational environment. The knowledge embodied through years and years of experience, which made possible for some nurses to recognize medicines at glance, appears useless now that the physical interaction with the closet for drugs has changed. This point further out the relevance not just of technology but of materiality *tout court*, so that organizational and working practices are always sociomaterial practices (Law and Mol, 1995; Orlikowski, 2007), and the body and its senses are always at stake.

Finally, I would like to focus on a linguistic detail, last example of adjustment and alignment of technology and daily work. Within the conversations going on into the ward, the Busterspeed is more often known as "the buster" (as, for instance, in the last excerpt presented), as well as some other human subjects are called with nicknames. Even more interesting, a few operators keep using the traditional expression "working with the closet" (legacy of the days when nurses had to open the closet and look inside to find medicines) to refer instead to the process of their interaction to the machine. In other words, the intertwining of technology with existing organizational and working practices takes form also through linguistic practices, contributing to make technology a proper participant to the organization.

Conclusion

Looking at technology, work and organization as practical accomplishments, in this paper I have focused on the experience of introduction, adoption and stabilization-in-use of the Busterspeed, a machinery for the automatized management of the therapy, in a (Italian) hospital.

The introduction of the machinery is the outcome of the willingness of the organization to improve safety and working practices, thus acquiring the level of excellence required by international standards (the Joint Commission International model). But the introduction of the Busterspeed is also the outcome of the medical literature that identifies in the management of drug therapies a possible *locus* of risk. Finally, the introduction of the machinery is the outcome of an organizational process managed by an interdisciplinary group of professionals, which identifies in a new technology the potential to standardize some of the working practices and increase individual and organizational accountability. In brief, and contrary to theories that interpret the introduction of technologies in organizations as the outcome of a purely rational process and cost-benefit calculation, the introduction of the Bustersped is the result of multiple logics, actors and practices, whose association is not given, but actively constructed at the organizational level.

By the way, as we have seen, the introduction of the new machinery sets out some unexpected problems. Some of them are 'simply' technical (and can be solved by technicians), but the most important ones have an organizational character. They are related to the daily work of clinicians, their habits, as well to the kind of technical infrastructure the Busterspeed presupposes. As for other studies (Mort et al., 2003; Hanlon et al., 2005), the new machinery seems totally detached from the organizational reality it is about to encounter, causing major interferences with working and organizational practices (as for the doctors having to queue in order to insert the prescriptions). This give raise to the constitution of two (contrasting) groups and it is important to notice how a passive opposition (the non-use of the machinery) is more effective that an active support (as for the doctors that spent time to insert the prescriptions of the opposing colleagues).

Not by chance, the Busterspeed has to be adopted by another community (in a different hospital department) to find its stabilization-in-use. Here, things are different not only because the medical community is willing to innovate its practice, but also because the machinery benefits from past experiences and has become more "infrastructured" in the concrete working practice (so that doctors and nurses have been all equipped with a tablet PC). Again, there are some difficulties and a reconfiguration of collective work related to the adoption of the new machinery and this brings to the light the presence of two different groups inside the community of nurses (the "traditionalists" and the "youngest"). This time, supporting the functioning of the new system, the "youngest" slowly marginalize the "traditionalists" and, shaping the new "computerized" practices, give form to a new community of practice.

In fact, it could be said that the stabilization-in-use of the Busterspeed is closely linked to the birth of this new community, at least for the invisible work nurses do in order to adapt the system to their organizing and working practices, as well as to adapt their practices to some of the changes brought by the Busterspeed. In this sense, it is worth noticing that the most "dramatic" change regards the dematerialization of some processes (as for the handling of the medicines) and, thus, the reconfiguration of the aesthetic knowledge (Strati, 2003, 2007) involved in everyday working practices. Maybe as a partial remedy, we have seen how nurses talk about the Busterspeed as it was a newcomer in the community, a "colleague" with which interact and coordinate for getting the work done.

It is worth noticing how in this overall process the issues of safety and of improving working practices somehow disappear, in favour of much more specific and organizationally situated aspects related to the adoption of the new machinery.

To recall the two questions posed at the beginning of this paper, this case illustrates how technologies play an active role in contemporary organizational settings, in a variety of ways: supporting and interfering with organizational and working practices; offering a solution to certain problems while causing new and unexpected ones; activating and dismantling groups of actors; calling into question professional and aesthetic knowledge. At the same time, technologies need to be performed by organizational and working practices, in that they become concrete only through their daily use. To quote John Law (1999: 24) "objects interpellate us", so that the continuous reproduction of their practical meaning and use preserve their stability. Otherwise (as in the first attempt of introducing the Busterspeed) they will be stabilized for their being practically meaningless and non-usable.

In this sense, the implications of a performative approach for the designing of technology, work and organization are clear. As from the analysis presented, such an approach fosters to look for the ways in which technology, work and organization are intertwined and constantly redesigned on the basis of the practices they entail, the problems they pose, and the actors with which they interact. In fact, to design a new technology means to design a community of users. This is why, in terms of organizational design, it is crucial for technologies to be acknowledged to users and to take into account the situated practices and working infrastructures they will encounter. And, for managers and designers, to be aware of the invisible work the adoption of the (new) technology will require and of the possible arrangements to which it will be subject in order to be effectively used.

References

Barley, S., Kunda, G. (2001), "Bringing Work Back In", *Organization Science*, 12 (1), pp. 76-95.

Berg, M. (1997), *Rationalizing Medical Work.* Cambridge: MIT Press.

Bruni, A. (2005), "Shadowing Software and Clinical Records: On the Ethnography of Non-Humans and Heterogeneous Contexts", *Organization*, 12 (3), pp. 357-378.

Bruni, A., Gherardi, S. (2007), *Studiare le pratiche lavorative,* Bologna: Il Mulino.

Bruni, A., Pinch, T., Schubert, C. (2013), "Technologically Dense Environments: What for? What Next?", *Tecnoscienza – Italian Journal of Science and Technology Studies*, 4 (2), pp. 51-72.

Carlile, P.R., Nicolini, D., Langley, A., Tsoukas, H. (2013), "How Matter Matters: Objects, Artifacts and Materiality in Organization Studies: Introducing the Third Volume of Perspectives on Organization Studies". in Carlile, P.R., Nicolini, D., Langley, A., Tsoukas, H. (eds.), *How Matter Matters: Objects, Artifacts and Materiality in Organization Studies.* Oxford: Oxford University Press.

Cooper R., Law J. (1995), "Distal and proximal visions of organization", in Bacarach S., Gagliardi P., Mundell B. (eds.), *Studies of organizations in the european tradition.* Greenwich: Jai Press, pp. 237-274.

Czarniawska, B. (2008), *A Theory of Organizing.* Cheltenham: Edward Elgar.

Garfinkel, H. (1967), *Studies in Ethnomethodology.* Englewood Cliffs: Prentice-Hall.

Gherardi, S. (1990), *Le microdecisioni nelle organizzazioni.* Bologna: Il Mulino.

Gherardi, S. (2000), "Practice-based theorizing on learning and knowing in organizations: An introduction", *Organization*, 7 (2), pp. 211-223.

Gherardi, S. (2006), *Organizational Knowledge. The Texture of Workplace Learning.* Oxford: Blackwell.

Hanlon, G., Strangleman, T., Goode, J., Luff, D., O'Cathain, A., Greatbatch, D. (2005), "Knowledge, technology and nursing: the case of NHS Direct", *Human relations*, 58 (2), pp. 147-171.

Heath, C., Luff, P. (2000), *Technology in Action*. Cambridge: Cambridge University Press.

Hernes, T. (2007), *Understanding Organization as Process. Theory for a tangled world*. New York: Routledge.

Jarzabkowski, P., Balogun, J., Seidl, D. (2007), Strategizing: The challenges of a practice perspective, *Human Relations*, 60 (1), pp. 5-27.

Latour, B. (2005), *Re-assembling the Social*. Oxford: Oxford University Press

Lave, J., Wenger, E. (1991), *Situated Learning. Legitimate Peripheral Participation*. Cambridge: Cambridge University Press.

Law, J. (1987), "Technology and Heterogeneous Engineering: The Case of Portuguese Expansion", in Bijker, W., Hughes T., Pinch T. (eds.), *The Social Construction of Technological Systems. New Directions in the Sociology and History of Technology*. MIT Press.

Law, J. (1994), *Organizing Modernity*. Oxford: Blackwell.

Law, J., Mol, A. (1995), "Notes on Materiality and Sociality", *Sociological Review*, 43 (2), pp. 274-94.

Law, J. (2002), *Aircraft Stories: Decentering the Object in Technoscience*. Duke University Press.

MacKenzie, D., Wajcman, J. (eds.) (1999), *The Social Shaping of Technology*. Buckingham: Open University Press.

Mol, A. (2002), *The Body Multiple: Ontology in Medical Practice*. Durham: Duke University Press.

Mort, M., May, C., Williams, T. (2003), "Remote Doctors and Absent Patients: Acting at a Distance in Telemedicine", *Science, Technology & Human Values*, 28 (2), pp. 274-295.

Mort M., Smith A. (2009), "Beyond Information: Intimate Relations in Sociotechnical Practice", *Sociology*, 43 (2), pp. 715-731.

Nicolini, D. (2009), "Articulating practice through the interview to the double", *Management Learning*, 40 (2), pp. 195-212.

Nicolini, D. (2012), *Practice Theory, Work & Organization: An Introduction*. Oxford: Oxford University Press.

Orr J. (1996) *Talking about Machines: An Ethnography of a Modern Job.* New York: Cornell University.

Pinch, T., Bijker, W., Hughes, T. (1987), *The Social Construction of Technological Systems.* Cambridge: MIT Press.

Rawls, A. (2008), "Harold Garfinkel, Ethnomethodology and Workplace Studies", *Organization Studies*, 29 (5), pp. 701-732.

Schatzki, T.R. (2006), "On organizations as they happen", *Organization Studies*, 27 (12), pp. 1863-1873.

Star, S.L. (1999), "The Ethnography of the Infrastructure", *American Behavioral Scientist*, 43 (3), pp. 377-391.

Star S.L., Strauss A. (1999), "Layers of Silence, Arenas of Voice: The Ecology of Visible and Invisible Work", *Computer Supported Cooperative Work*, 8 (1-2), pp. 9–30.

Strati, A. (1999), *Organization and Aesthetics*, London: Sage.

Strati, A. (2003), "Knowing in practice: aesthetic understanding and tacit knowledge", in Nicolini, D. Gherardi, S., Yanow, D. (eds.) *Knowing in Organizations.* Armink: M.E. Sharpe, pp. 53-75.

Strati, A. (2007), "Sensible Knowledge and Practice-based Learning", *Management Learning*, 38 (1), pp. 61-77.

Suchman, L., Blomberg, J., Orr, J.E., Trigg, R. (1999), "Reconstructing Technology as Social Practice", *American Behavioral Scientist*, 43 (3), pp. 392-408.

Suchman, L. (2000), "Organizing alignment: A case of bridge-building", *Organization*, 7 (2), pp. 311-327.

Timmermans, S., Berg, M. (2003), "The Practice of Medical Technology", *Sociology of Health and Illness*, 25 (3), pp. 97-114.

Wenger, E. (1998) *Communities of Practice: learning, meaning and identity.* Cambridge: Cambridge University Press.

Whalen, J., Bobrow, D.G. (2011), "Communal Knowledge Sharing: The Eureka Story", in Szymanski M.H., Whalen J. (eds.), *Making Work Visible. Ethnographically Grounded Case Studies of Work Practice.* New York: Cambridge University Press, pp. 257-284.

Whalen, J., Whalen, M., Henderson, K. (2002), "Improvisational Choreography in Teleservice Work", *British Journal of Sociology*, 53 (2), pp. 239-258.

DESIGNING ADMINISTRATIVE PRACTICES THROUGH ARTIFACTS:
PAPER-BASED REMEMBERING IN BACK-OFFICE WORK

Sari Yli-Kauhaluoma
Mika Pantzar

Introduction

Contemporary work is often hectic (e.g. Kuhn, 2006), full of disruptions (e.g. Staudenmayer et al., 2002), and even fragmented (e.g. Macpherson and Clark, 2009). One of the key challenges in modern work is the question of how to retain and retrieve required knowledge within the time limits imposed by the task at hand. This matter has attracted the attention of many scholars, particularly in the area of organizational remembering, after the publishing of a seminal piece of research by Walsh and Ungson (1991: 61), who studied and defined organizational memory as "stored information from an organization's history that can be brought to bear on present decisions." In general, gaining a greater understanding of storing, retrieving, and adapting knowledge in organizations has been found to be essential, for example, from the perspectives of organizational learning (e.g. Cacciatori, 2008), innovation (e.g. Kyriakopoulos, 2011), and organizational culture (Feldman and Feldman, 2006). Despite much effort, however, organizational remembering and its various temporal dimensions still require further examination (Casey and Olivera, 2011).

This study examines organizational remembering through a practice perspective (cf. Gherardi, 2000; Corradi et al., 2010; Feldman and Orlikowski, 2011), following Feldman and Feldman (2006: p. 862), who have developed a "conceptualization of organizational remembering as a collective, culture and time specific process and practice" and who emphasize that remembering is fundamental to the daily functioning of organizations. Moreover, this study recognizes that knowing is always material (Orlikowski, 2007) and that all everyday practices, including remembering, are "deeply bound in the material forms, artifacts, spaces, and infrastructures through which humans act" (Orlikowski, 2006: p. 460). The aim here is to examine how people in organizations perform retention and retrieval work, particularly through the use of material artifacts. The study rests on

an empirical examination of administrative work in a university back office with a focus on mundane material artifacts, physical paper documents, and the ways these material means are intrinsic to organizational
remembering in administration. The choice of the research site is justified
by an observation by Jelinek (1979: p. 162) that "administrative systems
are the mechanisms for impounding and preserving knowledge." To date,
however, university back offices as particular research sites have been
more or less neglected (e.g. Korczynski, 2004; Collinson 2006), although
administrators generally conduct vital and ubiquitous functions in modern societies (e.g. Wagenaar, 2004). Indeed, their importance, particularly
in university contexts, has been seen to have increased in recent years due
to ongoing institutional changes in higher education (e.g. Vogel and Kaghan, 2001; Szekeres, 2004, 2006).

The results of this study suggest that administrators engage in three
kinds of remembering practices to retain and retrieve administrative
knowledge over time: memoing, verifying, and backing-up practices.
These differ most importantly in terms of the duration of memory retention: in memoing practices, administrators use memory devices that are
short term, in verification they are medium term, and in backing up they
are long term. Overall, the study shows that remembering practices in
administration are closely connected to the materiality of things. This has
implications for the designing of future remembering practices based on
digitalization and the internet.

1. Remembering as an organizational practice

Analysis of organizational practices is important since "the practice constitutes the 'topos' that ties the 'knowing' to the 'doing'" (Corradi et al.,
2010: p. 274). Practices are carried out by both body and mind, and they
exist as sets of norms, conventions, ways of doing, know-how, and requi-
site material arrays (Schatzki, 2001). On the one hand, practitioners are
"captured" by practices that make demands on those who do them, while
on the other, practices are constituted through participation and defined
by the activities of those who "do" them. In other words, lively practices
generate the conditions for their own renewal (Shove et al., 2012). Following Schatzki (2001), Shove et al. (2012) suggest that the elements of practices can be condensed into three concepts: image, skill, and material.
When remembering practices emerge, spheres that originally seemed separate are influenced and transformed by new material objects and existing
competences become linked together. Once these links have been made,

practices become reinforced in repeated doings. For instance, a work contract can be seen as a stabilized remembering tool, a practice complex, which contains, in addition to material content, also symbolic content representing continuous commitments and competence related to formalized procedures. In other words, we simply suggest that the remembering practices (of a single office worker) are made by and through both their routine reproduction and the active integration of material, meanings, and forms of competence.

Every organizational practice, including organizational remembering, is always bound up with materiality (Orlikowski, 2007), and material means are constitutive of both organizational activities and identities (Orlikowski and Scott, 2008). Practice complexes (Pantzar and Shove, 2010), which are wider entities of practices – or, as Foucault would say, dispositions,[3] influence, condition, and enable the renewal of ideas, knowledge, and material objects, the very elements practices are made of. Problematically, as Reckwitz (2002) argues, the conceptual shift from "mental categories" to textual or discursive codes, however, has not yet led to a fundamental revision of the status of material entities, and today the material world is still interpreted through symbolic schemes. Reckwitz (2002) asks whether an alternative vocabulary would conceptualize materiality in a less intellectualist way than as "objects of knowledge". He rightly notes that Bruno Latour and Michelle Callon are to be thanked for offering in their "symmetrical anthropology" a theory that does not subordinate the material world to the world of thought. This means that things necessarily participate in social practices just as human beings do. Here, we suggest that in office environments the materiality of artifacts influences, but does not determine, which kinds of remembering practices are possible.

Wajcman and Rose (2011) state that in contemporary organizations, work is a complex entanglement of social practices and different kinds of material artifacts where the material properties of the artifacts play a crucial role in attempts to gain more understanding of existing and changing work practices. Cacciatori (2008), who has specifically examined the role of artifacts in organizational remembering, has discovered that even relatively simple artifacts can act as memory devices, depending on what

---

[3] According to Reckwitz (2002: 206), "in his 'genealogical' work Foucault begins to study those 'subject-forming institutional practices' which are not exclusively 'discursive', but which make use of novel artifacts."

knowledge representations they hold. Based on her study on Excel work-books, she (2008) argues that these kinds of memory devices can have a fundamental role in sustaining organizational procedures and formalized practices even in discontinuous project environments. Overall, as Øster-lund (2008) has shown, different types of documents, both paper based and electronic, constitute important material resources and serve, for instance, as essential communication and coordination and thereby also as memory devices in organizations.

In contemporary organizations, office workers apply many of the available modern technologies, from e-mail systems (Szekeres, 2006) to various software programs (e.g. Cacciatori, 2008; Gabriel, 2008), both to store and to retrieve organizational memory. Interestingly, however, constant encounters with a multiplicity of information can also cause information overload, challenges for the management of tasks, and requirements to create supporting personal knowledge systems to carry out tasks at hand in the given time limits (Bondarenko et al., 2010; Wajcman and Rose, 2011). Therefore, in addition to the vast variety of information and communication technologies, office environments can also contain a large range of different kinds of more traditional technologies in the form of paper documents, for instance, post-it notes or printouts.

An important reason behind the continuing use of paper, even when many documents are digitally available, lies in the material properties of paper. In this respect, paper documents are material artifacts which can act as visual reminders or cues at work (Lansdale, 1991). Moreover, Bondarenko and Janssen (2009) have shown that it is important for office workers to be able to encode relevant information in visual cues in physical documents and thereby to manage information in their physical workspace. Physical paper documents thus can have an important role in organizational remembering practices, but we do not know in detail how these traditional material artifacts contribute to retention and retrieval work, particularly in current digital office environments.

2. Back-Office administration in a university: a study
2.1. Research context

The context of this study is the work of administrative staff in the back-office services in a university. Since administrative staff in universities do not consist of a single uniform professional group (cf. Szekeres, 2004; Small, 2008), it is important to specify that in our study we analyze the work of those university administrators whose most important role is to deal with human resources, finance, bookkeeping, and academic administration. The administrators in back-office services in our study also conduct preparatory and secretarial work for committee meetings in academic settings. In more concrete terms, these administrators process the invoices, applications, and contracts that pour onto their desks, mainly from other university administrators, namely the academic service staff more often in closer contact with faculty members and graduate students. This means that, unlike the academic service staff, the administrators in back-office services are not located directly in various university departments or disciplines but rather in a separate department for administrative matters. We do recognize that the concrete tasks that the administrators in our study conduct daily can vary greatly; take, for example, the tasks of a bookkeeper or a register officer. Nevertheless, besides conducting back-office service work, administrators have three other important everyday characteristics in common. Therefore, particularly from the remembering perspective of this study, closer analysis is worthwhile.

First, all of the administrators in our study constantly confront and interact with a multiplicity of information and communication technologies in the course of their work. Each administrator's workstation is equipped with a networked desktop computer and either a landline telephone or a standard mobile phone. Only a few administrators possess a small printer in their office. For printing, a large machine is located in the corridor, which, besides printing, can also do other functions such as scanning. All administrators use the standard Microsoft Office programs, such as Outlook, Word, and Excel, and administrative managers in particular also take advantage of PowerPoint. Moreover, in addition to these general types of software programs, administrators mainly interact with more specialized office programs designed particularly for bookkeeping, finance, archiving, or personnel management purposes. At the time of the research, in the autumn of 2009, the university was preparing for a merger with two other universities, which took place at the beginning of 2010. From the perspective of administration, the forthcoming merger meant not only an outsourcing of some administrative tasks to a service center but also an intensification of preparations to apply electronic systems more extensively in administrative work. In general, an increase in modern technologies in office environments has been found to change the nature of the work itself (e.g. Eriksson-Zetterqvist et al., 2009; Wajcman and Rose, 2011), but the consequences of such a change regarding, for example, the remembering practices in offices still remain largely unexplored.

Second, besides their constant interaction with multiple modern office technologies, the work of the administrators in our study can be characterized as hectic, fragmented, and full of interruptions (e.g. Jett and George, 2003). Part of these attributes are a result of the increasing interaction with various technologies in the workplace (e.g. Barley et al., 2011), but as the existing literature (e.g. Small, 2008) has noted, ongoing changes in universities have also had an impact, resulting, for instance, in an "intensification of work, reduced resources, and increased expectations" (Szekeres, 2006: p. 143).

While the first two characterizations discussed above can well be argued to be typical in many types of work carried out in office settings, it is the third which makes our chosen research context particularly interesting from the perspective of organizational remembering. The nature of administrative work has been found to be twofold in that, on the one hand, administrators deal with various routine procedures (e.g. Collinson, 2006) which require handling various matters "correctly" – referring to prescribed processes done by the book and the clock (see Rämö, 2002). On the other hand, the tasks that administrators handle are complex and indeterminate, and they are required to act in a timely manner in the situation at hand (Wagenaar, 2004). In this setting where administrators face various kinds of complex demands from multiple sources, one of the key challenges for these administrators is how to retain and retrieve the required knowledge in time to accomplish the required tasks by the book and the clock (see Rämö, 2002).

2.2. Practice theory as a methodological lens

Our main research site was the administrative department of personnel and legal affairs in the institute in which we had a long working experience. Our research approach is close to the method of at-home ethnography (Alvesson, 2009) because we had natural access to the cultural setting that we aimed to study. Due to our working experience in the institute, we have participated in many administrative processes and have been in contact with many administrators, sometimes also with those engaged in back-office functions. In the study, the primary method of collecting data was to focus on what we heard in the field through engaged listening (Forsey, 2010), either in formal interviews or casual conversations. We conducted 14 in-depth interviews in total during a five-month period from September 2009 to January 2010 with both administrators in the department of personnel and legal affairs as well as their coworkers in the administrative service center to which some of the administrative back-service tasks had been outsourced. Moreover, we included five interviews in our analysis with informants outside the context of administrative work: two executives in private companies and three independent professionals – a journalist, a consultant, and an architect. Nicolini (2009) has suggested that zooming out from a certain context in the analysis of practices may crystallize the specificities of particular practices in the studied contexts. Thus, our aim was to reveal possible specificities of administrative work in a back-office setting in general and in remembering practices in particular.

At first, our ethnographic work focused on mundane materials, specifically paper, at work, and the original aim was to find in what ways people in offices explain the continued use of paper. We started our study by compiling an exhaustive list of practices related to the use of paper in a back office (Yli-Kauhaluoma et al., 2013). In the beginning, we anticipated that paper-related practices would be accounted for by conventional categories such as printing, copying, writing, or reading, and that nobody would be excited about relating these activities. To our surprise, our interviewees felt a strong need to explain their resistance to purely depending on digital documentation; people were very motivated to discuss the role of paper in their work. We also found that the categories of paper-related practices were more creative and specific than expected. The results showed that not only do socio-material aspects count but also the symbolic aspects and competencies to which the paper format was attached (see Shove et al., 2012).

Our original focus on paper as a material in administrative offices meant that in the interview situations we talked and asked questions about the kind of paper administrators use in their work, and about how and why they use it, for instance, instead of computers, software programs, or digital files. This approach proved fruitful since it allowed us to gain access to the key aspects and content of administrative work and to create an understanding of the essential tools that administrators either possess or create for their everyday lives in administrative offices. More particularly, it revealed to us the importance of mundane materials such as paper in everyday administrative work settings. In the interview situations, we also took photographs of our interviewees' offices. The aim of the photography was not to gather images (cf. Harper, 2003) of administrative offices for further analysis, but rather to take photographs that would help us to zoom in (Nicolini, 2009) on specific artifacts in administrative offices, such as binders, folders, or paper piles, enabling specific questions concerning the items and the practices related to them. The camera thus provided us an additional way to conduct interviews and to engage in participant listening (Forsey, 2010) at our research site. Moreover, in addition to interviews, we had numerous casual conversations in the institute relating to people's experiences and accounts of administrative processes.

In the analysis of our research material, we carefully read through our interview transcripts and field notes several times in order to gain an understanding of what administrators do in offices. After identifying several paper-related practices (Yli-Kauhaluoma et al., 2013), we then followed the suggestion of Nicolini (2009) and zoomed in on one specific administrative practice: remembering and its material accomplishments in space and time. Next, we carefully reviewed all our data to more closely analyze the practice of remembering. Careful re-reading and systematic coding of the data (see Eriksson and Kovalainen, 2008) resulted in three categories of remembering practices in administration. Importantly, we constantly interpreted and compared the emerging results against the existing literature.

3. Artifacts in office work: preliminary findings on paper-based remembering

Most of the offices that we visited during the research process were more or less full of paper. Various kinds of pieces of paper lay in different positions on or near office tables and shelves and in office cabinets. There were colorful post-it notes, separate sheets of paper, as well as piles of different kinds of paper. Following the practice-based perspective, we here focus attention specifically on processes and situations where organizational memory practices are enacted in administrative situations in back offices. Regarding the use of paper as memory devices in back-office administration, we were able to identify three different remembering practices in our analysis: memoing, verifying, and backing-up practices.

Following the scheme of Shove et al. (2012), we suggest that the three remembering practices recognized in our analysis form relatively enduring entities consisting of the specific skills of administrators, the images that the practices produce, and the material (here paper) through which the practices are entwined with other daily practices. In the case of missing elements (e.g. competence) or missing links between, say, material objects and images, permanent or shared remembering practices would be much less likely to develop and circulate widely. In a similar vein, we can suggest that the various remembering practices become more stabilized when they participate in the very reproduction of their own elements (e.g. the image of trust and continuity). We will now analyze each of the identified remembering practices in detail.

3.1. Memoing practices

One of key challenges of administrators in their hectic and fragmented work context is both to recognize all the incoming tasks and to remember to carry them out on schedule. With regard to other studies (Cacciatori, 2008; Gabriel, 2008), our results highlight that administrators use short-term memory devices, such as post-it notes, printouts, and paper piles with specific mnemonic qualities, to retain and retrieve their assignments according to their timetable. The process of the retention and retrieval of assignments with the help of short-term memory objects consists of four different kinds of activities: making notes of things to do or printing out assignments on paper; placing and keeping these somewhere visible; using the printouts or other paper documents as an instrument for a follow-up of the work process; and removing them, once processed, from the immediate work space.

Keeping track of all existing and incoming assignments is truly challenging in back-office administration because the work consists of a wide variety of scheduled assignments that administrators need to carry out daily, weekly, or monthly. Moreover, routine procedures can be interrupted by, for example, phone calls, e-mails, or the inquiries of and interaction with colleagues involving either new assignments or important information necessary to the accomplishment of the existing tasks. To keep track of the fragmented information in a hectic working environment, administrators make quick notes of things to do on paper.

> I have huge amounts of slips of paper [post-its] containing notes. Every time I talk on the phone with somebody, I make notes [on the conversation]. (Financial Secretary, female)

One of the key attributes of post-it notes or paper slips as memory devices lies in their simplicity, easy accessibility, and simultaneity. Most importantly, post-it notes and paper slips allow multitasking, which means that administrators are able to perform two or more tasks at the same time (see Stephens and Davis, 2009). In essence, small pieces of paper such as post-it notes allow administrators to keep up with the task and jot down keynotes (see Gabriel, 2008: 264) to remember later at the same time as they are concentrating on something more complex, such as talking on the phone or having a conversation with a colleague. Besides making notes, administrators also take print-outs of important e-mail messages or pages of electronic documents.

> "It is much better to have it on paper, because it then stays here. [Otherwise] it easily gets lost in my e-mail box. When someone sends you a message, you take a look at it and think that okay, this is something that I will not immediately start taking care of because it is complicated. I have to think about it first. [Besides] I have something else here that I have to rush with. [Therefore] if it remains in my e-mail-box and as I receive more and more messages, it just sinks lower, and lower, and lower [in the list] and then gets forgotten even if I try to mark somehow that it needs to be taken care of...On paper I have it here in a concrete form. Therefore, I also notice it much better, and it reminds me all the time that I need to take care of it somehow...Out of sight; out of mind." (Project Manager, male)

An important reason for taking print-outs thus is to keep track of, and to stay alert to, all the existing assignments in administration. Moreover, as the above quotation from an administrator suggests, these reminders also help administrators to both prioritize and organize tasks and play an important role when confronting complex tasks. Most important to note here, however, is that the physical location of the post-it notes and print-outs in back offices is a vital part of using these as memory devices. To act as a memory device, post-it notes and print-outs need to be both placed and kept somewhere visible in offices, and those we saw were often stuck directly on computer screens. Another visible location for post-it notes or print-outs was on desk surfaces close to the computer or telephone.

Visual reminders in paper form help administrators to keep track of their tasks not only in busy conditions but also in situations where they are dependent on the accomplishments of their colleagues or they face either boring or even unpleasant tasks. Particularly in the latter cases, there is a risk that these tasks will be put aside and left undone.

> *"You have to wait for someone else to do something else first. If the other person has had no time to do it, [the paper] kind of reminds me with its existence that you have not taken care of this yet."* (Department Secretary in the Financial Office, female)

> *"[I]f you have an unpleasant job to do and you in no way want to start working on it, you then just know that you really have to do something about it, even if you [wonder] why can't these tasks just go away from here."* (Project Manager, male)

Besides the careful placement of memos in offices, administrators also use color codes or other attributes to remind them of the importance of the documents.

> *"Often, it may happen if I have many meetings that I do not necessarily have time to open my mail. Therefore, I keep these envelopes in piles so that I know which of them I have not processed yet. ... And the red binder contains my most important papers."* (Head of Department, female)

When administrators then grab the post-it notes or their print-outs, it often indicates the first stage in processing a job. In this respect, a paper note can also be more than an active reminder of a specific assignment. The administrators suggest that they also use these reminders actively to follow up on their own processing of the job.

> *"Whenever I process [a complicated bill] or make any kind of calculations, I want to have a [print-out] because then I can follow up on my own progress. If I have the same information on the computer screen, I cannot mark as clearly what I have already accomplished. ... If I get a phone call interrupting my job and if I have used electronic [equipment], I am not so sure anymore [after the phone call] how far I had*

proceeded, even though it is the same image (on the screen)."
(Service Manager, male)

Finally, as soon as the job has been accomplished, the short-term memory devices are removed from the immediate work space. Administrators either throw them away or in some cases file the papers in a pile of paper.

> *"As soon as I have processed the case, I throw my notes away. Otherwise I would wonder the next day whether I have already done something about [the inquiries]. As soon as I throw the note away, I have processed the case."* (Financial Secretary, female)

To sum up, short-term memory devices such as post-it notes, print-outs, and encoded paper piles help administrators to recognize, prioritize, and organize their tasks. The visibility and location of these material means in administrators' physical office space is essential as administrators design their everyday working and organizational life with the help of these short-term memory devices.

3.2. Verifying practices

In addition to short-term memory devices, administrators also use memory devices that are longer-term in nature. The key difference between the short-term and longer-term memory devices is that while the former remind administrators of the tasks that they have to do – and in that sense are future oriented – the longer-term devices help administrators to remember what they have already done, and in that sense they are past oriented. Medium-term devices (paper copies) reference only periods of some weeks or, at most, a few months and are used in relation to verifying practices. The key aspect of paper copies as memory devices is that they show administrators that they have carried out the task and give the details of the accomplished task. Moreover, paper copies help administrators to retrieve the required information whenever it cannot be found in electronic files. The retention and retrieval of information for verifying purposes in the medium term includes both retaining original documents which have arrived in paper form and been scanned into the electronic administrative systems as well as making paper copies of those original documents that administrators must forward to their colleagues or other administrative units for further processing. Both types of documents are then kept in their personal files.

Administrators use a range of electronic systems, many of which link to various monetary transactions within the university, such as payment of wages and invoices. At the time of our study, the university was in the process of moving to an e-billing system, which means that the university would accept invoices only in electronic form. Nevertheless, some invoices still arrived in paper format. This happened, for instance, when bills were sent from abroad or when some private person sent an invoice, for instance, for giving a guest lecture. All the invoices in paper format, however, are fed into the electronic system, and this is one of the most critical phases in the complete payment system because errors or mistakes may easily happen. In cases in which an invoice does not enter the system electronically, it will be scanned into the system. The same is done for different kinds of receipts that still often are in paper format but have an important function in providing grounds for making certain payments from electronic systems, such as travel reimbursements. The electronic system is essentially the most vulnerable during the whole scanning process, in which errors may easily take place. In order to be prepared to encounter and tackle these problems, administrators retain the original paper documents for backup in cases of missing payments.

> "There are human mistakes, for example, either two receipts have been scanned one on top of the other, or the receipt number is not correct, or ... for some reason or other, [the receipt] has not gone into an electronic archive. ... The documents that have been scanned into the system are put in boxes for a while. We do not hurry to destroy them. ... In case the documents contain information that is not processed yet, they can then easily be found. Otherwise, we do not need to keep them." (Service Manager, male)

The extract above clearly points out that even scanning can be a complicated job and mistakes may happen, for example, because of negligence, incompetence, or errors in the system. It is in these cases that documents in paper format help administrators to go back to the original information, check it, verify it, or change and extend it when necessary.

Another example of paper copies functioning as a medium-term memory device concerns situations where administrators process a document which they have to send forward to their colleagues for further processing. In these cases administrators also take copies of some of those documents in paper format for their personal files. These copies help administrators not only to quickly retrieve the information in cases of questions or problems in an administrative process, but also to verify that the administrators have indeed carried out the given assignment.

> "I take a copy of the bill, just the front page, not the attachments. Only so I know that the bill has been here by me as proof. In case later somebody asks whether this bill has been here, I then know that it has been here, or if the bill gets lost, I know that I have had it and I have sent it forward."
> (Accountant, female)

This suggests that the reasons for taking and saving copies are twofold. On the one hand, the copies help administrators to correct, verify, or clarify issues in problematic situations that may emerge, for example, when there are mistakes, errors, or delays in the process or if documents are lost. In these situations, paper copies can help administrators accomplish their tasks according to the book and the clock (see Rämö, 2002). On the other hand, however, the role of paper copies is also to prove more specifically that administrators have done things correctly. In case someone asks an administrator about the current status of an administrative process or about some specific details concerning an administrative process, the copies can help administrators to answer these inquiries, even though the administrators no longer have the original documents but have forwarded them on. The copies then help administrators to show and even prove that they have carried out an administrative procedure, to demonstrate the exact date on which the task was performed, and to give details of the content of the performed tasks. In these situations, paper copies thus act simultaneously as proof with which to correct mistakes (see Porter, 2005) but also as material evidence of the performance of specific administrative tasks.

3.3. Backing-up practices

Besides using paper copies as medium-term memory devices to verify practices, administrators also apply long-term memory devices as back-up material at their work. Essentially, these long-term memory devices are original documents consisting in length from a single page to several pages, although they may even consist of several different kinds of document sets. The essential dimension of these documents is that they contain information which is either legislated for personnel management or which has undergone a long and complicated working process. The storage of those paper documents that are regulated by legislation is essentially simple to manage. The legislation gives strict guidelines for the administration of the storage of, for instance, work contracts in paper format to guarantee the existence of information for retirement records, despite the development of various technological programs and tools. The storage of those paper documents that are not under legislation is a much more complicated matter. From the perspective of the retention and retrieval of the information in the documents, administrators essentially face the following questions as they deliberate between the disposal and keeping of the documents: what documents should administrators keep and store, for what reason, for how long, and in what form?

So far, the question of the disposal of papers has mainly been seen either as a question of sustainability (e.g. Porter and Córdoba, 2009) or of technologies related to knowledge management (e.g. Hutchinson and Quintas, 2008). The results of our study, however, suggest that administrators often save and keep some specific paper documents to hold knowledge on the current state of affairs *just in case*. This means that throwing paper documents away can be a difficult task in administration since these documents may contain information that *may* be important in the future.

> *"When I started in this position, there were still papers from my predecessor in these cabinets. In the beginning I had no idea about what to do with these papers; [I did not know] whether they are necessary at all. So, I just kept them. And it is a good thing that I did not throw them away because I have also needed some of these papers."* (Head of Department, female)

"There are various kinds of reports which may perhaps have required a lot of work. You have managed to sort out the case and you have perhaps written up a report on the case which makes things easier, for instance, the next time you have to do the accounts. If it is a really exceptional project and the sponsors have atypical requirements, the [reports] are particularly important. I have saved, for instance, the documents of a project funded by EU structural funds. Currently, we do the accounts for this project. Fortunately, I have kept all [the papers] from different phases and various back-up memos, because [otherwise] I don't remember all the [documents] that we have sent to the sponsor." (Head of Department, female)

The keeping and storing of paper documents is then first and foremost a remembering issue. Administrators think carefully about what paper documents they will keep, since the paper documents can act as important memory devices to help them to better retrieve the required information in future cases.

"I do sometimes take a look at, well, in what meeting it was when we talked about that [matter] and what did we say about this matter and what kind of notes have I then made on that paper. I still have them [=proceedings] in that pile. ... In these office cabinets I even have older [proceedings]. .... I do not keep them forever, but perhaps the previous year or two, because they might contain matters that pop up again." (Project Manager, male)

The comment above reveals an important criterion for saving old documents, which is the current state of those matters that are discussed in the document. More particularly, the comment suggests that in cases when the document contains matters that are somehow unfinished, which means that administrators may need the information in the document in the future, then these documents are saved and put aside where they can easily be found again. An interesting question is how administrators know or how they decide that a matter is somehow unfinished. An additionally interesting notion in the comment above is the role of handwritten notes in the documents. Such notes cannot be found in the official files saved in the intranet, for example, and therefore the documents are only useful when they are kept in a form that includes the notes. The same applies to the attachments.

> *"The official minutes [of academic meetings] are stored in the registry...But, I also keep them here as a support for my own work. ... Sometimes I simply need to see how something has been formulated previously. The minutes do exist in an electronic format too in the intranet. But the attachments cannot be found there. Here [in paper format] I have the attachments too."* (Department Secretary, female)

Besides keeping the documents in order to better remember similar cases from the past, another important aspect of their retention in paper form is the question of connecting knowledge among different kinds of cases.

> *"If I have prepared something for a board meeting, as soon as I have finished [the proposal] and the board has accepted it, I throw those obscure papers away immediately. This is because when the matter has been processed to the end, you rarely need to go back to the details any more. Unless they are useful in some other [contexts] at your own work. Then [the information] just changes its form. The documents may, for instance, have a connection to the internal budget allocation, and therefore you need them in the negotiation processes."* (Head of Department, female)

The comment above emphasizes first and foremost the ability to see and make connections between matters. In general, previous research has pointed out that sharing knowledge across projects is extremely difficult exactly because it is hard to recognize that some existing knowledge might be useful in some other case or context (Newell et al., 2006). The critical aspect in the above comment by a head of department, however, is that connections are not made just between any type of matters, but instead between matters in the administrators' own work. This means that the ability to evaluate the usefulness of information in different contexts might require at least some kind of knowledge of the content of those matters that are to be connected.

As soon as administrative staff have made decisions on whether to keep and save certain documents or not, they face the next challenge of how to store the papers in practice. A head of department comments on the use of traditional binders for archiving purposes:

> *"If I put the matters into binders, I feel that they will stay there forever. Therefore, I have various nebulous piles. Well, some of them I could throw away, but I simply do not have the time to go through them. ... When you start looking at the papers, you [need to consider] whether the document is useful and where [you ought to] put it. ... And, typically if you throw something away, that piece of paper will be missed in a couple of weeks because it contains exactly the essential piece of information on a matter that is being clarified."*
> (Head of Department, female)

The extract above makes two particularly important points. First, it raises the question of the locus and type of the archive, with a key issue being the question of access. In principle, papers in binders are easily accessible. More importantly, however, the question seems to be whether papers in binders are sufficiently "attractive" in that format that administrators would feel like accessing them. Another related issue here is whether people can remember all the documents that they have in their binders. Simple and obscure piles on a table in the office might help people remember matters more easily. The other relevant aspect in the head of department's comment is that archiving papers takes time: sorting papers and filing them is a difficult task because it is not necessarily easy to decide whether some of them will be useful in the future or not. So far, the basic answer in knowledge management literature on the issue of archiving documents has been the use of information and communication technology systems, which, however, from the perspective of the retrieval of information, may not necessarily be the best solution (see Hutchinson and Quintas, 2008).

> *"There are documents related to the preparations of various projects. For instance, as we started to set up the Service Center, there were many papers and documents that were written. Many of those documents can already be disposed of, and I have already thrown away a lot since the Center func-*

tions quite well. In principle, I gained the materials electronically, but since [many documents] came from different persons and in different phases... at least I have not figured out what the most systematic way would be to archive [the documents] electronically. If I were to set up an [electronic] folder called "The Service Center" it should include many other folders. ... A search among many folders is really difficult. In these cases, it is easier to have all the documents concerning a particular matter in one pile. ... I remember the important documents according to their layouts." (Head of Department, female)

Ultimately, then, our study suggests that people in offices want to keep and save some of their paper documents in case these might prove useful in the future but that this is not an easy task. Keeping and archiving documents requires constant reflection on whether a task remains somehow unfinished or whether the information in the document is transferable and thus applicable in some other context. Questions related to access to and the form of documents are essential when administrators apply long-term memory devices in their work. Organizing large paper-based backup material can be time and space consuming. Table 1 summarizes the developments described above.

	Material	Image	Skill	Key citations
Short-term memoing practices	Post-it notes, print-outs, paper piles in specific places (locations) or with mne-monic quali-ties	"The order of things"	Fast scanning, multitasking, keeping within a schedule, prioritizing	"Out of sight, out of mind."
Mid-term verifying practices	Paper copies to be shared with others	"Avoiding errors"	Sharing, prov-ing, guarantee-ing, correcting	"I take a copy of the bill.... In case later some-body asks whether this bill has been here,... or if the bill gets lost, I know that I have had it and I have sent it forward."
Long-term backing-up prac-tices	Original doc-uments and document sets	"Complex and overlap-ping archiv-ing systems"	Archiving, completing, transferring,	"I do not keep them forever, but perhaps the previous year or two, because they might con-tain matters that pop up again."

**Table 1: A schematic presentation of the three kinds
of remembering practices**

Conclusion

This article focusing on back-office work took remembering practices as the unit of enquiry. Practice theory was used as a theoretical lens through which we approached remembering in an office context. Our main concerns were the constitutive elements, material artifacts, and to a lesser extent, the skills and images of remembering practices (Table 1). The elements of remembering practices integrate differently when we shift from individual memo practices to more collective verification and back-up practices. We only partially focused on the relations between practices and the ways practitioners were carriers of a practice (i.e. patterns in which practices recruit new people or are reproduced). Nicolini (2012: p. 219) offers a set of "sensitizing questions" that offer an "invitation to see" into the world of practices. An invitation to reiterate between two basic movements is essential: on one hand to *zoom in* on the accomplishments of practice and on the other to *zoom out* of their relationships in space and time. As Nicolini (2012: p. 221) emphasizes, "the study of practices always begins in the middle of action; in other words, what are people doing and saying?"[4]

Indeed, our case of back-office administrating offers an empirical example of applying the processes of zooming in and out. Empirically, the case contains the challenge of uncovering double invisibilities. On one hand, many of the paper-based documents were kept hidden by the administrators and, thus, were invisible to us. This was because the documents contained detailed, confidential information on matters of personnel and financial administration. Consequently, we had to first and foremost rely on talking and participant listening (see Forsey, 2010) in our endeavor to produce empirical data on the back-office administrative practices related to paper-based documents. On the other hand, many of the paper-based documents in the back office were so ordinary or mundane that they were invisible not only to us researchers but also to the administrators themselves. The act of photographing in connection with the conversational interviewing proved to be an essential means of seeing these paper-based documents, thereby offering possibilities to zoom in and out while operating in the field.

---

[4] We need several ontologically and methodologically coherent packages of theory and method in order to gain a better understanding of the various details and aspects of practices and their linkages with each other in the world we live in (Nicolini, 2012: 217).

However, our analysis extends the notion of zooming in and out to *zooming back and forth*, thus pondering empirical access not only to spatial but also to temporal dimensions of practice. The temporal dimension is essential when thinking about organizational remembering. Metaphorically, the difference is that of "photograph" (zoom in and out) and "movie" (zoom back and forth). The administrators in our case were constantly thinking about the questions of how long and where to keep particular paper-based documents in order to be able to access these if and when necessary.

A design aspect which deserves more emphasis is how digitalization and internet-related practices such as browsing, tagging, and digital recording change remembering practices. To address this issue, we must differentiate between *practice as performance* and the relatively stable and widely understood *practice as entity*. Here, we were mainly interested in performance, or the ways in which remembering takes place in office work.

To extend the notion of practice to zooming back and forth implies that the entity we call remembering is approached in terms of more encompassing historical developments and future potential. The perspective of zooming back and forth generates questions such as:

a. How and which kind of ideas, objects, and skills become historically integrated into practices of organizational remembering? (In which way do historical paths differ in back-up practices from memo practices?) What is required for digital document management, for instance, to be stabilized into an identifiable entity?

b. How do practices related to verifying practices, for instance, start to integrate with other practices, and how does the emerging "ecosystem" of remembering capture its practitioners? How does digitalization change the practice complexes situated in an office?

c. How do practices of remembering generate and reproduce their own constituent elements (e.g. trustworthiness)? Does digital document management generate and reproduce new types of skills or ideals?

The materiality of artifacts, spaces, and infrastructures through which humans act matter in short-term, mid-term, and long-term remembering in organizational life. To influence the design of either work or technology in organizations, the distinction between paper-based and digitally aided remembering practices should first be properly understood. This is very crucial if and when administrative practices are closely connected to the materiality of things, as our findings suggest. The affordances of digital document management are very different from those of paper document management (Sellen and Harper, 2003). The affordances of paper are related to its capacity to be portable and sharable and its quick access. The affordances of digital document management are quite different: the capability of storing a large amount of information in a small place, widespread access to information storage, remote access to information storage, the fast searchability of an information storage platform, and the capabilities for the flexible and systematic viewing and sorting of content and its dynamic updating or modification (Sellen and Harper, 2003).

Digitalization, specifically the internet, extends the limits of the office to a larger network that any office can belong to. The internet has changed human relationships, communication, and society. With regard to remembering practices, new practices such as browsing, searching, and tagging profoundly challenge institutions which are based on codifying and classifying knowledge, such as the office. Weinberger (2007) takes an example from library science, which was built around classifying books according to the strict and unchangeable Dewey Decimal Classifying System (developed in the 1870s by Melvil Dewey). In libraries worldwide, books are organized on the shelves according to this ancient system. Essentially, then, it is a law of physical geography that dictates the place of a book in a single library. This resembles our ethnographic findings in which the position (and size) of paper piles in an office could be seen as a kind of extended brain.

Future archives are likely to be less limited by physical geography and more limited by the limits and possibilities of cloud services, servers, and computers situated even outside of the office. This also means that the division of labor within an office will change, possibly increasing the responsibilities and power of data scientists integrating, analyzing, and separating data. The image of trustworthiness will gain more emphasis when the system becomes less transparent. The use of memos could remain quite the same, even though verification and back-up practices may change radically.

The skills needed in a digital office are certainly changing. Some workers are being replaced by algorithms, and compared to a paper-based back-up system, the risks and methods of protecting memory will be different. Perhaps memory failure in a digital office is less common, but the consequences are more dramatic because the back-up storage is closely connected to the whole system and the risk of a cascading crisis is larger.

The modular structure of archives is less subject to total collapse (due to the fact that back-ups in paper format are widely and independently distributed). In fact, it is possible that in the future digital archives will be backed up with paper archives, which are less influenced by hackers or military attacks (e.g. a magnetic pulse). Furthermore, continuous changes in software do not cause harmful effects to material archives. Overall, the understanding of historical developments is fundamental as we think about the future potential and risks.

References

Alvesson, M. (2009), "At-home Ethnography: Struggling with Closeness and Closure", in Ybema, S. Yanow, D., Wels, H., Kamsteeg, F. (eds) *Organizational Ethnography*. London: Sage, pp. 156-174.

Barley, S. R., Meyerson, D. E., Grodal, S. (2011), "E-mail as a Source and Symbol of Stress", *Organization Science*, 22 (4), pp. 887-906.

Bondarenko, O., Janssen, R. (2009), "Connecting Visual Cues to Semantic Judgments in the Context of the Office Environment", *Journal of the American Society for Information Science and Technology*, 60 (5), pp. 933-952.

Bondarenko, O., Janssen, R., Driessen, S. (2010), "Requirements for the Design of a Personal Document-Management System", *Journal of the American Society for Information Science and Technology*, 61 (3), pp. 468-482.

Casey, A. J., Olivera, F. (2011), "Reflections on Organizational Memory and Forgetting", *Journal of Management Inquiry*, 20 (3), pp. 305-310.

Cacciatori, E. (2008), "Memory Objects in Project Environments: Storing, Retrieving and Adapting Learning in Project-based Firms", *Research Policy*, 37 (9), pp. 1591-1601.

Collinson, J. (2006), "Just "Non-academics?": Research Administrators and Contested Occupational Identity", *Work, Employment and Society*, 20 (2), pp. 267-288.

Corradi, G., Gherardi, S., Verzelloni, L. (2010), "Through the Practice Lens: Where is the Bandwagon of Practice-Based Studies Heading?", *Management Learning*, 41 (3), pp. 265-283.

Eriksson, P., Kovalainen A. (2008), *Qualitative Methods in Business Research*. London: Sage.

Eriksson-Zetterquist, U., Lindberg, K., Styhre, A. (2009), "When the Good Times Are Over: Professionals Encountering New Technology", *Human Relations*, 62 (8), pp. 1145-1170.

Feldman, R. M., Feldman, S. P. (2006), "What Links the Chain: An Essay on Organizational Remembering as Practice", *Organization*, 13 (6), pp. 861-887.

Feldman, M. S., Orlikowski, W. J. (2011), "Theorizing Practice and Practicing Theory", *Organization Science*, 22 (5), pp. 1240-1253.

Forsey, M. G. (2010), "Ethnography as Participant Listening", *Ethnography*, 11 (4), pp. 558-572.

Gabriel, Y. (2008), "Against the Tyranny of PowerPoint: Technology-in-Use and Technology Abuse", *Organization Studies*, 29 (2), pp. 255-276.

Gherardi, S. (2000), "Practice-based Theorizing on Learning and Knowing in Organizations", *Organization*, 7 (2), pp. 211-223.

Harper, D. (2003), "Framing Photographic Ethnography: A Case Study", *Ethnography*, 4 (2), pp. 241-266.

Hutchinson, V., Quintas, P. (2008), "Do SMEs do Knowledge Management?: Or Simply Manage What They Know?" *International Small Business Journal*, 26 (2), pp. 131-154.

Jelinek, M. (1979), *Institutionalizing Innovation*. New York: Praeger.

Jett, Q. R., George, J. M. (2003), "Work Interrupted: A Closer Look at the Role of Interruptions in Organizational Life", *Academy of Management Review*, 28 (3), pp. 494-507.

Korczynski, M. (2004), "Back-Office Service Work: Bureaucracy Challenged?", *Work, Employment and Society*, 18 (1), pp. 97-114.

Kuhn, T. (2006), "A "Demented Work Ethic" and a "Lifestyle Firm": Discourse, Identity, and Workplace Time Commitments", *Organization Studies*, 27 (9), pp. 1339-1358.

Kyriakopoulos, K. (2011), "Improvisation in Product Innovation: The Contingent Role of Market Information Sources and Memory Types", *Organization Studies*, 32 (8), pp. 1051-1078.

Lansdale, M. W. (1991), "Remembering about Documents: Memory for Appearance, Formal, and Location", *Ergonomics*, 34 (8), pp. 1161-1178.

Macpherson, A., Clark, B. (2009), "Islands of Practice: Conflict and a Lack of "Community" in Situated Learning", *Management Learning*, 40 (5), pp. 551-568.

Newell, S., Bresnen, M., Edelman, L., Scarbrough, H., Swan, J. (2006), "Sharing Knowledge Across Projects: Limits to ICT-led Project Review Practices", *Management Learning*, 37 (2), pp. 167-185.

Nicolini, D. (2009), "Zooming In and Zooming Out: A Package of Method and Theory to Study Work Practices", In Ybema, S., Yanow, D., Wels,

H., Kamsteeg, F. (eds.) *Organizational Ethnography*. London: Sage, pp. 120-138.

Nicolini, D. (2012), *Practice Theory, Work and Organization. An Introduction*. Oxford: University Press.

Orlikowski, W. (2006), "Material Knowing: The Scaffolding of Human Knowledgeability", *European Journal of Information Systems*, 15 (5), pp. 460-466.

Orlikowski, W. (2007), "Sociomaterial Practices: Exploring Technology at Work", *Organization Studies*, 28 (9), pp. 1435-1448.

Orlikowski, W. J., Scott, S. V. (2008), "Sociomateriality: Challenging the Separation of Technology, Work and Organization", *The Academy of Management Annals*, 2 (1), pp. 433-474.

Østerlund, C. (2008), "Documents in Place: Demarcating Places for Collaboration in Healthcare Settings", *Computer Supported Cooperative Work*, 17 (2-3), pp. 195-225.

Pantzar, M., Shove, E. (2010), "Temporal Rhythms as Outcomes of Social Practices: A Speculative Discussion", *Ethnologia Europaea*, 40 (1), pp. 19-29.

Porter, C.O.L.H (2005) "Goal Orientation: Effects on Backing Up Behavior, Performance, Efficacy, and Commitment in Teams", *Journal of Applied Psychology*, 90 (4), pp. 811-818.

Porter, T., Córdoba, J. (2009), "Three Views of Systems Theories and Their Implications for Sustainability Education", *Journal of Management Education*, 33 (3), pp. 323-347.

Reckwitz, A. (2002), "The Status of the 'Material' in Theories of Culture: From 'Social Structure' to 'Artifacts'", *Journal for the Theory of Social Behavior*, 32 (2), pp. 195-217.

Rämö, H. (2002), "Doing Things Right and Doing the Right Things: Time and Timing in Projects", *International Journal of Project Management*, 20 (7), pp. 569-574.

Schatzki, T. (2001), "Introduction: Practice Theory", in Schatzki, T., Knorr-Cetina, K., von Savigny, E. (eds.) *The Practice Turn in Contemporary Theory*. London: Routledge.

Sellen, A., Harper, R.H.R. (2003), *The Myth of the Paperless Office*. Cambridge: The MIT Press.

Shove, E., Pantzar, M., Watson M. (2012), *Dynamics of Social Practices*. New York: Sage.

Small, K. (2008), "Relationships and Reciprocality in Student and Academic Services", *Journal of Higher Education Policy and Management* 30 (2), pp. 175-185.

Staudenmayer, N., Tyre, M., Perlow, L. (2002), "Time to Change: Temporal Shifts as Enablers of Organizational Change", *Organization Science*, 13 (5), pp. 583-597.

Stephens, K.K., Davis, J. (2009), "The Social Influences on Electronic Multitasking in Organizational Meetings", *Management Communication Quarterly*, 23 (1), pp. 63-83.

Szekeres, J. (2004), "The Invisible Workers", *Journal of Higher Education Policy and Management*, 26 (1), pp. 7-22.

Szekeres, J. (2006), "General Staff Experiences in the Corporate University", *Journal of Higher Education Policy and Management*, 28 (2), pp. 133-145.

Vogel, A., Kaghan, W. (2001), "Bureaucrats, Brokers, and the Entrepreneurial University", *Organization*, 8 (2), pp. 358-364.

Wagenaar, H. (2004), "'Knowing' the Rules: Administrative Work as Practice", *Public Administration Review*, 64 (6), pp. 643-655.

Wajcman, J., Rose, E. (2011), "Constant Connectivity: Rethinking Interruptions at Work", *Organization Studies*, 32 (7), pp. 941-961.

Walsh, J. P., Ungson, G. R. (1991), "Organizational Memory", *Academy of Management Review*, 16 (1), pp. 57-91.

Weinberger, D. (2007), *Everything is Miscellaneous: The Power of the New Digital Disorder*. New York: Times Books.

Yli-Kauhaluoma, S., Pantzar, M., Toyoki, S. (2013), "Mundane Materials at Work: Paper in Practice", in Shove, E., Spurling, N. (eds.) *Sustainable Practice: Social Theory and Climate Change*. London: Routledge, pp. 69-85.

STUDYING PRACTICES TO INFORM DESIGN:
ORGANIZATIONAL ISSUES AND LOCAL ARTIFACTS

Alessandra Talamo
Barbara Mellini
Stefano Ventura
Annamaria Recupero

Introduction: on the role of artifacts within professional communities

An artifact is an object designed and tailored on a specific human activity, which did not exist before that activity and cannot be understood apart from the human activity in which it is used and for which it has been, at least partially, conceived (Vygotsky, 1978).

The concept of artifact plays a key role in understanding how professional communities are developed and professionalism is exploited within them (Norman, 1988; Simon, 1996; Wartofsky, 1979). As described by Halverson and Zoltners (2001), artifacts refer to procedures and policies intended to shape or reform existing practices in the institutional context. Therefore, the authors assume that by shifting from the institutional context to the situational context, an extremely heterogeneous combination of artifacts that shape practice can be found.

To better understand the interplay between artifacts in the situational context, Halverson (2003) proposes to categorize artifacts based on their origin, assuming that three types of artifacts can be found into professional contexts: received artifacts, inherited artifacts and locally designed artifacts.

- *Received artifacts* are those adopted and implemented at a local level and are based on professional policies. They are received from identifiable external sources, such as state and regional authorities or professional development providers.

- *Inherited artifacts* constitute the given institutional aspects of the situation of practice. A key issue to define inherited artifacts is that they have shaped and institutionalized some working practices over time.

- *Locally designed artifacts* are designed by local actors to address emergent concerns in the organization. They can come to be recognized as inherited artifacts through turnover in leadership or staff composition

The network of received, inherited and locally designed artifacts embeds both the meaning of daily practice and the professional perspective it sustains. This network contributes to shape practices and routines that build up the role of professionals within their organizations. Halverson (2003) describes this network in terms of "system of practice" (Halverson, 2003), conceived as the representation of how the local network of artifacts facilitates the flow of professional practice. *"The system of practice moves beyond a mere context for practice to describe the dynamic interplay of artifacts and tasks that inform, constrain and constitute local practice"* (Halverson, 2003: p. 7).

To look at the distribution of different information across these three categories of artifacts is a crucial point to understand how professional practice is depicted within the working context according to or diverging from the institutionalized view of a profession and to explore and exploit the strong relation between professional identity and the design of tools that support work.

Within this chapter, the case of nurses and tools to support nursing is taken as example. The specificities of professional change in nursing will be presented together with two ethnographic studies on nursing carried out into two wards in Italy, thus enabling the understanding of the complex interplay between institutional change, professional practice, local artifacts and design (Mellini, 2014, Mellini and Talamo, 2014).

1. Professional change in nursing: a definition of professional identity neglecting professional practice

By the '80s, worldwide in the healthcare domain a push towards the raise the professional standing of nursing was devoted to the improvement of autonomy, power and respect for the occupation (Iley, 2004).

According to this, a series of legal reforms opened up to the introduction of senior-level clinical roles for nurses and nurse-led services (i.e. nursing clinics), where enhanced clinical responsibilities for nurses were foreseen, as much as a substitution for certain roles traditionally fulfilled by doctors (Robinson et al., 1997; 2006) had a spread. This gave rise to roles such as nurse specialist, nurse prescriber and nurse consultant (Currie et al., 2010).

The challenges of professional building for nurses were mostly related to the construction of a professional identity around which members of an occupation, as multifaceted as nursing is, might converge. It was mostly under the influence of North American theorists that the new occupational mandate for nurses was built up worldwide: it bases on a holistic bio-psycho-social model of nursing which places the quality of the relationship with patients at the heart of nursing's claims to specialist expertise. Thus, nursing is defined as a therapy in its own right and it is nurses' "therapeutic use of self" (Travelbee 1966, p. 18) that help people to get better.

Together with professional change, even professional tools have been institutionalized to support the formal practice of the new nursing. It is the case of the Nurse Record (NR), the tool that was introduced to sustain professional renewal and that has, therefore a special relevance in this complex scenario of change.

It is a cultural artifact, product of the new professionalism, built through the legal reforms on nursing to support some of the nurses' key attributes. In particular, it sustains nurses accomplishing a distinct practice based on a separate discipline as with respect to medicine. Making a step forward, it also supports that the practice of nursing has to be documented in autonomy, through dedicated tools (separated from medical tools) that make nurses' work visible and accountable.

In this light, the NR should be considered not as "just a tool", but as the materialization of some institutional instances on nursing, playing a key role in the process of nurse professional building. In fact, the NR is considered worldwide the most important tools for nursing: it is an indispensable tool to systematize information on nursing in a specific theoretical perspective.

It brings into the wards a theoretical model of nursing to be adopted and to be followed in order to accomplish patient care in a consistent way that is shared among the professional community, being based on the application of a structural and functional orientation to health problems. Although there are different templates, we can state that NR is developed around the nursing plan. The nursing plan can be defined as a nursing strategy through which the nurse identifies and threat patient's problems, thus taking in charge the patient and his health needs. Together with a new professional mandate focused on patients, a patient-centered tool to address the instances raised by change, is released.

This model, that looks at nursing as a professionalism which relies mainly on the professional-client intimate relationship (Dingwall et al., 1998) has not been received uncritically. However, the idea of nursing as a profession founded on an intimate relationship with the patient (see, for example, Newman 1986; Parse 1981; Watson 1979) remains the dominant professional ideal, as well as the "to care" process is considered at the core of nurse profession (Currie et al. 2010; Allen, 1997).

To start deepening the issue of what does it mean to do nursing in practice, it is worth pointing out that (although disregarded in the definition of the new nursing) the context in which nurses work, as well as the intertwining of nurses' work with that of other professionals they interact with, play *de facto* a crucial role in defining nurses' role into the wards (and therefore nurses' professional identity). In fact, although relevant changes invested the practice of nursing after the previously mentioned reforms, to look at nurses as professionals engaged exclusively in dual therapeutic relationships with their patients does not provide an accurate picture of the multifaceted roles experienced by nurses into the complex healthcare system scenarios.

Given the institutional moment that is investing the nurse profession, the new structure given to work by the introduction of the NR and the reframe of nurses professional identity, we started an ethnographic research in order to understand how institutional change was depicted in organizational contexts and translated into practice thanks to new artifacts designed to support it.

The research transformed over time into an information for design study, translating findings into insights on nursing in practice that could be used by those who want to develop technological tools to support the work of these professionals. The research grounds on cultural psychology basic assumptions as with respect to organizations and groups at work, and it relies on ethnographic methods and perspectives on knowing (Bruni, Gherardi, 2007). It aims at reconstructing technology as a social practice (Suchman et al., 1999), investigating artifacts when they are in use and maintaining the attention focused on how they relate with situated work and professional identity.

2. Bundles of practices in nursing: an overview of ethnographic studies

Despite most of contemporary organizational literature on nursing is now centerd on professional roles and identities in relation to the new professional building in several National Healthcare Systems, there is a fragmented body of literature based on ethnographic studies of nurses' practices. A key reference to frame the discussion on nurses' concrete practices is a review of ethnographic studies on nurses' work made by Davina Allen (2004).

The review identifies eight interrelated bundles of activity that shed light on the complexity of nurses' role within the hospitals. It stresses the fact that although some *"dirty work"* (Hughes, 1984) is normal when one passes from the institutional formulation of a professional mandate to the professional license experienced in the workplace division of labor, this tension between public and workplace jurisdiction is triggered for what concerns nurses practices. In fact, Allen (2004: 273) describes "the work that nurses undertake by virtue of their structural location within contemporary healthcare systems" as "at odds with the profession's culture and ideals, focused as it is on the quality of relationships with individual patients".

In line with this statement, the bundles of activity traceable in this literature review are almost all focused on nurses' pivotal position in healthcare systems that "naturally" shapes the role of nurses in the form of an organizer and mediator for the organization.

The first important nurses function that literature reveals is that they perform *management and mediation of the multiple agenda and discourses* which shape contemporary healthcare systems.

The second bundle of activities is the management of patients' movements inside and outside the hospital ward/structure in order to keep the service in good "shape".

The third one is that *"*one of the most efficient ways of processing people and managing patient flows is through the use of routines and standard operating procedures. Standards, routines and timetables provide staff and patients with templates for action and a structure of what is to be expected within certain temporal boundaries" (Allen, 2004: 274). Standardization and routines are in fact an ever-present feature of contemporary healthcare systems and nurses work in practice involves *articulating individual patient needs with hospital routines.*

The fourth bundle of activity deals with *organizing the work of others, especially doctors,* in order to ensure continuity of care and to: a) make doctors' work organization fit with nursing activity, or b) to re-arrange their own agenda when some pieces of doctors' work are missing, not to negatively affect patients (Allen 1997). The fifth bundle of activities refers to nurses *managing information flows,* passing on information, making relevant telephone calls and assessing, interpreting and communicating relevant information to doctors so that they can make a diagnosis.

Moreover, nurses spend a lot of their time in the *record-keeping* of clinical documentation. This work on compiling official documentation emerges as a crucial one in defining nurses' identity since the NR makes certain elements of nursing visible and keeps others marginalized and the fact of having this part of work written down contributes in fixing just a part of nurses work experiences.

Another group of activities that is treated in the review is that nurses have also a function in *prioritizing care and rationing resources.* Two studies also point out that often nurses are requested of *mediating occupational boundaries,* by plugging gaps in service provision if no other services is available.

The framework pictured by Allen offers quite a dissonant representation of nursing activities as with respect to the professional mandate, and at least in part, it claims for a new vision of nursing that starts from the ostensive aspect of local routine practices (Rerup and Feldman, 2011). Moreover, the mismatch between professional mandate and the wider range of actual practices and professional license provokes a sort of uncertainty in nurses when they are requested to answer the question of what they do in practice or of what their job is about.

This bundles of practice will be kept into consideration and used as reference for analyzing research data in the following paragraphs to better understand and conceptualize the frequent shifts in positioning that are required to nurses at work.

3. Nurses routines in practice: a brief description of the two hospitals where the research took place

The data presented in the following sections are part of a data corpus composed of field notes and pictures collected between February 2011 and July 2013 within 2 emergency departments and a plastic surgery ward of two Italian hospitals during 20 sessions of observation and shadowing of about 4 hours each.

3.1. Refusing the nurse record: exploring professional change by observing the introduction of a tool

The research started with the objective of supporting the introduction of the electronic nurse record in a Complex Operative Unit (COU) of a hospital in Italy considered a center of excellence for what concerns the treatment of burns and complex injuries. It is composed of two Departments (an Intensive Care Unit and a Plastic Surgery ward for a total of 28 beds), plus a Day Hospital, an Emergency Room for first aid and two operating rooms. The wards host adults and children, admitting them both in a matter of urgency and through scheduled hospitalizations.

The context of the research was selected because of the supposed incoming introduction of the electronic Nurse Record (NR) in a Unit that did not even use the paper version of the NR. The research started in a moment perceived as organizationally crucial by the hospital management because of the possible implications of the introduction of the Electronic NR on nurses work. The research aimed at understanding how the introduction of this tool could change actual nurses practices and to support its re-design in case needed.

While the observations took place, it became clear the relevance nurses gave to organizational tasks, where the lack of official supporting tools and the effort needed was perceived as frustrating and dysfunctional. Due to the fact that the introduction of the NR wouldn't have supported this kind of tasks (being a documentation tool), they decided to make a strong opposition to its introduction and to push the research in the direction of getting insights to report to designers from the local informal artifacts they used to pursue their organizational tasks. The priority given to organizational activities as with respect to the documentation of nursing emerged at the very first stage of the research as a crucial organizational model of this COU for what concerns doing nursing.

After six months of fieldwork, once the key bundles of nurses' practice were identified, a focus was put on organizational instances and on how they were accomplished through informal tools locally developed by nurses. New research questions specifically focused on the use of informal tools arose:

- Which types of information are embedded into informal tools?

- Which tasks they support?

- Which logics they convey/embed?

- How their study can be beneficial to the development of IT tools for nurses?

- Together with these questions, others that couldn't be fulfilled within this context showed up:

- Does the electronic NR already support these organizational practices in the contexts where it is in place?

- Which is the faith of informal tools once the electronic NR is introduced?

At this point, in order to have a clearer picture of the kind of information the NR in its electronic form could support, and of the type of organizational shift it could bring, the research was extended to another context.

3.2. Adopting the nurse record: deepening the relation between bundles of practice and artifacts in use

The second research context was another Complex Operative Unit of a different Italian hospital and it was chosen since it had the electronic NR in use from five years. This COU is composed by an Intensive Care Unit (12 beds) and a Post-Surgical Intensive Care Unit (3 beds).

Patients that occupy the Intensive Care Unit beds are critical patients (often in a not vigil status) that generally remain hospitalized for long periods of time. On the contrary, Post-Surgical patients are admitted in the ward in the morning hours between Monday and Friday, after a surgical intervention that implied a general anaesthesia, and they are released after a few hours (as soon as the effects of anaesthesia are gone) to be moved to their respective wards depending on the type of surgery they had. Then, although the average number of beds is 15, there is a huge difference between the work needed for post-surgical and intensive patients.

The total number of nurses in the ward is 21 (17 shifters, 3 non shifters) plus the nurse in charge. Also in this context, as well as in the previous one, together with the officially based staff, there are some professionals that can be considered as stable collaborators to the daily routine of the wards. The working team is described by the nurse in charge as composed of the doctor, the nurse, the physiotherapist, the psychologist, the nutritionist.

The objective of this second part of the research was to have the chance to observe if and how the introduction of the electronic NR could have an impact not only on nursing assistive tasks, but also on coordination and management practices. Grounding on the findings from the previous context, the focus of these observations was the relation between tools in use and bundles of practices, with a special attention to the implications coming from the NR on organizational tasks performed through the use of informal artifacts.

4. Practice-based observation of nursing: organizing data for recognizing the baseline of nurses' practices

In this section, a brief overview on how practices are carried out in the observed contexts is presented.

Based on bundles of activity already identified in literature (Allen, 2004; Currie et al, 2010) and on nurse professional mandate statements (DM 739/94), we can identify three macro areas of work where nurses undertake their professional action: *information breaking, planning and coordination; implementation of nursing* and *documentation keeping.*

Below, these three macro-areas of work are at first described as a whole, and then broken down into the activities observed in the two contexts. Major issues will be discussed across the two contexts in order to highlight common traits and relevant differences that contribute to give meaning to professional activities at a local level.

- Information breaking, coordination and Planning

  The activities included in this macro-area are related with anticipation, coordination and management. They comprise the tasks necessary to make the ward as a whole work and they are managed entirely by nurses. They include, for example, the activities of planning drugs orders or request blood exams and expert consultancies; but they are also related with the organization of space and time routines (i.e. organize the fast for the patients that have to make blood tests the day after, or sort the drugs in the closet in a way that allows other nurses to find them), as well as with the generation of alerts referred to important issues arose during the shift (i.e. to point out the entrance of a new patient in the ward, etc.).

Part of this activity is performed through the use of official documentation. Specific official forms or IT dedicated systems are set for each typology of request needed to ask for a service or for an asset (i.e. one dedicated form for asking for cardiologic consultancy, one for radiologic consultancy, an IT system for blood requests, an IT system for medical radiological reports, etc., for a total of about 15 forms and 2 IT systems).

Another part of this work is done through the creation of informal artifacts for the accomplishment of articulation practices (Gerson and Star, 1986).

A peculiarity of this bundle of activity is that it has a strong organizational focus, where the ward as a whole has to be treated as the unit of analysis in order to provide patients with the best healthcare service. Within the ward, planning and prioritization of activities should be made in order to make patients' needs fit with the agendas of several professionals.

Moreover, the ward has to interact with external structures that have their own agendas and a specific structure of work that nurses need to know and to artfully manage if they want their daily duties accomplished at the end of the turn.

• Implementation of nursing

This area refers to the patient-centerd activities of implementing nursing and relates with the "caring" process in strict sense, that is to assist the patient and to provide to his/her needs. This activity is usually split in two parts: on one side, there is the technical part of work, related to nursing specialized procedures (i.e. parameters' monitoring, drugs administration, catheter positioning, bronchoscopy, tracheostomy); on the other side there is the holistic care of the patient, that includes mostly hygienic and nutritional care and deals with the mission of "taking care" (in opposition to that of "curing").

- Documentation (Record Keeping)

In this area activities such as data entry and information recording are included. This part of work can be resumed essentially in record keeping. Both from literature and fieldwork, it emerges that nurses spend a lot of effort in documenting practices. To fill the NR (when it is in use) or the medical record (task that is often performed also on behalf of the doctor) is considered by nurses as a work per se. Moreover, this bundle of activity deals with the representation of work offered inside and outside the wards, with all the implications it has in terms of professional identity. At least partially, this is also the reason why nurse and medical records have been the most studied and digitalized artifacts in hospitals. In fact, apart from the records, it is rare for Italian hospitals to have an integrated system to collect the entire patient documentation. This leads to another part of work that is to collect the different paper or electronic/printed forms from different systems (such as x-ray reports, results of blood tests, etc.) and to include them in the clinical record, together with the day-to-day updates (i.e. clinical parameters' report, etc) as a crucial part of documentation. This is a patient-centerd work, in the sense that documentation is filled and assembled individually for each patient, aiming at tracing his/her clinical history.

In the following paragraphs, the cases of the two observed units will be presented and local practices will be discussed on the basis of these three macro-categories. The analysis will offer quite a wide perspective on nurses practices, because the organization of work is structured in very different ways between the two contexts as with respect to the three identified bundles of activity.

4.1. Refusing the nurse record: the intertwining between two different visions

As previously described, the Complex Operative Unit that was investigated at first did not use the NR for documenting nursing. In fact, despite the pressures of the management, all the attempts of introducing the tool failed because it was not perceived as a priority by the staff.

It is relevant to say that, this state of the art on the introduction of the NR is quite common in a large part of Italian hospitals, where the effective work of nurses' professionals is often not yet aligned with the institutional/legal path.

A specificity of this context is that nurses use to work with a strong focus on organizational issues, privileging the opportunity to be always aware of the actual workload of the ward as a whole. This means that nurses spend a lot of effort in their daily activities to get the pulse of the situation of the ward, focusing on different agendas to organize the working day in the making. This is particularly true for the nurses that work out of the shift system and that therefore have a much structured role in organizing agendas.

An overview of nurses' activity within their working day will help in understanding the ways in which work is distributed here within the three macro-areas identified above. The picture below depicts a typical working turn of nurses, and shows the main differences in the tasks accomplished between shifters and non-shifters[5].

We chose to use the morning turn as example for several reasons since it is the turn when the activity in the ward is more intensive both from an organizational and from an implementation point of view and also because it is the turn in which the nurse in charge works and therefore some managerial activities use to take place. Practices are divided into front stage and back stage activities as with respect to nursing care, carried out within the dual relationship with the patient and conceived at the heart of nurses' professional agenda by the statements of the new professional mandate. The time flow is streamlined represented by the horizontal line at the top of the table. It is relevant to say that, although some activities are rather fixed in time (i.e. therapy administration, doctor visits or board requests), in this ward activities are usually temporally positioned during the turn in a contingent way, based on a daily prioritization of emergent needs.

Activities that typically belong to shifter nurses are grey bordered, while activities that are exclusive of non-shifter nurses are black bordered.

---

[5] According to the ILO (1990), working in shifts is "a method of organization of working time in which workers succeed one another at the workplace so that the establishment can operate longer than the hours of work of individual workers" at different daily and night hours. Under a rotating three shift system, workers might be assigned to work shifts that vary regularly over time; these are called "rotating shifts" because they rotate around the clock (e.g. from a shift in the morning, to one in the afternoon, to one at night). Nurses in the ward use to work in rotating shifts. Some nurses, usually due to disease or personal reasons are taken out of the rotating shifts and have fixed working hours.

In fact, although there is a frequent overlap between bundles of activities and type of focus (organizational activities are often ward focused, while implementation and documentation practices are patient focused), some coordination or documentation activities can be accomplished with a different focus depending on the objective for which they are carried out. In example, discussing with colleagues at the beginning of the working turn may be devoted to know more information on the patient in order to assist him/her at best, but also to evaluate the daily workload of the ward and to coordinate with the team.

As it emerges from figure 1, non-shifter nurses are more involved in coordination and documentation tasks than the shifter, but they also practice nursing in strict sense. Their work is somehow that of the "writers" of the ward. Given the very heterogeneous nature of activities and their implications in coordination and documentation processes, a continuous translation of information in order to make them fit with the objectives to be reached is required. Shifts of focus between the ward and the patient are continuously needed and this is quite well highlighted in the figure by the colorshade of the activities: the compilation of the medical record has a patient centerd focus, but the scheduling of medications is centerd on the ward. Some specific activities, as the therapy organization, need a double focus to be accomplished, since their focus shifts from the ward to the patient along the therapy process.

Shifter nurses are more involved in patient care. As it emerges from the activities that are exclusive of shifters, they are the ones that usually perform hygienic care and the most part of medications, patients' feeding and parameters check. This is because these activities usually are temporally positioned in the hours when non-shifter nurses have to deal with orders, consultancies and requests.

It is also relevant to point out that shifters participate to the organization of activities together with non-shifters. They are always able to know "what's going on" in the ward and to artfully manage formal and informal documentation to get information on the work to be accomplished and to be updated on activities that have been already done.

From the UOC without the NR:
Outline of activities carried out in a working turn

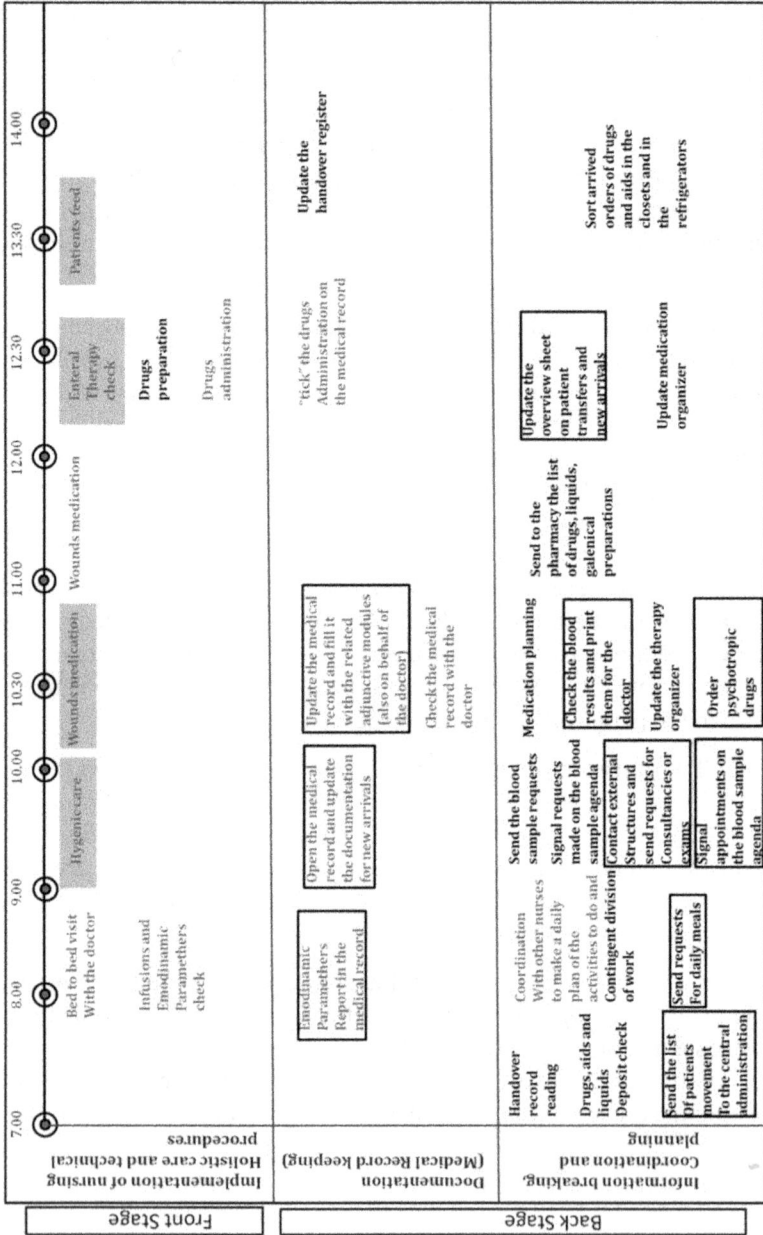

	7.00	8.00	9.00	10.00	10.30	11.00	12.00	12.30	13.30	14.00

Implementation of nursing procedures / Holistic care and technical (Front Stage)

Bed to bed visit With the doctor

Infusions and Emodinamic Parameters check

Hygienic care

Wounds medication

Wounds medication

Patients feed

Enteral Therapy check

Documentation (Medical Record keeping) (Back Stage)

Emodinamic Paramethers Report in the medical record

Open the medical record and update the documentation for new arrivals

Update the medical record and fill it with the related adjunctive modules (also on behalf of the doctor)

Check the medical record with the doctor

"tick" the drugs Administration on the medical record

Update the handover register

Drugs preparation

Drugs administration

Information breaking, Coordination and planning (Back Stage)

Handover record reading

Drugs, aids and liquids Deposit check

Send the list Of patients movement To the central administration

Coordination With other nurses to make a daily plan of the activities to do and Contingent division of work

Send requests For daily meals

Send the blood sample requests

Signal requests made on the blood sample agenda

Contact external Structures and send requests for Consultancies or exams

Signal appointments on the blood sample agenda

Medication planning

Send to the pharmacy the list of drugs, liquids, galenical preparations

Check the blood results and print them for the doctor

Update the therapy organizer

Order psychotropic drugs

Update the overview sheet on patient transfers and new arrivals

Update medication organizer

Sort arrived orders of drugs and aids in the closets and in the refrigerators

□ Activities that are exclusive of non shifter nurses　　▨ Activities focused on the single patient

▨ Activities that are exclusive of shifter nurses　　■ Activities that involve a focus on the ward as a whole

Figure 1: Outline of a working turn in the COU without the NR

4.2. Adopting the nurse record: Not a dual vision anymore, but two separated visions

The history and nature of the NR define it as an object that has a strong relation with nurse working routines in the wards. In fact, since it reconstructs nursing around the nursing plan centerd on patient's needs, it also contributes in the re-organization of some traditional inter and intra professional balances. An example of this is given by the second research context, where shifter nurses' work is strongly focused on a patient based, NR guided agenda, while non-shifters are fully dedicated to the organization of work.

In this COU nursing is strongly "standardized" and performed in quite a different way as with respect to the previous context. Each shifter has 2 dedicated patients out of the 12 patients of the ward. Together with nurses that are responsible of the same patients during other turns, they compose a mini-équipe that guarantees to the patient a continuous and stable nursing based on the in-depth knowledge that the team has of its patient's problems and needs. The working model adopted here is strongly centerd on the patient and on the satisfaction of his health needs, as well as it is stated in the professional mandate.

Shifters daily practices, result exclusively focused on the patient, both in the field of implementation and in that of documentation and coordination. In fact, the few coordination activities carried out are always centerd on the patient and concentrate in the first and last hours of work. For this reason, shifter nurses in this context don't have a double perspective on the patient and on the ward.

Differently from what emerged from the first context, here implementation and documentation of nursing go always together and are accomplished by shifters: this is because, since the NR is an official tool and its compilation is mandatory, the documentation of actions undertaken on the patient must be made by the same professional who implemented it and that has the legal duty to report the work done.

In addition, here the organization "per time flow" is strictly followed and the scheduled activities are usually accomplished within the given temporal bonds. Partially, it is the structure of the NR itself that imposes a very strict agenda on nursing. In fact, as soon as the turn starts, the nursing daily plan has to be established together with the doctor, and then nurses will proceed per nursing objectives and will re-evaluate patient's health status each 30 minutes until the end of their turn.

The nurse in charge also explained how the NR, once introduced into her ward, contributed to support nursing based on the new professional vision it embodies. This is possible because it sustains specific logics of action, gives priorities and promotes a model of nursing based on the construction of a one-to-one relationship between nurse in turn and patient. This way of conceiving nursing completely reshapes nurses' profession and sustains new paradigms of collaboration with the rest of the multi-professional team.

By the way, although here it is much less visible than in the previous COU, organizational work is not an activity that can just be skipped or avoided. Here it is not distributed anymore within the whole staff, yet it is performed by the nurse in charge and by nurses out of shift. It has the effect of producing a split in two in nurses profession based on the type of activity undertaken, as the nurse in charge describes in the following excerpt:

> "We organized the work this way: shift nurses work on patients and compile the NR. They don't have to do anything else. Here they are a little bit spoiled, because my colleagues non shifters and I, we deal with everything else. Want an example? If they don't have the uniform, they don't have to call the cloakroom; I have to".

The nurse in charge defines, mildly argumentative, how the dual vision requested to nurses to be operative, that was already identified in the previous context, here results in two separated roles of nurses. It seems that we have two different professions as with respect to the tasks accomplished within the Unit. As well as in the first context organizational work was perceived as highly valuable, here, on the contrary, it is conceived as "ancillary" to the work of shifters. The dual vision on work tasks resists only in the work of non-shifters, who try to "give the line" to shifters by getting information on patients from shifter nurses and by helping them with complex procedures. The added value of conciliating holistic care with organizational tasks is lost, and what remains in the representation given by the nurse in charge is a sort of "maternage" by the non-shifters to the shifters (labelled as "spoiled").

As it emerges from the comparison of Figure 2 and Figure 3, shifter workers are responsible for nursing and for holistic care: they always work within the dual relationship with the patient, in coordination with the mini-team devoted to nursing for the same patients. Non-shifter workers are those that do "the rest", that is organization, management and information breaking. Their focus is almost always centerd on making the ward work as a whole, and their work on the patient is occasional and limited to effective contingent needs.

However, it is relevant to point out that differently from shifters, non-shifters maintain a double vision on the patient and on the ward thanks to some key tasks (bordered in Figure 2) that are centerd on the patient and that allow coordination. These activities are those where non-shifters interact with shifters, thus gaining a sort of oversight on the tasks to be accomplished. Thus remaining the only ones maintaining the double focus needed to interpret and communicate ward's needs and to give a list of priorities in action to their colleagues. Therefore non-shifters are described as the ones who make things work, and their job is pictured as follows by the nurse in charge:

> "My colleagues out of the shifts and I we are in charge of making nursing smooth. Because here we are in an emergency department and we have to organize things in a way that allows our colleagues, even in emergency, especially in emergency, to have everything well prepared" (Fieldnote, May, 16th 2013)

The work of non-shifters is to ensure the continuity of work, to coordinate activities, to maintain things in order, to anticipate or deal with malfunctions, to interact with external structures. It is about, with the words of the nurse in charge "making nursing smooth".

The way nurses' activities are carried out in this COU helps in having a better understanding of the relation between nurses roles in the wards and professional mandate. If it is true that at an institutional layer the core activity of nurses is nursing, not only we can see that nursing is just one (although probably the most relevant) of the activities performed by nurses at work, but also that some nurses (those that are non-shifters) don't use to deal with nursing at all.

This complete separation between nursing and the activities needed to make nursing work, establishes here, *de facto*, two separated sets of activity (as well as roles and licenses) within the same profession.

From the UOC with the NR in place

Outline of activities carried out by shifter nurses in a working turn

	7.00	7.15	8.00	9.00	10.00	10.30	11.00	12.00	12.30	13.30	14.00

Front Stage

Holistic care and technical procedures
Implementation of nursing

- Infusions and Emodinamic Parameters check
- Active participation to the visit with the doctor
- Hygenic care Patient 1
- Hygenic care Patient 2
- Emodinamic Paramethers check
- Gas check
- Enteral Therapy check
- Drugs preparation
- Preparation And change of Aerator
- Preparation And change of CVC
- Preparation And change of Perfusional lines
- Surgical wounds medication
- Therapy administration
- Emodinamic Paramethers check
- Patient arrangement And preparation For relatives arrival

Back Stage

Documentation (Nurse Record keeping)

- Writing down Of the emodinamic paramethers
- Writing down Of the emodinamic paramethers
- Therapy Administration "Thick"
- Writing down Of the emodinamic parameters
- Writing down of the handovers: Now documentation of all Relevant clinical notes

Information breaking, Coordination and planning

- Briefing e Handovers with the Nurse of the Previous turn At patient beds
- Record reading
- Visit with the doctor And daily planning
- Coordination Of the area Cleaning Without leave The patients
- Welcome of Patient's relatives And discussion On eventual requests
- Briefing and Handover with the Nurse of the Subsequent turn at Patient bed

◼ Activities focused on the single patient *

■□ Activities that involve a focus on the ward as a whole **

□ Activities that imply a double perspective and allow coordination **

*All the activities focused on the single patient are accomplished by each nurse on his/her two patients

** Shifter nurses are not involved in activities that have have the ward as focus and therefore they don't even have a double perspective

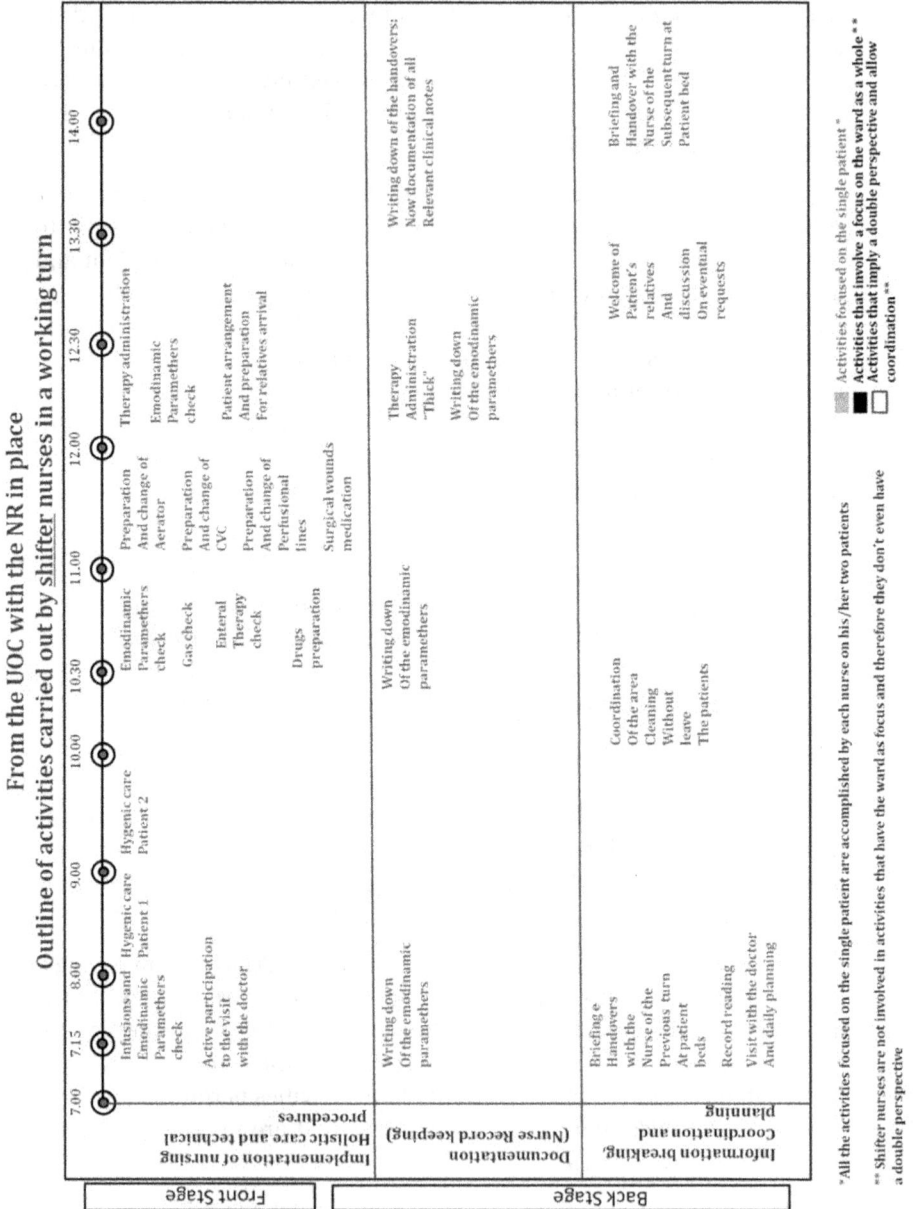

Figure 2: Outline of a shifter nurse working turn in the COU with the NR

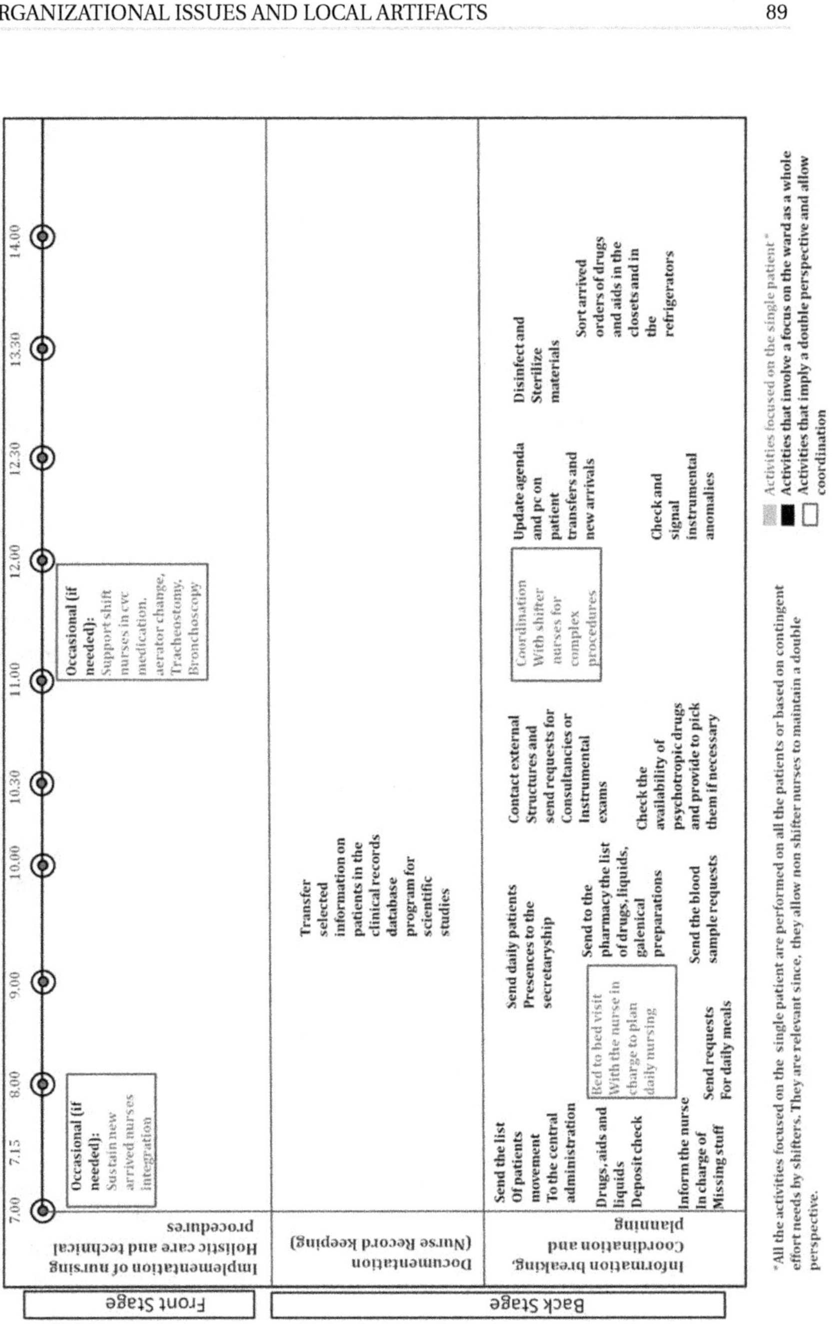

From the UOC with the NR in place

Outline of activities carried out by non shifter nurses in a working turn

Figure 3: Outline of a non-shifter nurse working turn in the COU with the NR

4.3. A comparison between the two contexts: what do nurses do at work?

To frame the discussion on the peculiarities of nurses' bundles of activities within and between the two COUs will provide some key information, relevant for the understanding of nurses' daily work practices, and of their relation with professional identity and professional tools.

- Information breaking, coordination and Planning

  The two COUs are strongly different in the way they plan activities and distribute the workload between professionals. Planning is mostly situated and contingent in the COU without the NR, where, day by day, nurses are assigned to tasks mainly based on ward needs (although the role of shifters and non shifters has an impact on the daily division of tasks). Opposite, there is a firmly structured organization of both practices and roles in the COU with the NR, where, based on their being shifter or non shifter, the given agenda of nurses completely changes.

- Implementation of nursing

  The two COUs have two very different models of accomplishing nursing in strict sense. The COU without the NR conceives nursing starting from the ward necessities and then stresses the need for an always situated distribution of the work on patients (it means that if needed a nurse can work one day with a patient and the day after with another one) based on two main issues:

  i.   Competence and attitude of nurse in accomplishing specific procedures: the nurse that is more competent/fast/efficient in doing a procedure is the one that usually does it the most. Some professionals prefer to accomplish a task instead of another and, when possible, nurses find a way to pander to each other;

  ii. Equally distributed work based on the daily ward workload: this division is made by professionals through informal coordination tools. Since all nurses have a general vision on the ward, they confront themselves on the daily workload and divide the tasks in autonomy, trying to keep the work equally distributed across the days and between professionals. This means that a patient may be nursed by two or three professionals each day based on his needs, on ward needs and on professionals competence.

In the COU with the NR nursing is more a one to one activity, where the nurse always works on the same two patients, generally for their whole hospitalization. The nurse is responsible for all the activities on his patients and for none on the others. Obviously this changes if an emergency occurs, since all the staff is called to help.

- Documentation (Record Keeping)

  The two COUs have a very different documentation in use. Whilst in the COU without the NR the official documentation on the patient is essentially composed of the Clinical Record and of adjunctive paper forms (plus 2 electronic systems for blood samples and radiographies), in the second context they have an electronic NR which is integrated with the medical record (that also offer the possibility to embed blood sample results and consultancies). Moreover, in the COU without the NR, the compilation of the medical record is a task usually performed by nurses that are also responsible of organizational activities (usually accomplished by non shifters through the use of written forms), since they have a clear vision on the whole ward and may help the doctor in accomplishing his documental work. In the COU with the NR the compilation of the NR is a duty of the nurse that delivers the professional service on the patient, since it is the documentation of an activity of which the nurse is responsible in first person.

From this overview it emerges that once entered in the wards one can find the bundles of activity presented in the baseline more or less intertwined depending on the organization given by professionals to their daily work. Moreover, the routines that they institute in separated contexts are much different both in their ostensive and performative nature. If it could be said that they compose in a certain way the range of competences and the field of action of these professionals, one should also consider that the different shapes of nurses' work are never explicit in the professional mandate, nor in the official documentation. This means that there is an adjunctive invisible workload for nurses in the wards (that of organization of practices) that somehow has to be accomplished.

This need to work on very divergent and additional tasks lead professionals working in the same context to produce a contingent internal division of work. Starting from being a very situated and negotiated order, it becomes over time an explicit professional positioning as with respect to the mandate.

It happens then that each nurse, based on the work he accomplishes in the wards (and on the activities he perceives as more relevant) has a different vision on what nursing is about, thus producing, as it emerges from the literature in the field, very dissonant representations on nursing and re-shaping through routines the schema proposed by the institutional professional renewal.

5. The artful process of making the flow work: backstage professionals and invisible tools

A key issue that emerges from the analysis of nurses' work is that planning and coordination are essential in order to make work efficient.

When the nurse in charge of the COU with the NR says that their work is "making nursing smooth", she is pointing out a key focus of nurses on *workaround*. In the COU without the NR this workaround is perceived as the primary work by non-shifter nurses, while in the COU with the NR it is considered as "dirty work" (Hughes, 1984). This is due to the fact that different practices are interpreted at a local level based on the organizational routines and the organizational models within which they are accomplished (Rerup and Feldman, 2011), that drastically change the perception professionals have of their work.

What remains similar in the two COUs is that planning and coordination work is unofficial in both contexts. In the COU with the NR this practice is stressed at the limits and appears even more problematic, since here some nurses don't do nursing at all in favour of planning and coordination work. This way not only an invisible professionalism is instituted together with backstage professionals entitled to accomplish invisible work. They are the only ones that are able to maintain a double perspective on nursing activities, giving other nurses the agenda to accomplish work when unforeseen events occur.

The point is that "to make nursing smooth" means to work at the border between the ward and the central administration of the hospital, dealing with patients and costs, making organizational routines fit with the work on the single patient and vice versa. Still using as reference the words of the nurse in charge of the COU with the NR, this work is about "organizing things in a way that allows our colleagues, even in emergency - especially in emergency – to have everything well prepared".

This *articulation work* (Starr, 1999) is based on increasing the level of awareness on some processes that are considered critical. This is done through the situated planning of contingent organizational mechanisms (Heath and Luff, 1992; Bardram, 1998; Button, Sharrock, 1997) and emerges as a key competence of some nurse professionals in both the wards. This task is accomplished through the organization of agendas, spaces and tasks and it is built up by structuring work based on a dual perspective: on one hand by focusing on patient's care and on his needs by personalizing the cure process; on the other hand by paying a specific organizational attention to ward's functioning, standardizing procedures and protocols and keeping in mind the bonds of the hospital structure.

This dual perspective is distributed differently among professionals in the two COUs, but it is crucial for both of them, since it relates with the infrastructural functioning of hospitals. Moreover, this dual perspective is not embedded in the official documentation in use, as it is pointed out by the nurse in charge of the second context:

> *"Here everything goes its own way. The laboratory has its own system. The radiologists have their own system. The pharmacy has its own system, but then we still have four different types of paper forms depending on the drug used for special medications".*

Together with these systems and modules, there are also those for the canteen, the movement of patients, the medical aids, the replacements of nurses absent, the organization of procedures and the sterilization of materials.

Moreover, there are the agendas of each structure that a nurse needs to know to plan and coordinate efficiently patient care.

> *"You have to take appointments, ask for consultancies...it is a huge work to keep it together...We also have a computerized medical records archive for longitudinal studies. And this is another system which is different from the integrated record and it's even other work because I have to rewrite data on the patient...fortunately just a part of that data!"*

On one hand, it is highlighted a portion of work that deals with compiling documentation, that is not related with the work required by the NR; on the other hand, it is showed that this is a transactional area potentially "at risk", because it implies the reconciliation of rhythms, routines and different objectives, tasks that are not supported by official documentation

Now, if we go back to the concept of "system of practice" and we look at how it works in nursing, we see that *received artifacts* are focused on the patient and have a polysemic institutional nature (i.e. the clinical record as well as the NR have at the same time clinical, legal and economic implications). Moreover, they don't embed a vision that allows nurses to look at the ward as a whole. To this aim nurses develop *locally designed artifacts* that, on the contrary, have no visibility at an institutional level, neither are included in the official workflows, but that are crucial for professionals to manage the contingencies of practice and make the institutional flow work. *Locally designed artifacts* are used to fill the gaps of the official documentation, which – in the case of nurses- is to do *articulation,* to *anticipate* and to *coordinate* the work, by focusing on the re-built of the bridge between patient needs and ward requirements.

Considering the strong link between unexploited nurse roles, coordination and locally designed artifacts in the observed contexts, in the next paragraphs the discussion will focus on these locally designed tools and on how they contribute at a micro-level in shaping nurses' daily work and professional identity. They offer a complementary perspective to the one proposed by the professional mandate and strengthened by the NR. Therefore, by analyzing the artifacts locally designed by nurses to accomplish this invisible work, the logics of action that enable nurses to maintain the flow of activities are highlighted and exploited. Evidences are provided by the description of how tacit knowledge is reified and embedded into objects by the professionals themselves (Button and Sharrock, 1995).

6. Building a bridge between patient's care and ward's organizational instances: the case of the therapy organizer

Some critical processes in hospitals stress at its limits the link between the two focuses of nurses' practices. The therapy is one of those complex processes because of the following reasons:

- It is composed by sub-phases that are logically contiguous, but occur delayed in time;

- It is performed by different professionals;

- It implies the involvement of structures that are separated from the ward to take place (e.g. the laboratory, the pharmacy and the hospital canteen);

- It needs to be always organized in advance to be performed correctly.

In the first research context, in order to accomplish this complex activity, nurses created a highly operational locally designed tool: the therapy organizer. It responds to the need of dealing with a critical process in the clinical field: the one that goes from therapy prescription to therapy administration.

In the following sections we will describe how this tool is structured and how it works, showing the need for a tool supporting nurses' dual focus on the patient and on the ward. In the end, the management of therapy within the second context of the research will be discussed in comparison with the first one.

6.1. Structure and functions

The therapy organizer (Figure 4) is a mediation artifact that helps nurses in the management of the whole process that goes from a drug prescription (medical task centerd on the patient), to the drug order (nurse task centerd on the ward), to the sorting of the drugs into the carts (nurse task centered on the ward), to the administration of the drugs (nurse time oriented task centerd on the patient).

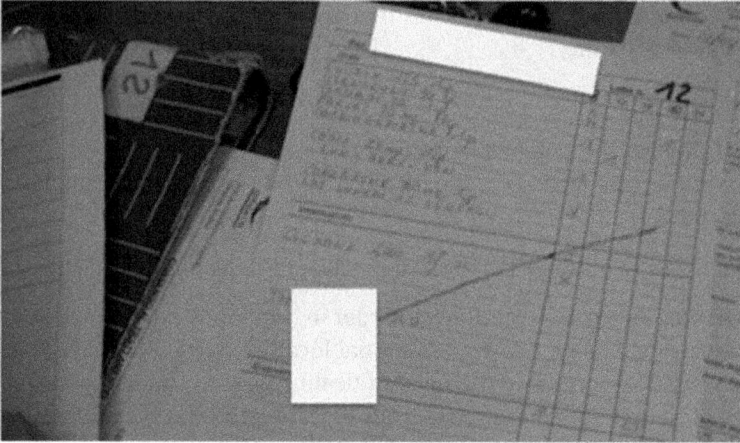

Figure 4: A picture of a therapy organizer page

Since frequent shifts of focus are necessary to accomplish the therapy organization for the whole ward, the therapy organizer is structured in a way that makes nurses able to manage it in an integrated way:

- it resumes in a unique tool all the therapies prescribed by the doctors for all the patients in the ward (and written down in their clinical records);

- it organizes the information for the administration phase;

- it helps in the drugs order when an overview of the used drugs is required;

- it provides criterion for sorting drugs in the carts and in the closet, assuring consistence between tools.

The therapy organizer makes it possible to reconcile these different phases of the therapy process thanks to the dual nature of its structure, that reflects the duplicity of nurses' professional vision:

- On one hand, it is composed by cards (one per patient in the ward) where time, dosage and route for administration are the organizing criteria. On each sheet it allows to see the therapy for the single patient at a glance, based on the number of bed occupied by the patient, and thus also giving to nurses a reference for his position in the ward;

- On the other hand, the sheets are kept together in an organizer: a concise and lightweight tool of maximum 15 sheets (one per bed) that offers a vision on all the therapies to administer in the ward, always positioned on the therapy cart in order to allow them to check on the drugs to order, to prepare and to administer.

It is useful for deepening the understanding of how this tool works, to start from the narration of how it relates with the therapy section of the clinical record. In fact, contingently to the drugs prescription made by the doctor on the Clinical Record (CR), information are transcribed by nurses and slightly modified basing on their needs on the therapy organizer, as shown in the example below:

> *"Anna, one of the non-shifter nurses, waits for dr. Bianchi to sit down at the desk in front of her. She starts passing to him, one by one, the medical records based on the number of bed occupied by the patient. He quickly takes a look to the laboratory results of the day that Anna has printed and left in evidence in the medical record to make them immediately visible. The doctor checks then which drugs the patient assumed during the last week, and decides to not change them, writing an "R" (for "replicate") at the current date. Then he passes to the next CR."*

> *"For this patient, there is the necessity of writing again down the whole therapy, since a week is passed from the day he was admitted to the hospital and the clinical diary, where the therapy section is comprised, has expired. Instead of transcribing it by the old clinical diary, he asks Marta, another nurse, to take the therapy organizer and to read the old therapy from there. Marta takes the organizer, finds the page and reads the therapy for the doctor. He decides to change the dosage of an analgesic and writes it down on the clinical diary. Marta, in parallel on the therapy organizer, rubs out the old therapy and writes the new one in pencil. Anna asks her: "you wrote down that the elastomer has changed? Do I need to check?" Marta answers: "I wrote down everything"."*

The example above describes the dialogue between the two tools (the CR and the therapy organizer) and opens up the discussion on how the structure of these tools supports different objectives strictly related to the

work of different professionals and to different tasks within the same process.

6.2. Professional "visualization" of information on the patient

To better understand why nurses and doctors use different tools to display
the same information it is worth to compare the structure of the therapy
organizer with the therapy section in the clinical record.

The therapy section in the CR (figure 5) provides a weekly view of the
therapies employed.

Date Day	Mon	Thu	Wed	Tue	Fri	Sat	Sun
OBSERVATIONS AND TERAPY							

**Figure 5: Graphical representation and peculiarities of the therapy section
in the CR**

This view helps the doctor in having a longitudinal perspective on the
therapeutic decisions made by his colleagues. Moreover, the proximity
within the CR itself of all the other clinical information and laboratory
examinations can guide his medical reasoning (e.g. laboratory tests in
evidence). Type of drug, dosage, method and timing of administration are
compressed into a single box, not always easy to read because of the lack
of space associated to the need of a comprehensive approach for orienting
the clinical reasoning.

Completely different is the goal of the single therapy sheets in the organizer: they serve to nurses to organize all the information related to the
administration of drugs.

As already pointed out, each sheet (figure 6) collects information on a single patient, and the sheets are organized in the notebook in ascending order based on the number of bed.

Patient				Bed number	
Oral	6/8	12	18	20/21	24
Intramuscolar					
Intravenous					
Medications					

Figure 6: graphical representation of the therapy sheet in the therapy organizer and overview of its peculiarities

The vertical reading of the sheet allows nurses to have a view on the drugs taken by each patient on the basis of the route of administration (oral, intramuscular, intravenous). The horizontal reading displays the times at which each drug should be administered (6.00, 12.00, 18:00, 20:00, 24:00). Changes in the time of administration are also pointed out in order to equally distribute workload among turns (from 6.00 to 8.00 and from 20.00 to 21.00).

The therapy is crayon written (since it is an informal tool, it does not have to meet the requirements of official documentation), in order to allow the continuous updating of routine changes in the prescription: "we are not interested in the historical part of the therapy, we are interested only in the present, on what it is written in the folder that we have to administer today", says one of the nurses in order to explain the use of the pencil on the therapy organizer.

Once the drug is administered, the successful or unsuccessful administration is reported by "ticking" on the CR. This means that an informal tool is used for organizing the work and the return to the official tool is due for reporting the work done.

6.3. Professional "visualization" of information on ward needs

The therapy organizer is more than the single sheets it is composed of. As we already anticipated it is able to support work thanks to its very nature of organizational tool. By keeping all information on the therapy within one sole tool, it constitutes the *fil rouge* of the therapy process into the wards. First, it is highly manageable as with respect to the CRs. By having in one sole organizer all the information on all the therapies of the ward nurses avoid to bring all around within the department the CRs of all patients, that are binders of documents which, with the persistence of the patients in the ward for long periods, become heavy, bulky and impractical (see Figure 7).

A Clinical Record   **The whole Therapy Organizer**

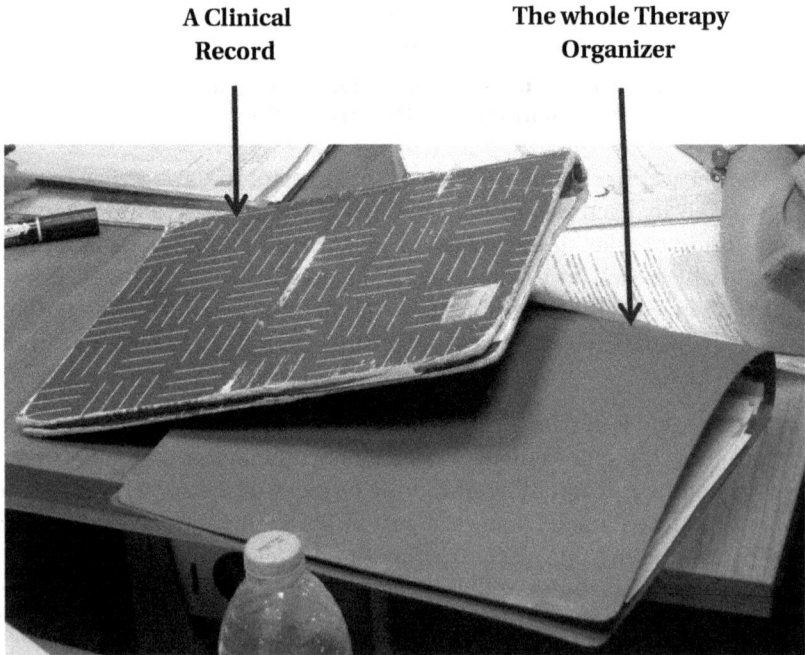

Figure 7: Picture comparing the dimensions of a clinical record and of the therapy organizer

Second, the therapy organizer is strategically positioned within the ward (see figure 8). As it is an "activity oriented" tool, it is key positioned where the activity/ies related to the therapy process take place: on the mobile therapy cart (used to prepare and to administer drugs), near to the therapy closet (where drugs to be administered are sorted) in the nursing room (where the drugs order took place).

In fact, as already anticipated at the beginning of the paragraph, the therapy organizer is used not only to administer therapies (although that one is its primary function), rather it is involved in the whole therapy process and constitutes the main reference for everything related to the therapy (see Figure 8).

Therapy organizer positioned on the therapy cart

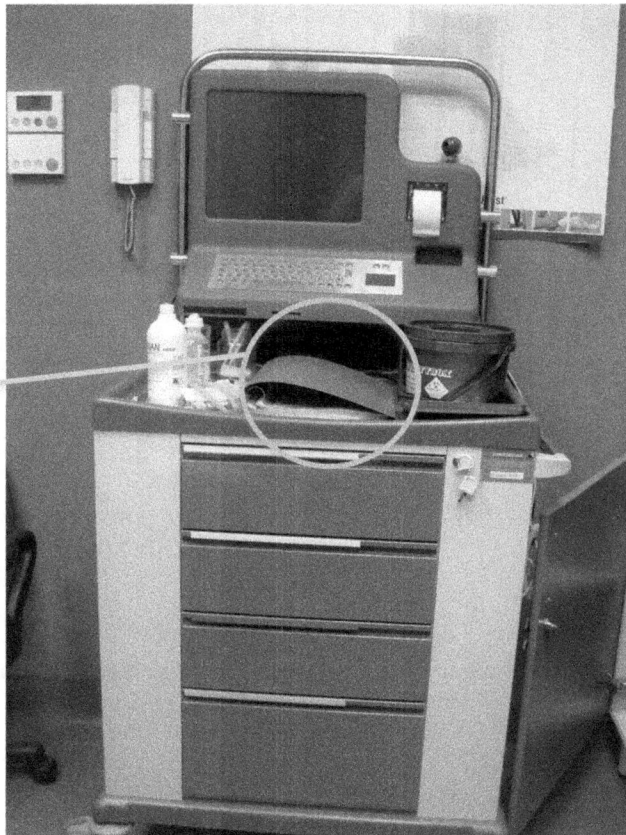

Figure 8: The therapy organizer positioned as usual on the therapy cart

6.4. Use and interaction with other tools

By interacting with other official and unofficial tools, and by supporting nurses' cognitive shift between one vision and the other, the therapy organizer brings consistency between interlaced practices that would otherwise be disjointed. Going through a description of the therapy process may clarify how this tool works (see figure 9).

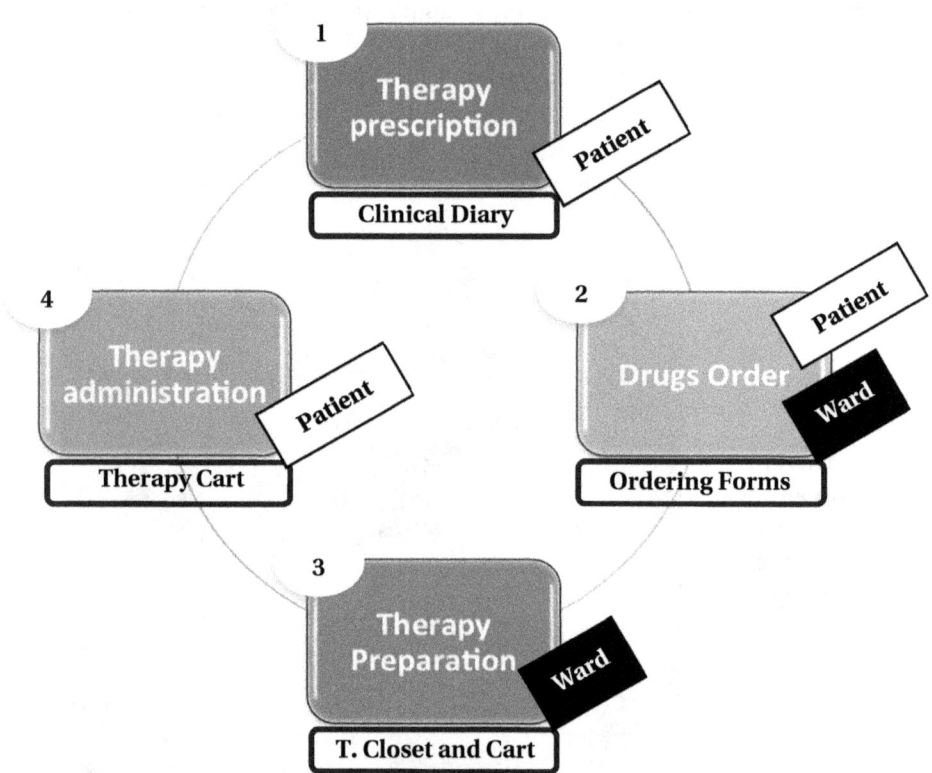

Figure 9: A graphical representation of how the therapy organizer supports the therapy process in interaction with different tools and allowing the shift of focus between the patient and the ward

1. The first step, as we already saw, is to transcribe (and slightly modify) information on therapy from the CR. Moreover, information from the therapy organizer are often used by the doctor as reference to re-transcribe them back to the CR when a new clinical diary is prepared.

The focus is here on the single patient, but, single patient after single patient, information on therapy are grouped within one sole tool.

2. At this point, when the drugs order has to be performed based on the prescribed therapies, the therapy organizer, used as a whole (by counting the dosages of each drug needed for the ward) gives nurses an overview of the drugs prescribed to perform the order. Once the order arrives, drugs are sorted in the therapy closet using as main criterion that of the therapy organizer (way of administration) together with a specific tacit expertise related to the frequency of use of each drug in the ward (see Figure 10). The vision adopted by nurses in this phase is on the ward as a whole, rather than on the single patient.

3. Right before the drugs administration, when nurses need to prepare the drugs cart, they again refer to the therapy organizer in order to have a clear idea of drugs and aids necessary for each administration (eg. CVC, elastomer, gauze, etc.). This phase becomes even easier given the fact that a continuity has been built during time within the previous phases, when the prescription was transcribed and the order was sorted out according to the drugs administration criteria. Again the leading vision is here on the ward.

4. Nurse's eye comes back on the patient during the administration phase, when cart and organizer on the hand, the single sheet is used to check dosages, and time of infusion.

Criteria of a drug position as with respect to other drugs:
1. **Way of administration:** same way of administration, same place
2. **Type of drug:** same drug, same place
3. **Space-saving:** in the end, someway, all the drugs should enter in the closet

Criteria of a drug position as with respect to the structure of the closet:
1. **Frequency of administration:** most frequent is the use of a drug, most external is its position in the closet
2. **Frequency of the way of administration:** most frequent is the way of administration, most external drugs administered through it are positioned
3. **Alphabetical order:** top-down A to Z positioning

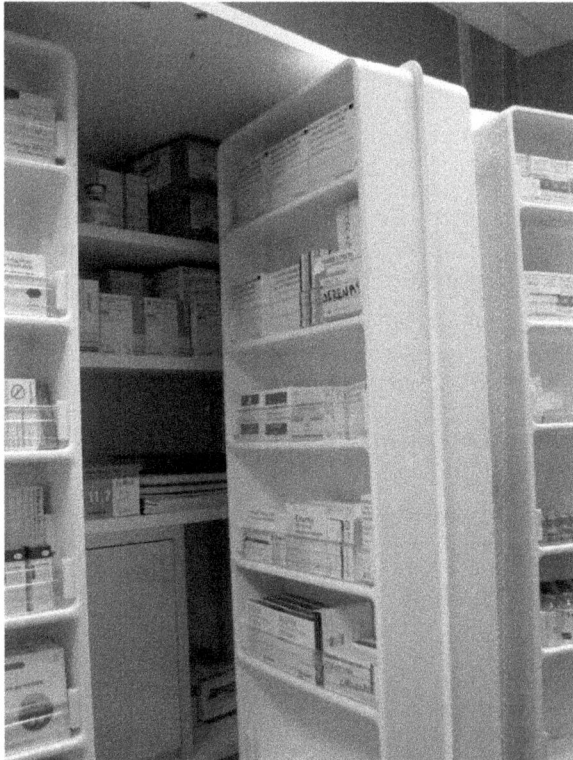

Figure 10: A picture of the therapy closet together with the shared criteria for drug positioning within the ward

As it emerged from the passages described above, the therapy organizer builds up a continuity between the therapy as a unique process and its objects, and this is possible only because of its very nature of twofold tool that relies in its capability of embedding and maintaining together the two focus of nurses' work.

6.5. Changes in the organization of therapy coming from the introduction of the nurse record: the therapeutic data single sheet

How does this process change with the introduction of the Electronic NR? Being focused on nurses responsibilities as autonomous workers, the structure of the NR has a specific section dedicated to therapy administration. This section, integrated with the section for medical prescription of drugs is called "Therapeutic data single sheet".

This sheet, drawn based on the operational scenario of therapy administration embeds two sections to be compiled by doctors and nurses, thus resuming the complexity of the therapy process. This is done thanks to the flexibility in allowing different visualizations of information provided by electronic systems. Therapy is written by the doctor on the therapeutic data single sheet, which is part of the integrated (nurse/medical) record, considering that data written on the prescription are, from a legal perspective, a medical responsibility.

The therapy administration is carried out by nurses and then "ticked" on the same sheet in dedicated boxes that are electronically signed, thus assuring the individual responsibility of the professional on the work done. This way, transcriptions, which are considered as the first cause of errors in healthcare, are avoided and formal responsibilities on the therapy process are reflected in the official tool used for documentation.

The presence of this inter-professional sheet within the NR opens up a window on the effective role and on the power of the NR in fostering and exploiting nursing as an autonomous profession into the wards. Moreover, being not only a reporting tool but also an operational tool, the therapeutic data single sheet is able to hold together the functions that in the first ward were covered by the medical record (for the prescription part), and by the therapy organizer (for the administration part), not only creating a link between the work of different professionals, but also embedding the functions of the official artifact (medical record) and the informal one (therapy organizer). We can affirm that the use of the therapeutic data single sheet introduces an upgrade in the way the therapy prescription and administration (phases 1 and 2 of the therapy process) are document-ed and managed as with respect to the transcription of information made in the first context on the therapy organizer from the medical record.

However, the organizational part of the process, focused on the ward, where orders are accomplished and carts prepared, is missing. This is not taken into consideration because the NR does not aim at supporting this part of nurses' profession and keeps disregarding the work not focused on the patient.

What happens then when drugs need to be ordered and sorted into carts and closets?

The therapy organizer is re-built by nurses. It is rebuilt informally and kept hidden, like it is for the invisible organizational work they do into the wards. Re-designed starting from the therapeutic data single sheet of each patient in order to support the organizational part of the therapy activity. The sheets are extracted from the records, printed and assembled together every time drugs are ordered or sorted for the ward.

Here we are again at the point in which a substantial part of nurses work is disregarded. But if the therapy organizer has a sort of recognized accountability within the first ward, here its function is split into two arti-facts: one of them (the therapeutic data single sheet) is considered at the core of nurses profession, while the other one (the informal patchwork made by nurses to coordinate activities) is even more pushed into the backstage region of nursing than in the first context.

Institutions design inherited artifacts to be sent into the wards to re-design nursing, while nurses design local artifacts to retro-act on the pro-cess of design that their profession is experiencing. Ostensive and per-formative aspects of routines are shaping professional change through a sort of "design battle" played by the means of strategic production and use of artifacts.

The relevance of the design of professional tools can't be disregarded by organizational research as artifacts are at the core of professional activ-ities. Moreover, if adequately informed, developers and stakeholders in the domain can have a benefit of a research that aims at supporting de-sign. For these reasons, in the conclusions some insights from the field-work are translated into implications for the design of IT tools for support-ing nurses' work from an activity oriented perspective.

Conclusion

Our research started from the ethnographic study of the everyday work of nurses in different organizational settings in order to provide guidelines for designing prototypes of digital tools and services to support their work.

We look at the case of nurses since it provides us with a special focus at the same time both on professional change and technological introduction of institutional tools. The dynamics between technologies introduction and new practices creation has been a long-standing problem in understanding institutional change, and it requires the importance of materialism and agency to be weighed up (Leonardi and Barley, 2008; Orlikowski and Barley, 2001; Pentland and Feldman, 2008; Labatut et al. 2012). Studies from institutional literature (Cohen, 2007), workplace studies (Luff, Hindmarsh and Heath, 2000; Suchman, 1997) and routines studies (Pentland and Feldman, 2008; Labatut et al. 2012) address the relation between institutional change and modifications in practice based on two shortcomings: the interaction between routines and higher-level entities; and the understanding of artifacts and technologies' roles in routine dynamics as with respect to change.

The study of artifacts in action is relevant to the comprehension of change since it highlights the relation between institutional instances and daily organizational practices, thus emphasizing the active role of users in shaping practice and meaning through the use of technologies. Therefore, technologies can be interpreted and used in ways that contradict the intentions of the designers (DeSanctis and Poole, 1994), and this multiplicity of uses professionals made of artifacts generates variety within routines (D'Adderio, 2009), creates new routines, and transforms schema, thus contributing to foster professional change.

In the case studies examined in this chapter, the way informal tools are designed and used by nurses highlights a need for the design of tools supporting the hard work done by nurses on organizational practices due to the lack of integration between the core activities carried out in the wards (planning, implementation, documentation). Some unexpected research findings showed off the production and self-management by nurses of several operational tools for coordination to fill this gap of the official documentation in reflecting real practice. In addition to electronic systems, paper forms, clinical record and the NR, nurses made a wide use in the wards of local tools in support of the management of organizational resources/constraints. This population of informal tools has the specific goal of building a bridge between the patient and the hospital and to combine working rhythms and spaces for the entire professional team.

The example of the therapy organizer highlights the complex management of data made by nurses, providing evidence of their effort in reworking several times the same information according to different activities. This work does not disappear once the official documentation system introduced by the NR is in place. Because of this, certainly nurses of both contexts could profit from digital tools offering interoperability and information integration. Assuming a design perspective, the data presented show that the strongest point in favour of digitalization in these contexts is the ease of selection, adaptation and use of key information it allows. In fact, if integrated and interoperable IT tools could be introduced, they would fill the gap on official documentation that is at the present moment quick fixed through locally designed tools. Through interoperability it would be also easy to have automatic shifts in the visualization of key information according to specific aims/tasks that have been identified and that seems to be crucial to guarantee the efficiency of working practices.

By default, the automatic adaptation in the visualization of official information for different purposes would diminish nurses' workload, avoiding the huge amount of time required to nurses to produce un-official organizational documentation. Together with the decreased workload, the possibility to have organizational tools embedded into official documentation would produce positive effects also on risk management by reducing the risks connected to information transcription and by assuring that official documentation has no gaps.

The ethnographic study of nurses shows that it is not sufficient to design tools starting from official professional mandate, since doing so does not always lead to artifacts which helps users (nurses) to make their own work smoother. Rather, sometimes it seems that users actively refuse digital tools which they do not recognize as helpful in deploying they daily work, as in the case of the hospital where the use of NR has been hindered.

Observing nurses' work made it possible to unveil invisible tools that they do consider necessary to smooth their practices. That is to say that the "discovery" by user researchers of locally designed organizational artifacts highlights areas for design which are still uncovered. One of these areas regards the shift of perspective from patient-based to ward-based information required to nurses and it should be regarded by system designers with much attention since it also deals with the potential reduction of risks in care management.

Studying practices before systems are designed is a core activity social researchers can perform to help two activity systems (the one of professionals and that of developers) to engage in the cross-cultural process of production of artifacts that embed the tacit knowledge and expertise of both of them (Mellini et al., 2014). Given the complexity of the process in place, a cultural mediation between the two is needed. This is crucial not only to guarantee a better practical result in introducing technologies in working contexts. In fact it mostly deals with the possibility that the introduction of a technology is seen as an innovation process from the activity system in which it takes place: it is about ensuring that professional identities and knowledge are not spoiled in change of "blind" digitalization or dematerialization.

References

Allen, D. (1997), "The nursing–medical boundary: A negotiated order", *Sociology of Health and Illness*, 19 (4), pp. 498-520.

Allen, D. (2004), "Re-reading nursing and re-writing practice: towards an empirically based reformulation of the nursing mandate", *Nursing Inquiry*, 11 (4), pp. 271-283.

Bardram, J. (1998), *Collaboration, coordination and compter support: an activity theoretical approach to the design of computer supported cooperative work*. PhD. Thesis. Aarhus University, Computer Science Department.

Bruni, A., Gherardi, S. (2007), *Studiare le pratiche lavorative*. Bologna: Il Mulino.

Button, G., Sharrock, W. W. (1995), "Practices in the work of ordering software development", in Firth, A. (ed.), *Negotiations In The Workplace: Studies of Language in the Workplace*. New York: Pergamon, pp. 159-180.

Button, G., Sharrock, W.W. (1997), "The production of order and the order of production", in Hughes, J., Prinz, W., Rodden, T., Schmidt, K. (eds.), *Proceedings of the Fifth European Conference on Computer Supported Cooperative Work*. Kluwer: Dordrecht, pp. 1-16.

Cohen, M. D. (2007), "Reading Dewey: reflections on the study of routine", *Organization Studies*, 28 (5), pp. 773-786.

Currie G., Finn R., Graham M. (2010), "Role Transition and the Interaction of Relational and Social Identity: New Nursing roles in the English NHS", *Organization Studies*, 31 (7), pp. 941-961.

D'Adderio, L. (2009), "The influence of artifacts and distributed agencies on routines' dynamics: from representation to performation", in Becker, M. C., Lazaric, N. (eds.), *Organizational routines: Advancing empirical research*. Edward Elgar: Cheltenham, pp. 185-222.

De Sanctis, G., Poole, M. S. (1994), "Capturing the complexity in advanced technology used: adaptative structuration theory", *Organization Science*, 5 (2), pp. 141-147.

Dingwall, R., Rafferty, A. M., Webster, C. (1998), *An introduction to a social history of nursing*. London: Routledge.

Gerson, E. M., Star, S. L. (1986), "Analyzing due process in the workplace", *ACM Transactions on Office Information Systems*, 4 (3), pp. 257-270.

Giorgi, S., Talamo, A., Mellini, B. (2012), "Putting again the Culture "in the Middle": in Search of Meanings in the UX Research", *Proceedings of CHI'12*, May 5–10, 2012, Austin, Texas, USA. ACM 978-1-4503-1016-1/12/05.

Halverson, C. A. (2002), "Activity theory and distributed cognition: or what does CSCW need to do with theories?", *Computer Supported Cooperative Work*, 11 (1), pp. 243-267.

Halverson, R., Zoltners, J. (2001), "Distribution across artifacts: How designed artifacts illustrate school leadership", *The American Educational Research Association Conference*, Seattle, WA.

Halverson, R. (2003), "Systems of practice: How leaders use artifacts to create professional community in schools", *Education Policy Analysis Archives*, 11 (37), London: Sage.

Heath, C., Luff, P. (1992), "Collaboration and control: crisis management and multimedia technology in London Underground control rooms", *Computer Supported Cooperative Work*, 1 (1), pp. 69-94.

Hughes, E.C. (1984), *The Sociological Eye*. New Brunswick-London: Transaction Books.

Iley, K. (2004), "Occupational changes in nursing: The situation of enrolled nurses", *Journal of Advanced Nursing*, 45 (4), pp. 360-370.

Labatut, J., Aggeri, F., Girard, N. (2012), "Discipline and Change: How Technologies and Organizational Routines Interact in new practice creation", *Organization Studies*, 33 (1), pp. 39-69.

Leonardi, P. M., Barley, S. R. (2008), "Materiality and change: challenges to building better theory about technology and organizing", *Information and Organization*, 18 (3), pp. 159-176.

Luff, P., Hindmarsh J., Heath, C. (2000), *Workplace studies: recovering work practice and informing system design*. Cambridge: Cambridge University Press.

Mellini, B. (2014). *Showing off the invisible. An ethnography of practices and artifacts and its implications on the design of IT tools for nursing.* Ph.D. Thesis, Dipartimento di Psicologia dei Processi di Sviluppo e Socializzazione, Sapienza Università di Roma.

Mellini, B., Talamo, A. (2014), "Uno sguardo nella cassetta degli attrezzi dell'infermiere. Oggetti che organizzano le cure", in Pipan, T. (2014), *Presunti colpevoli. Dalle statistiche alla cartella clinica: indagine sugli errori in sanità*. Milano: Guerini e Associati.

Mellini, B., Giorgi, S., Talamo, A. (2014), "Soglie, scene, spazi e artefatti come strumenti di conoscenza dell'organizzazione", *Studi Organizzativi*, 1, pp. 97-125.

Newman, M. (1986), *Health as expanding consciousness*. St Louis: Mosby.

Norman, D. A. (1988), *Psychology of everyday things*. New York: Basic Books.

Orlikowski, W. J., Barley, S. R. (2001), "Technology and institutions: what can research on information technology and research on organizations learn from each other?", *MIS Quarterly*, 25, pp. 145-165.

Parse, R. R. (1981). *Man–living–health: A theory of nursing*. New York: Wiley.

Pentland, B. T., Feldman, M. (2008), "Designing routines: on the folly of designing artifacts, while hoping for patterns of action", *Information and Organization*, 18 (4), pp. 235-250.

Rerup, C., Feldman, M. S. (2011), "Routines as a source of change in organizational schema: the role of trial-and-error learning", *Academy of Management Journal*, 54 (3), pp. 577-610.

Robinson, S., Murrells, T., Clinton, M. (2006), "Highly qualified and highly ambitious: Implications for workforce retention of realising the career expectations of graduate nurses in England", *Human Resource Management Journal*, 16 (3), pp. 287-312.

Robinson, S., Murrells, T., Marsland, L. (1997), "Constructing career pathways in nursing: Some issues for research and policy", *Journal of Advanced Nursing*, 25 (3), pp. 602-614.

Simon, H.A. (1986), *The science of the artificial*, Cambridge: MIT Press.

Star, S. L. (1999), "The ethnography of infrastructure", *American Behavioral Scientist*, 43 (3), pp. 377-391.

Suchman, L. (1997), "Centers of coordination: a case and some themes", in Resnick, L. B., Saljo, R., Pontecorvo, C., Burge, B. (eds.), *Discourse, tools and reasoning: essays on situated cognition*. Berlin: Springer-Verlag, pp. 41-62.

Suchman, L., Blomberg, J., Orr, J., Trigg, R. (1999), "Reconstructing technology as social practice", *The American Behavioral Scientist*, 43 (3), pp. 392-408.

Talamo, A., Mellini, B., Giorgi, S. (2011), "Ergonomia Sociale", in Di Nocera, F. (ed.), *Ergonomia cognitiva*. Carocci, pp. 251-281.

Talamo, A., Ventura, S., Giorgi, S., Ceriani, M., Bottoni, P., Mellini, B. (2013), "Do the gestures you think of", *Proceedings of the Biannual Conference of the Italian Chapter of SIGCHI on CHItaly '13*, New York: ACM.

Travelbee, J. (1966), *Interpresonal Aspects of Nursing*. Philadelphia: FA Davis.

Vygotsky, L. S. (1978), *Mind in society: The development of higher psychological processes*. Cambridge: Harvard University Press.

Wartofsky, M. W. (1979), *Models: Representation and scientific understanding*. Boston: Reidel.

Watson, J. (1979), *Nursing: The philosophy and science of caring*. Boston: Little Brown.

SECTION 2

Designing Technology, Work and Organization in Emerging Organizational Settings

DESIGNING A NEW CHAIR, TRANSGRESSING ORGANIZATIONAL BOUNDARIES

Laura Lucia Parolin

Introduction

In past decades, we have witnessed a growing interest in users' contribution to the design of technological artifacts. For example, starting from the remarkable volume by Lucy Suchman (1987), the perspective of the technology-in-use in organizational studies has led to a progressive blurring of the distinction between design and use (Orlikowski, 1992).

If it is true that the design of an artifact is an endless articulation process – as it is plunged in a network of relationships and uses, that determine newer and newer configurations (Shove et al., 2007) – it is also true that some forms of stability and "closure" of the artifact are reached before it is set on the market through the definition of its parts, materials, relationships, and the fixing of the production process (Storni, 2012). This becomes particularly clear with artifacts interfacing the industrial (re)productive system, i.e. with industrial design.

Curiously, scholars who have focused on design practices (Law, 2002; Yaneva, 2005, 2009; Vinck, 2003) have rarely been interested in the activities that take place out of the traditionally foreseen sites, like design studios. However the interpretative keys offered by Science and Technology Studies for unpacking design practices are indifferent to the boundaries of design studios. They actually offer the possibility of following the processes of progressive transformation of the thing designed up to its use by the users. The development of the entire process of an artifact's articulation – from its ideation up to the (relative) stabilization of its commercialization – seems to be a field requesting further investigation (Storni, 2012). At the same time, the complex and articulated characteristics of production in manufacture industry make the longitudinal research into the entire process of creation of an artifact an almost impossible task.

When does the design activity start and when does it end? Who are the actors involved? Where can we outline its boundaries? In order to answer to these questions this chapter focuses on the development of a new product (a chair) in the industrial setting. By directing attention to industrial design, I will show what happens in production sites as the project of a new product (a chair) leaves the studio of the designer. I will not only focus my attention on the production sites but also on the supply chain relationships, so to trace the articulation process of a new artifact across organizational boundaries. After introducing briefly STS works on design practices, I will illustrate the case of the creation of a new model for a chair by focusing on the mediations that take place in the suppliers' production sites. I will thus introduce the concept of the "network within" (Parolin and Mattozzi, 2014) to illustrate this process of (continuous) (re)articulation of the network of relationships that makes an object part of a broader system formed by human and non-human actors that enter the relationship with it. By doing so, I will shed light on mutual relationship between design, work, and organization.

1. STS and design practices

Since their origin, STS have been interested in the stabilization processes of technological systems (Bijker et al., 1987; Hughes, 1999) and their description (Akrich, 1992; Akrich and Latour, 1992). The roots of this are taken from the Social Construction of Technology (SCOT) approach, which illustrated a number of relatively predictable steps, including how relevant social groups (such as users) interact with technologies to "closure" their initially malleable potentials (Bijker, 1995).

Despite the influence STS have on a wide range of disciplines, including design studies (Fallan, 2008), empirical works centered on the unpacking of design practices are relatively few (Storni, 2012; Volontè, 2014). As a consequence, although there is a growing interest for STS to meet design studies[6], an actual cross fertilization between these two epistemic cultures (Cetina, 2009) has not taken place yet (Coletta et al., 2014; Volonté, 2014)[7].

---

[6] Besides being the title of Storni's work, "unpacking design" was the general theme of two recent colloquia, one by the *European Group on Organization Studies* (EGOS, Helsinki 2012) and the other in occasion of the joint meeting between the *Society for the Studies of Science* (4S) and the *European Association for the Study of Science and Technology* (EASST – Copenhagen, 2012). This further confirms the general interest in Organization Studies, as well as in STS, for design issues.

Among the most influential works in the world of artifacts' design, it is important to mention those studies that have shown the design practices of engineers, architects, and designers (Suchman, 2000; Law, 2002; Yaneva, 2005, 2009; Vinck, 2003), using professional studios as the point of departure[8]. However, only rarely have the relationships between a studio and what lies outside of it been explored: for example, the various transformations of what has been designed, from concept to prototype, to product, to artifact in use, and to waste; or the articulations of the relationships with production departments, external suppliers, or with construction sites (in the case of architectural studies).

By studying what takes place at professional studios, this literature has illustrated the interactions with other actors and agents who take part in the process of articulating a new artifact. John Law (2002), for example, shows how aircraft designers use prototypes and experimentations to decide what they have to take into account to determine the appropriate project for an aircraft wing. Through different tests and simulations of gusts of wind designers study the wing's reaction to turbulences and define factors that might affect gust responses. These factors are materially heterogeneous, in that they may refer to technical features (such as the size of the wing), but also to international standards, protocols, and so on (Law 2002).

Also in architectural practices models are used "to gather a number of things – human and non-human actors, and their concerns, requirements, and disputes – and to 'accommodate' them into objects that can be subjected to design experiments" (Yaneva, 2005: p. 872). In her research on architectural design practices, Albena Yaneva shows how architects are involved in a comprehensive dialogue with materials through movements of scaling up and scaling down. In so doing, architects move between two alternative states of the building that are simultaneously archived and kept: a state of being "less known" and a state of being "more known". The building emerges, becomes progressively visible by the scale trials that bring it into existence.

---

[7] It seems instead consolidated by information system design, where CSCW traditions and participatory design have reached by now a consolidated role (Engeström and Middleton, 1998; Greenbaum and Kyng, 1991; Oudshoorn and Pinch, 2003; Suchman, 2002).

[8] See also Farias and Wilker (2015) in aknowledgement of the crucial role of studios in cultural production.

The stabilization process of a new object is - therefore - not a linear, progressive process that starts out with an ideal intuition that defines once and for all the final object. Studies as the ones carried out by Law and Yaneva show how design practices can be interpreted as a kind of socio-material practice, through which the new object slowly emerges. In architectural studios, or in engineer's design department, object's controversial nature is made visible (Latour, 2005: p. 80), so that it becomes possible to (re)trace objects as "matters of concern" (Latour, 2009).

The controversial nature of objects in design practices is also at the center of Cristiano Storni's attention (2012). Referring to Brown (2001; 2004), Storni suggests to frame a "thing" as an undefined entity that stands behind an object. According to Brown, the word "thing" is an entity that is "in course of a definition", and therefore vague and problematic. In other words, the concept of "thing" does not refer to the mental image of an object that has not yet materialized, which precedes it. Following Storni (2012), the design process itself can be described as an oscillation between two poles, the "objectifying" and "thinging" tensions that vie against each other until one configuration succeeds in stabilizing and imposing itself on the other possible alternatives. Conceived as an oscillation between different tensions, design shows its temporary character, always open to new re-articulations in virtue of the characteristics of the materials and actors involved (users included). In this sense, design can be conceived as a (re)definition process of a certain "thing" that – by using approximations and temporary objects, like samples, models, and prototypes – experiments and tries out materials, bodies and the relationships among them. Another implication is that authorship cannot be attributed to an independent and isolated subject who works in his own studio, nor just to human actors. Design, instead, has to be understood as a complex and distributed network of heterogeneous elements (humans and non-humans) and practices.

Referring to these literature and through an empirical case, in the rest of the paper I will show how unpacking design practices leads to the tracing of a long chain of articulations and re-articulations involving things, concepts, materials, words, sketches, renderings, bodies, and habits. While (re)tracing the articulation process that translate a "thing" into an "object", I will underline the emergence of a new network of actors that sets new relationships between materials, bodies, knowledge, skills, and production modalities within and among boundaries.

2. Research, context and methodology

The data I am introducing were gathered from the ethnographic observation of a company specialized in the furniture sector and of its supply chain. In particular it is focused on the very moment of the production of a new product, and, thus, on the relationships between the company and its supply chain. The study was carried out interruptedly over a period of approximately two months during the spring of 2008 and was part of a broader study on inter-organizational relationships in the Brianza manufacturing district.

An initial period of investigation on the field was carried out in the production department where many products were assembled by using semi-finished products and where several technicians (in charge of assembling the new product production practices) work. In that period, I shadowed (Czarniawska, 2007) Stefano – one of the buyers of the production department, in charge of planning the production of a new product – in his meetings with some suppliers. But my fieldwork came to a sudden stop when the managers of the company – worried for the infringement of their industrial trade secrets – did not sign the formal authorization for the research. In the moment in which the authorization was denied, I had already had access to some of the sub-suppliers' workshops. With the agreement of the actors involved, I therefore decided to continue my research outside the boundaries of the firm, by focusing on two of the suppliers I previously met. This "accident" gave me the opportunity to focus my attention on the translation practices that take place through organizational borders and to concentrate on how things and design practices travel across organizational boundaries.

3. The case of the Calepina chair[9]

Furniture manufacturing firms in Brianza, the area where this story takes place, have close ties with the Milan International Furniture Fair, where new products are shown. It is frequently the feedback given by insiders that decides of the fate of a new product (i.e. their being included in a catalogue) and identifies the strengths and weaknesses of a product. The sta-

---

[9] This same empirical case is descripted in Parolin (2010a; 2010b). It also appears in Parolin and Mattozzi (2013; 2014) for different theoretical and interpretative purposes (namely, to elaborate a model to describe interactions among bodies, corporeal knowledge and innovation processes).

bilization of products is only partially reached before their being exhibited at the Fair, where they are often introduced as pilot series[10].

In the case of Calepina chair, the question of some kind of closure of the chair (although temporary) and the relevant production process reached Stefano's desk several months before the Fair. The new model of the chair originated thanks to the design by a well-known architect who had already worked with the company. After some time spent at the Research & Development unit, the new Calepina chair was a combination of rendering images, 3D objects, prototypes, samples of materials, texts, and verbal descriptions. Those material and non-material objects made up Calepina as a "thing".

As I will show, at that time some properties of the new chair were defined (like the standard of the tubular used for the frame or the type of leather used for the cover), but others were still vague, or inscripted and embodied in different instances of the "thing". The "thingness" (Storni, 2012) dimension of Calepina reached – thanks to Stefano's mediation and the travel ability of provisional objects – the suppliers' shop floors. Not only technical specifications or prototypes to be reproduced arrived on the suppliers' shop floors, but a plurality of elements and proprieties of the new chair that needed to be tuned. Physically carried by Stefano to the suppliers' shop floors, various elements of Calepina as a thing (renderings, prototypes, texts, verbal descriptions, etc.) spoke for its properties.

As I will show in the next paragraphs, the polyphony of the material and non-material objects that made up Calepina, allowed for the re-articulation of the semi-finished products on the shop floors. When Stefano went to the suppliers and showed them some of the artifacts of the Calepina project, what he was asking for was not the production of a complete semi-finished product with detailed technical specifications, but its re-articulation. The suppliers played a crucial role in the re-articulation of the semi-finished product through provisional objects and other elements by viewing Calepina as a thing that had reached their shop floors. As the readers will see, the (re)articulation of semi-finished products followed the indication of elements and properties of the thing which were not lodged in the prototype of the same semi-finished artifacts but in the in-

---

[10] Since this is a niche market, production is carried out in small batches. This allows for continuous improvements to be made even to products that are already on the catalogue.

stances (renderings, technical description, samples, and discursive practices) that traveled with it.

3.1. Focusing on the relationships between materiality and bodies

Giovanni is the owner of a small metalwork company that produces semifinished and finished objects in steel, aluminium, and other metal alloys. The company, inherited by Giovanni, was founded in the early '50s to build frames for bicycles and motorcycles. In the early '60s, the activity moved to the construction of metal structures for furniture manufacturing. Although they cannot produce large quantities of products, Giovanni's company has machinery that allows them to cover the entire production cycle, from cutting, degreasing, bending, and soldering tubes and profiles, to painting, zincing, nickeling, and chroming. In addition, their supply network can find tubes and profiles with special features, which makes it possible for the company to manufacture personalized products. Giovanni's company is therefore noteworthy for its productive flexibility, which is a welcome asset for furniture companies that manufacture small batches of limited series. Part of the work of Giovanni's company has been in production for years, while other jobs come from commitments for a temporary period only, such as pilot series or special editions.

Stefano hired Giovanni to prepare the frame for the new Calepina chair in production. He did it because he knew he could count on his skilled experience in working metal frames for furniture. When he actually went to Giovanni's company, he took certain artifacts related to the Calepina project with him: various renderings of the project, a sample of the leather and a prototype of the chair's metal structure. As he exhibited the work, Stefano commented on the images and on the prototype to illustrate the features of the design: a tubular metal frame, a seat made of a combination of materials to offer both support and softness with a complete covering in soft leather.

What Stefano asked Giovanni to do was to intervene "as you deem best". As the rendering was the reference for the visual aspect of the chair, it meant to (re)articulate the chair by tuning it with the frame. When Giovanni compared the images in the renderings, as Calepina's "spokesperson" (Callon, 1986) for the way the leather and the structure interacted, he realized that the structural configuration of the prototype would not grant the visual impact conveyed by the rendering. As he explained, the drop in the covering over the leg of the chair was "soft yet taut" in the renderings. The same effect would not have been reached by covering the prototype in leather.

The structure of the frame had empty spaces where the tubes intersected, which would have affected the behavior of the covering. A soft, malleable material such as leather to cover Calepina (to which he referred through the samples) would have loosened over time in the presence of the empty spaces. Although he did not have the covering at hand, Giovanni noticed the problem because of his knowledge of the metallic structural relationships and the sensitivity of the materials used for the covering. Giovanni had a "professional vision" (Goodwin, 1994) that allowed him to see the prototype not as a combination of soldered metal tubes, but as a structure made of full and empty spaces, and it was the full and empty spaces in the frame that did or did not provide support for the leather covering, which tended to suit the frame over the course of time.

He therefore worked on re-articulating the structure of full and empty spaces to affect the behavior of the leather, thereby aligning the material transformation of the prototype to the visual image offered by the rendering. In order to fill the empty spaces between the soldered tubes, Giovanni added a small metal plate to re-articulate the relationship between the frame and its cover. The leather would therefore remain taut instead of loosening and folding.

The relationship between the leather and the frame had therefore been reframed, and the problem of the loosening leather was solved. However the application of the plates to the tubes set new problems for the production process that allowed for imperfections being caused in the final product. The application of a metal plate to the tubular structure required special care during the soldering process because it introduced residual material that could have been perceptible (to touch or the eye) underneath the covering. Giovanni replaced the metal plates with a piece of metal tube that had been flattened at one end so that it adhered to the leg (also made of tubular metal): the area of contact between the two tubes created gaps (empty spaces) that could use the material required for the soldering. By using the empty spaces created by the contact between the two cylindrical structures of the metal tubes, there was no longer the risk that the material left over after the soldering process could interfere with the covering. In this way, Giovanni succeeded in re-articulating the frame while also taking into account the network formed by the frame in relation to the covering.

This re-articulation of the semi-finished product did not deal with the frame of the chair alone but it re-articulated the whole Calepina by (re)arranging the relationship between its material features (structure and covering, metal, leather, full or empty spaces, etc.).

3.2. Focusing on the human and non-human bodies' relationship

In parallel with Giovanni's work on the metal structure, Stefano involved another supplier for Calepina who worked through its half-finished product. In this case, too, the company was well-known, and had previously supplied semi-finished products to the firm. Stefano asked this supplier to re-articulate the seat of the chair. The founder, Carlo, is a chemist who once worked for one of Europe's largest chemical industries that sell some of the most widely distributed synthetic polymer kits used in molds. When he returned to Italy, he first worked as an employee for one of Brianza's most important furniture companies, and then started his own company producing semi-finished synthetic polymer products. The distinctive feature of his company is to know how to use basic chemical elements (rather than the most widely distributed pre-packaged kits) and, thus, to create ad hoc mixtures to use in molds.

When Stefano went to Carlo, he took with him some of the renderings for the new chair, some samples of materials, texts, and a prototype of the Calepina seat, made of a thin layer of wood covered with a plastic material to spoke the shape of the semi-product. When introducing the prototype, Stefano underlined how its consistency was not satisfactory. Stefano asked Carlo to create a seat for the chair that was soft but strong enough to support the weight of the user at the same time. The renderings, the unsatisfactory prototype because of its consistency, the designer's requests regarding the materials to be used, and the overall effect provided by the chair were a bulk of inputs that had to be specifically articulated in Carlo's work to stabilize the semi-finished product.

The features of the chair requested from Carlo related to the sensorial capacity of softness and support coexisting together. Carlo's main task was therefore to translate two characteristics into a composition of the chair that, as the use of the adversative conjunction "but" shows, had been thought to be incompatible: soft but supportive (Parolin and Mattozzi, 2013).

Carlo followed the suggestions offered by the designer as written in the texts; he initially concentrated his attention on the two materials: metal and polymers and their relationship. Such relationship between the materials was to be found in their juxtaposition: the metal core was meant to grant support, while - a to be defined mixture of - polymers had to reach the quality of softness. This juxtaposition was expressed through a number of variants as the result of different compositions of the foams in various layers and metal grids.

Carlo carried out tests, and made an assessment of a variety of combinations of metal grids and polymers based on the relationship of co-penetration rather than of juxtaposition by applying various "sensitivity tests"[11] he performed with his own body. Out of the sensations experienced by his contact with each combination, he gradually modified the grid, which increasingly resembled a metal fabric; once inserted into the mold it was penetrated - rather than covered - by the polymer foam. However, none of these developments led to the outcome he was looking for, based on Stefano's suggestions. While he was exploring the materials and their relationship, Carlo inserted some felt into the mold. As he observed how it behaved, he thought he could eliminate the metal. Because of its porosity, felt absorbs resins, and becomes more rigid. With the help of resins[12], and based on their composition, quantity, and spread, and on the type of felt used – its thickness, density, etc. – felt can support the user without losing its characteristic to suit the body. The felt plus resin relationship as a structural agent for the semi-finished product was introduced into the mold.

In the course of his tests he tried the various configurations of materials and experimented with the sensations they gave him. Finally, Carlo changed his strategy: rather than trying to make the metal grid sensitive, he sought to give a pressed material the supporting character, which was reached as the outcome of its reaction with resins.

---

[11] Although Latour (1987) only focuses on "trial of strength", Parolin and Mattozzi (2014: p. 374) have suggested that one might also talk of "trial of sensitivity", especially with technical tools in scientific laboratories, which are the main topic of Latour's analysis (Latour, 1987).

[12] It should be noted that felt "assisted" by applications of synthetic resins was already known to both Carlo and Stefano for its structure-creating characteristics, a well-known furniture manufacturer developed an armchair without a load-bearing frame.

However, as it had already occurred in the case of the "solution" offered by the metal plates to fill the empty spaces by Giovanni's structure, the identification of the materials and their own relationship that provided the sensation was not yet sufficient to give stability to the network that brought to the semi-finished product. The new pairing of materials (the relationship between the two materials) could give the sought for sensation, but the semi-finished product out of the mold was not well done. As Carlo explained to me: "When polyurethane is poured into a mold, it takes the shape of the mold as it expands. But if we have a material, which is what we need here, that once in contact with the polyurethane creates wrinkles and bubbles, then it is of no use... and they all showed up once upholstered".

Certain aspects of the work (the distribution of the material inside the mold), with its re-articulated relationships and materials, became problematic. The introduction of a material that was not (yet) rigid into the mold made it difficult to grant the consistent behavior of the foam. The non-uniform distribution of the material created imperfections in the semi-finished product, which was not acceptable, given the type of covering used (particularly sensitive to the materials underneath it). Two new solutions were introduced to better control the behavior of the materials inside the mold: the mold was made to tilt, so that the spread of the polymer mixture inside it would be assisted by a mechanical movement, and a film was placed over the felt to form a barrier against the liquid material. The re-articulation of the Calepina artifact across boundaries involved not only the materials and the relationships in-between one with the other, but also the working processes and the productive modalities.

4. Designing in-between boundaries

The case study I have introduced highlights how it is not possible to relate to design as the authorial expression of a single person who – through a cognitive process – decides all the aspects qualifying a new artifact. Design is rather a process that implies the partaking of human and non-human actors, things, inscriptions, material and non-material objects in a shared and distributed dimension. This process within the industrial design field I observed has necessarily to cross the borders that separate design studios from production sites. As we have already seen in the case introduced, Calepina's elements and properties are in fact redefined by meeting new actors and places (R&D department, suppliers, production processes, product standards, etc.).

We have noticed that tests on the materials and on their relationships take place even on the suppliers' shop floors, in the moment in which re-articulations of the semi-finished emerged as the outcome of experiments and translations. When we first met Calepina at the production department, we examined the sketches, renderings, 3D models, several samples of materials, the technical tests, standard directions, and prototypes. These different instances coexisted in the definition of the "thing" Calepina. Thus its material assemblage at that time was not clearly outlined. Although through Calepina's passage to the R&D department several prototypes had been added, the chair did not lost its "thingness". Prototypes did not substitute other instances of the project (renderings, samples, technical tests, etc.) but were rather added to them. This further material translation was not useless or voiceless since it embodied inscriptions that became the spokesperson for Calepina's properties. We can see it in the case of the prototype of the seat produced by the R&D department that, although it was not an adequate translation of the searched for feeling, it offered the needed characteristics for the definition of the mold.

What becomes evident is how such practices located at the production sites and spatially distributed across organizational boundaries are part of the design process. The plurality of instances that left the designer's studio travel to the various departments of the company up to reach the suppliers' shop floors where new articulations underwent tests with the aim of modifying again Calepina's properties. The properties of the new object were inscribed in texts, images, samples, lodged in models and in prototypes. Each one of these instances had several characteristics of the new chair inscribed, which remained vague and undefined in their polyphony. The traveling of the renderings, together with the prototypes and the verbal requests regarding its properties, allowed for Calepina's thingness to reach the suppliers' shop floors. And it was the characteristics of such instances raised to Calepina's spokesperson to orchestrate the re-articulation of the semi-finished on the suppliers' shop floors.

The re-articulations on the shop floors of the suppliers had – as a reference – several properties (and more precisely the relationships between bodies) that were not inscribed in the prototypes. On the first shop floor we saw how Giovanni's re-articulation of the semi-finished aimed at an alignment of the structure with the covering plus structure relationship inscribed in the rendering. On the second shop floor, the re-articulation of the elements of the seat and their relationship was aimed at reaching an effect that was expressed in the "soft but supporting" locution.

The image of the rendering that reached Giovanni's shop floor, showed a relationship between structure and covering that required a certain behavior of the leather (taut and without folds). By using the rendering as a "spokesperson" (Callon, 1986) of such a relationship, Giovanni re-articulated the whole of what was void and full in order to work on the behavior of the leather. The material-like quality of the prototype was in fact a "matter of concern" (Latour, 1996) as the "sort of structure" became evident when referred to the prototype. Yet, the request: "develop it as you deem best". On Giovanni's shop floor, the prototype had the status of an artifact in search for stabilization. In order re-articulate it, Giovanni focused on its relationship with the covering. A relationship between frame and covering already inscribed in the rendering but in search for its material translation. Giovanni reopened the same metal structure to act on the frame-covering relationship to better grasp the action of the leather to tune it with the rendering. It was by acting locally on the frame that he modified the relationship between frame and covering of Calepina. He embodied inside the frame the relationship between frame and covering which had been previously inscribed in the rendering. As a result, the materials used for Calepina and their relationships formed a more cohesive network.

The same happened with Carlo. If the prototype had to be the spokesperson for the shape of the chair, the design of the mold, as the consistency and the properties of the foam were still "matters of concern" (Latour, 1996). What drove Giovanni to a search for materials and relationships for the semi-finished product was the "soft but supporting" locution. It referred to the sensitive quality of Calepina that had to be embodied (and thus translated) into the semi-finished product.

On Carlo's shop floor, the prototypes, the technical descriptions, and the verbal requests (Cooren, 2010) for Calepina's sensorial qualities opened up a network of materials and relationships still to be defined. Carlo's work initially concentrated on two possible materials: metal and polymers in a juxtaposed relationship. This first literal translation (metal to support, and polymers for softness) of the effect of the user's body was jeopardized by the repeated sense of dissatisfaction with the sensation he experienced on his own body. What he experienced on his own body was the behavior of the seat that differed from the verbal indication expressed with the locution used by Stefano. It was therefore replaced by his study on the penetration relationship of polymers with metal grids. With this new translation (based on an inter-penetration relationship) various tries were carried out, but they did not live up to the sensitivity test of Carlo's body. As previously seen, it was only by eliminating the metal grid, and replacing it with felt, that the action of the seat on his body satisfied him; the translation of the sensitive property of the "soft but supporting" locution was reached. It was thanks to a research on the materials and on their relationships to build the seat that Carlo succeeded in re-articulating not only Calepina's semi-finished but its entire relationship with the user's body.

Also in this case, as we have already seen with the rendering used by Giovanni, the re-articulation took place within a broader network than the simple material elements (and their relationships) inscribed in the same semi-finished. Carlo intervened on the relationship between the materials that made the semi-finished by keeping in mind the "soft but supporting" locution. Moreover, the re-articulation of the semi-finished, re-articulated the entire relationships that Calepina had with the user's body. The verbal request "soft but supporting" brought Carlo to focus his attention on the relationship between the user's body and the seat by setting the used materials and their relationships to a loose network in search for definition. Carlo succeeded in "betraying" the materials – as foreseen by the initial project – because they were not "sensitizable" (Parolin and Mattozzi, 2013). As already highlighted in the case of the frame, by working locally on the semi-finished (by working on the materials and their relationships, and by testing them), the supplier acted on the relationship that he had set with the other bodies that made up Calepina's network. If by re-articulating the structure, the relationship it set with the covering was re-articulated, in the case of the seat, it was the same relationship with the body of the user to be re-articulated.

5. Designing as the deployment of a network

What I would like to underline in the present chapter is how the present case can help us define the design process as the emergence of a new "actor" (the artifact) through a process of making the network of relationships that constitute it.

It is useful here to introduce the concept of the "network within", in that it allows for a consideration of this reticular dimension of artifacts. The expression "network within" was suggested in a previous work (Parolin and Mattozzi, 2014) to refer to the network of materials, bodies, and their reciprocal relationships that build an object. By referring to the "network within" of an artifact we can also show the relationships that makes an object part of a broader network formed by (human and non-human) actors that enter in a relationship with it.

In this sense, the artifact's design process can be retraced not only by tracing the sites where the re-articulations of Calepina have taken place (design studio, R&D department, production department, suppliers' shop floors, etc.), but also by highlighting the importance of the actors (human and non-human) involved in its reticular-actor dimension.

Taking into consideration the "network within", it is possible to account for the translations an actor faces, i.e. the ways in which the network that sustains a certain actor is re-articulated when entering in relationship with other actor-networks. This also draws attention to the fact that when a semi-finished (like the structure) is modified, the relationship it sets with other semi-finished (like the covering, for example) changes, or how the relationship with the body of the user is re-articulated.

The case introduced here shows that a metal layer for the seat was among the initial actors taken into consideration. It disappeared in the course of the research on softness, and was replaced by a piece of felt, which created a different relationship with the polymers compared to the metal. Not only did a new actor – felt, which became rigid because it was impregnated with polymers – emerge, but there was also a different articulation of the network within of the Calepina chair. This outcome was not foreseeable, it was instead produced by the specific relationship between Carlo, the prototype and the materials [13].

At the same time, through the re-articulation of the network within, also human actors (like Carlo, Giovanni, and Stefano) are re-articulated. Carlo, for example, at the end of the development process of the prototype of the seat is not exactly the same Carlo that was at the beginning of such development. The relationships that defined him have changed: he is now in relationship with a knowledge and competence linked to softness, as well as to the production of a certain kind of seat that implies a new relationship between felt, polymers, resins, and mold. He learnt by knowing in practice materials, bodies and their relationships.

---

[13] In the same way, also the productive modalities as the tilting property of the mold could not be foreseen a priori, in terms of the behavior of the (new) coupled materials inside the mold.

Conclusion

The aim of the present chapter has been to trace the process of (re)articulation of a new artifact across organizational boundaries, that is out of the studios of the production site, out of the company, and along the supply chain.

By following Calepina's travel across boundaries, I have highlighted the role of instances (rendering, samples, technical descriptions and prototypes) in the design process, as well as in its distributed dimension. The (re)articulations of the semi-finished can thus be referred to renderings and to locutions, as the spokespeople for Calepina. That is, the re-articulation of the semi-finished influences the entire "network within" of Calepina, i.e. it acts on the relationship it entertains with other bodies (covering, and body of the user). What happens on the shop floors, is thus part of a (re)articulation process of the artifact that contributes to the stabilization of the network relationship between materials and bodies that make up the object and other bodies that will interact with it. I have shown how the new product that came out of these relationships could emerge as the actor-network set by the relationships between some materials, bodies, sensations, etc., and from their following re-articulations. However, tracing of the design process requires also an outlook on the transformations that have occurred to knot-actors as networks in themselves. It means to follow and to account for the ways Carlo, Giovanni and Stefano have changed by entering in a different relationship with materials, bodies, and sensations. It is what in organizational learning debate is known as situated learning or knowing in practice (Gherardi, 2006; Nicolini, 2012; Nicolini, et. alt. 2003). The concept of "network within", thus, allows to trace the site-distributed emergence of the actors that participate to the artifact, but also the transformation produced thanks to the design process that has been triggered.

References

Akrich, M. (1992), "The de-scription of technical objects", in Bijker, W.E., Law, J. (eds.), *Shaping technology - building society. Studies in sociotechnical change.* Cambridge: MIT Press, pp. 205–224.

Akrich, M., Latour, B. (1992), "A summary of a convenient vocabulary for the semiotics of human and nonhuman assemblies", in Bijker, W.E., Law, J. (eds.), *Shaping Technology/Building Society Studies in Sociotechnical Change,* Cambridge: MIT Press, pp. 259-264.

Bijker, W. (1995), *Of Bicycles, Bakelites, and Bulbs: Toward a Theory of Sociotechnical Change.* Cambridge: MIT Press.

Bijker, W. E., Law, J. (1992), *Shaping technology/building society: Studies in sociotechnical change.* Cambridge: MIT Press.

Bijker, W. E., Hughes, T. P., Pinch, T., Douglas, D. G. (1987), *The social construction of technological systems,* Cambridge: MIT Press.

Brown, B. (2001), "Thing Theory", *Critical Inquiry,* 28 (1), pp. 1-22.

Brown, B. (2004), *Things.* Chicago: University of Chicago Press.

Callon, M. (1986), "Some elements of a sociology of translation: domestication of the scallops and the fishermen of St. Brieuc Bay", *Power, Action, and Belief: A New Sociology of Knowledge,* London: Routledge, pp. 196-223.

Cetina, K. K. (2009), *Epistemic cultures: How the sciences make knowledge.* Cambridge: Harvard University Press.

Coletta, C., Colombo, S., Magaudda, P., Mattozzi, A., Parolin, L. L., Rampino, L. (2014), *A matter of design. Making society through science and technology.* Milano: Politecnico di Milano Press.

Cooren, F. (2010), *Action and agency in dialogue: Passion, incarnation and ventriloquism.* Amsterdam: John Benjamin Publishing.

Czarniawska B., (2007), *Shadowing: And Other Techniques for Doing Fieldwork in Modern Societies.* Copenhagen: Copenhagen Business School Press.

Engeström, Y., Middleton, D. (1998), *Cognition and Communication at Work.* Cambridge: Cambridge University Press.

Fallan, K. (2008), "De-scribing Design: Appropriating Script Analysis to Design History", *Design Issues,* 24 (4), pp. 61–75.

Farías, I., Wilkie, A. (eds.) (2015), *Studio Studies: Operations, Topologies & Displacements*. London: Routledge.

Gherardi, S. (2006), *Organizational Knowledge: The Texture of Workplace Learning*. Oxford: Blackwell.

Goodwin, C. (1994), "Professional Vision", *American Anthropologist*, 96 (3), pp. 606–633.

Greenbaum, J. M., Kyng, M. (eds.) (1991), *Design at work: cooperative design of computer systems*. Hillsdale: Lawrence Erlbaum Associates.

Hughes, T.P. (1999), "Edison and electric light", in MacKenzie, D., Wajcman J. (eds.), *The Social Shaping of Technology*. Buckingham: Open University Press, pp. 50–63.

Latour, B. (1987), *Science in action: How to follow scientists and engineers through society*. Cambridge: Harvard University Press.

Latour, B. (1996), *Aramis or the Love of Technology*. Cambridge: Harvard University Press.

Latour, B. (2005), *Reassembling the Social: An Introduction to Actor-Network-Theory*. Hampshire: Oxford University Press.

Latour, B. (2009), "A cautious Prometheus? A few steps toward a philosophy of design (with special attention to Peter Sloterdijk)", in Hackney, F. Glynne, J. Minton, V. (eds.), *Networks of Design. Proceedings of the 2008 Annual International Conference of the Design History Society*. Boca Raton: Universal Publishers, pp. 2-10.

Law, J. (2002), *Aircraft stories: Decentering the object in technoscience*. Durham: Duke University Press.

Nicolini, D. (2012), *Practice Theory, Work, and Organization: An Introduction*. Oxford: Oxford University Press.

Nicolini, D., Gherardi, S., Yanow, D. (2003), *Knowing in organizations: A practice-based approach*. Armonk: ME Sharpe.

Orlikowski, W. J. (1992), "The Duality of Technology: Rethinking the Concept of Technology in Organizations", *Organization Science*, 3 (3), pp. 398-427.

Oudshoorn, N., Pinch, T. (2003), *How users matter: the co-construction of users and technology (inside technology)*. Cambridge: MIT Press.

Parolin, L. L. (2010a), "Sulla produzione materiale. Qualità sensibili e sapere pratico nella stabilizzazione degli artefatti", *Tecnoscienza - The Italian Journal of Science and Technology Studies*, 1 (1), pp.39-56.

Parolin, L. L. (2010b), "L'innovazione nelle relazioni tra i nodi di un network. Il caso dei fornitori artigiani nell'industria del mobile", *Studi Organizzativi*, 2, pp. 55-74.

Parolin, L. L., Mattozzi, A. (2013), "Sensitive translations. Sensitive dimension and knowledge within the Italian furniture production sector" *Scandinavian Journal of Management*, 29 (4), pp. 353—366.

Parolin, L. L., Mattozzi, A. (2014), "Come meglio credi. Conoscenza tacita e innovazione nel distretto del legno-arredo della Brianza", *Polis*, 28 (3), pp. 365-392.

Shove, E., Watson, M., Hand, M., Ingram, J. (2007), *The Design of Everyday Life*. Oxford-New York: Berg.

Storni, C. (2012), "Unpacking Design Practices The Notion of Thing in the Making of Artifacts", *Science, Technology & Human Values*, 37 (1), pp. 88-123.

Suchman, L. A. (1987), *Plans and Situated Actions: The Problem of Human-Machine Communication*. Cambridge: Cambridge University Press.

Suchman, L. A. (2000), "Organizing alignment: A case of bridge-building", *Organization*, 7 (2), pp. 311-327.

Suchman, L. A. (2002), "Practice-Based Design of Information Systems: Notes from the Hyperdeveloped World", *The Information Society*, 18 (2), pp. 139-144.

Vinck, D. (2003), *Everyday Engineering: An Ethnography of Design and Innovation*. Cambridge: MIT Press.

Volonté, P. (2014), "Design Worlds and Science and Technology Studies", *Tecnoscienza - The Italian Journal of Science and Technology Studies*, 5 (2), pp. 5-14.

Yaneva, A. (2005), "Scaling Up and Down Extraction Trials in Architectural Design", *Social Studies of Science*, 35 (6), pp. 867–894.

Yaneva, A. (2009), *The Making of a Building: A Pragmatist Approach to Architecture*. Bern: Peter Lang.

DESIGN EXHIBITION THROUGH TECHNOLOGICAL INFRASTRUCTURING

Teresa Macchia

Introduction

This chapter will take the reader through the procedures of creating knowledge in the context of museums. In these pages we describe the design of an exhibition, as an *everyday, ongoing, temporary, contextualized* and *shared* process, which takes place between museum staff, visitors, objects and museum exhibition environment. Thus, *design* starts from a professional framework and manages to embrace the social activity enriching knowledge in the context of museums.

Hence, in order to underline the complexity and the ongoing feature of designing and temporary shaping a museum exhibition, we adopt the concept of *infrastructuring*. This concept helps to organize thoughts and connections around sociomaterial practices, relationships, and design processes in museums. Moreover, while the sociomaterial perspective emphasizes the complexity of placing people and technology together (that is *social* and *material*), the *infrastructuring* takes into account the sociomaterial point of view and connect to the environment. It, then, intermingles relationships and processes that arise and exist in time and in a certain context. Furthermore, *infrastructuring* deals with the exploration of making and doing, and includes an open process of contextualized making (Star and Bowker, 2002; Karasti and Syrjänen, 2004).

In the context of museums we talk about *infrastructuring* as a process to think about. Nevertheless, the process of *infrastructuring* is intrinsic in the domain of educational institutions like the museum itself. It is stimulating, creative and it shares knowledge among experts and non-experts (Star and Griesemer, 1989; Edwards et al., 2013). Thus, in this chapter we will focus on the role of technology in the process of creating knowledge, and will refer to it as Technological Infrastructuring (TI).

In order to describe the *infrastructuring* in a museum, we consider the museum institutions as Cultural Infrastructures (CI) that, once they are set up, they evolve through the interrelation and blending of people and artifacts. Therefore, even though curators and museum experts are traditionally the designers of an exhibition, visitors and everyday museum staff contribute to the *infrastructuring* process. This can be achieved through the appropriation of the exhibit itself in order to create knowledge. In this respect, visitors and museum staff appropriate and interpret the space through its usage. In the STS tradition, the concept of *appropriation* refers to the moment in which actors become users, start experiencing the environment, and own the technical objects (Silverstone et al., 1992). Additionally, the *appropriation* implies dynamics of design processes that are related to specific contexts in which different actors and objects are involved (MacKenzie, 1996). Creating and designing an object requires empathy and advices from groups of people brought together by the object itself or by the space.

In this regard, STS tradition incorporates the figure of designer and user following three main lines (see, for example, Odshoorn and Pinch, 2008): the continuity of the innovation over the process of diffusion of technologies; the innovation as a result of information transfer over the users; and the involvement of users in the formal design process. Therefore, the role of actors involved in the process of experiencing and constructing objects develops and changes through collaboration and cooperation in actual contexts. In fact, innovations and changes happen because actors are willing to modify the object and the related context (Latour, 1996).

Following the general perspective about the concept of appropriation, each change is a local and interrelated experience between actors, objects and context, which contribute to continuous reframing of objects in their context. Thus, changes include human, non-human and the environment, as components of the same process. In this respect, the interdisciplinary tradition of STS that focuses on "origins, dynamics, and consequences of science and technology" (Hackett et al., 2008), fulfils the need to understand complex and articulated environments. To support and help understanding design and introduction of technologies in the museum, we will be looking at what introducing technology into such an environment implies.

In order to understand the implication that technology has on the environment, we adopt the concept of *Technologically Enhanced Environ-*

ment (TEE). A TEE is a space configured by the introduction of technologies that support people's actions and interactions in a space designed to fulfil specific goals (Kaptelinin, 2012). Thus, the introduction of technology is about inserting elements meant for *"the aggregation of capabilities, facilities, skills, knowledge and organization required to successfully create a useful service or product"* in a space (Branscomb, 1995). Following this line of thought, we focus on museum spaces enriched by technology that is meant to engage visitors and also provide information. More precisely, we focus on museum spaces that provide information through unconventional objects and unconventional visiting experiences. Furthermore, we link the concept of TEE with the concept of Technologically Dense Environment (TDE). The latter refers to the stratification of contents in an organizational environment in connection to the capacity of making these components work together (Bruni, 2013).

While TDE focuses on relational features, technologies, practices and know-how of the organizational context, the concept of TEE refers on the constant actions to design organizational space that supports the construction of the above mentioned TDE. Thus, the concept of TEE includes the features of TDE, and emphasizes the process of designing organizational spaces.

In museum, the introduction of technologies creates new opportunities for visitors and museum staff to discover multiple ways to experience the exhibition environment in order to create knowledge. In this regard, the appropriation of the exhibition includes the mutual production of knowledge in the process of using and experiencing it. Thus, the appropriation blurs the predetermined roles of museum staff and visitors, and modifies the traditional predefined, formal and separated museum roles. As a result of the research conducted in the Museum of Science of Trento (Italy) – MUSE – this chapter describes the process of appropriation of museum TEE through the activity of *infrastructuring*. Hence, *infrastructuring* is about collaborating and collectively (re)designing the exhibition, underlining the dynamics of interrelations and connections in the context of the museum.

In these pages we will consider experiences we had at the MUSE, in which people are connecting to each other by touching and appropriating objects. Furthermore, we report the experiences we had in an exhibit that is a representation of a typical alpine forest.

This chapter is structured as follows: we first propose an overview of the museum as a CI. Then we interweave the concept of design and that of *infrastructuring* to contribute to the *ongoing* temporary visiting design process. We continue these conceptual lines presenting cases that exemplify the *ongoing* temporary design. At the end of the chapter we reiterate the concept of *infrastructuring* in a museum environment that is a design process that is embedded in the context itself. That happens through the active participation of visitors.

1. Understanding museum dynamics

A recent trend in museum studies seeks to find new ways of understanding designing exhibitions, since the visit is considered as a situated and complex process as well (MacDonald, 2007). Following this trend that emphasizes the response of visitors to museum stimulus, we seek to bring visiting experiences to a higher design level in which visitors, spending time and acting and performing in the museum, are the designers of their own experience. The process of outlining what happens in the museum environment triggers the adoption of generalizations about the context itself that might be far from the representation of the actual complexity of museum exhibitions; these exhibitions are characterized by human and non-human interactions. The interactions that occur in the museum among visitors, museum staff, museum spaces, objects and technologies refer to the creation of knowledge and understanding of the exhibit. Thus, the analysis of these dynamics requires an intellectual tool that underlines the ongoing and contextualized features of a museum exhibition.

The concept of Infrastructure provides a set of instruments for analysing and describing the ongoing and persistent character of *infrastructuring* process (Karasti and Syrjänen, 2004). Thus, *infrastructuring* incorporates the dynamics that connect features and activities of human and non-human in the social framework. The social framework includes actors, practices and dialogues that happen through an ongoing process during a specific period of time (Clarke and Star, 2008). Additionally, Gibson (2005) describes *framework* as a box that contains a universal set of variables to describe phenomena. For us, the meaning of framework is useful for a better understanding of the concept of Infrastructure that, indeed, inscribes the social framework, the actors, the features and the practices, in and through the institutions.

Observations in the museum demonstrate repetitions and constancies, which, in the beginning, might seem peculiar and even eccentric. However, participating in the museum's everyday life you learn how to distinguish between dynamics that look like as they belong to a specific situation but that in fact may represent general conditions. Consequently, some of the dynamics observed during the time spent at the MUSE, stimulate further thinking about the process of the appropriation of the exhibition to create new knowledge.

The creation of *things* is specific to the designer profession, since designers create products or representations of products (Shön, 1983). As Shön describes (1983) the design process, the creation of *things* happens under various conditions, and through different variables, such as norms, materials, relationships and language interpretations. Thus, design is related to the creation of tangible things, like products, artifacts, buildings, and that of immaterial things, such as policymaking, organization practices and knowledge. The design process is commonly connected to professionals who are in charge of creating something, with or without the support of non-design-experts. Moreover, design is about breaking the relationship with the past and looking at something new (Latour, 2009).

We adopt the concept of infrastructure as a conceptual tool for understanding the creation of knowledge in the context of a museum. Hence, we consider the museum a CI and the creation of new understanding about the museum context as Infrastructuring knowledge.

2. Infrastructure and infrastructuring

The everyday notion of infrastructure is commonly related to structures that stand on the background and allow connections between parts, e.g. transportation *infrastructure*, water *infrastructure*, communication *infrastructure*, etc. In other words, we commonly describe infrastructures as systems that operate within a social, organizational configuration to provide natural or artificial resources. However, studies and discussions about this topic underline the fuzziness and richness behind it. Indeed, since Star and Ruhleder, (1996) with a critical eye, introduced the topic on the academic scene, an increasing number of scholars keep their attention on this concept. They focused on information systems overall that are meant to carry and create it through an association of elements (See Star and Ruhleder, 1996; Bowker and Star, 1999; Karasti et al., 2008; Pipek and Wulf, 2009).

Other points of view such as the Active Theory (Nardi, 1996), take into account the introduction of technologies in human activities. Additionally, discussions about *Infrastructure* need to take into account a robust network of people, artifacts, materials that generates innovation in the context of reference (Edwards et al. 2007). Thus, *Infrastructure* is an apparatus for supporting a collective need to *communicate, move* or *inform*, which is contextualized, ready to be used and practically responsive. Accordingly, we describe the *infrastructure* as embedded and embedding social practices and contextual elements that shape the meaning and the function of the *infrastructure* itself. To familiarize the museum with the concept of *infrastructure*, we propose to emphasize the cultural role played by museums, in order to prompt a set of characteristics that belong to museums. As mentioned above, we describe these institutions as CI.

The notion of *culture* is related to a society and it is about what people have to know, or perceive, and believe to know, to adequately relate to the other members of the society (Ingold, 2001). Nevertheless, institutions mediate the production of culture through formal or informal rules that support and direct social behaviour. In this respect, museum institutions are meant to preserve and provide tangible and intangible heritage, bestowing and stimulating culture, knowledge and social identity (Bennet, 1995). We rather talk about CI in order to emphasize the cultural character of this infrastructure, and we implicitly recognize practices, languages and signals that are commonly understood and followed by a community.

In this regard, CI refers to practices, relationships, tools and contexts that allow keeping and stimulating culture over time. About this Marcotte and Bernier (2011), referring to the cultural public sector and seeking a definition to support the cultural polices, divide CIs into those for producing and spreading culture, and those for communicating culture. Following their classification, we consider museums as both material and communicative CI since they respond to different needs: communicating, producing and spreading culture. In addition, the role of museums is to stimulate reflectiveness and creativity among people. Both reflectiveness and creativity are social activities and processes that imply the creation of new meanings and outcomes (Boud, 2006) through sharing dialogues and contents. Additionally, we integrate the CI in a tangible, physical and geographical area since it is a result of real actions.

In these particular circumstances, museum institutions allow the production of knowledge, providing spaces and technology to communicate it. This point of view on museums connects and follows the literature on infrastructure, in which we embed the visiting experience as an *infrastructuring* process. The *infrastructuring* process is meant to emphasize the role of museum institutions in stimulating the interaction between human and non-human. Thus, *infrastructuring* is a process designed to create and appropriate the space through interacting, doing, making, using objects and technology. In the setting of MUSE the process of *infrastructuring* is very often about touching and experimenting scientific objects or natural phenomenon representations that combine and enrich previous knowledge with new information. In this perspective, *infrastructuring* is an intellectual tool for understanding the dynamics of the museum experience. Various authors adopt this concept to analyze different topics. For example, while Star and Bowker (2002) propose guidelines and directions to study the theme of infrastructure, Karasti and Syrjänen (2004) focus on community design and processes through everyday materials. Moreover, Binder et al. (2011) consider *designing things* as an ensemble of enduring sociomaterial relationships. And, Marttila and colleagues (2013) concur and add the concept of commons.

The common aspects among the different interpretations lie in the description of *infrastructuring* as an ongoing and relational involvement of people in the process of modifying the existing state of things and creating something new. We also agree with this interpretation of infrastructuring that is an ongoing process characterized by social practices that involves visitors and museum experts. In this way, museum experts are called to represent and explain complex natural facts to laymen. Consequently, *infrastructuring* is a process of interpreting and modifying an exhibition with and for its visitors. Thus, this concept provides useful guidelines for understanding museum of science exhibitions as dynamic and evolving environments that happen through actions, interactions and stimulation of knowledge using technology.

At a practical level, Infrastructuring implies a set of actions, relationships and dialogues, that take place in a museum and that are meaningful through the use of technology in that space.

Since the aim of this chapter is to examine the concept of design as an ongoing, temporary situated activity that takes place in a given setting, we consider design to be a description of micro-situations in which phenomena occur (Olsen and Heaton, 2010) and a report of everyday ethnographical museum experience. That will explain the concept of designing exhibitions through the interrelation between human, non-human and a context.

3. Entering the field

We use ethnography to explore and keep informed of the museum context. Indeed, ethnography stresses on practices and social behaviours as they are, rather than as they are meant to be or they should be. Ethnography is included in the ethnomethodological approach that studies the everyday life (Silverman, 2008). The adoption of such approach for investigation intends to avoid misconception and to cross out a priori prejudices. Additionally, ethnomethodology deals with founded and practical conditions and actions that become actual and ethnographic analysis of the phenomenon (Garfinkel, 1967). Nevertheless, entering the context with the intention to grasp knowledge from the context itself can bring the researcher to unexpected situations related to the subculture they are studying.

We got access to the museum after negotiations via e-mail, over the phone and during meetings. First we got access to a new area for children. The museum management wanted to have an impartial report about their latest creation, which we concluded after a two-month research at the MUSE. Thanks to visitors and the museum staff, we had a very good and insightful experience. We reported back to the museum management about the activities and the observations collected there every two weeks. Even though these months have been rich and fruitful, we were looking for some more data and, at the same time, the museum management needed more information about another children area. Therefore, they suggested that we should research another children area. The two areas are different for the following major reasons: (1) the first investigated area was designed for babies and young children up to five years old, while the second one is for elementary school children; (2) because of the presence of babies, the first area is protected by glass walls; (3) the area for babies and young children is digitally interactive and proactive, while the area for older children is mainly analogical. Even though, both museum areas gave us an interesting insight, in this chapter we will focus on the second children area observed, the one for school children. Thus, we stress on the different and multiple types of technology that characterize a TEE.

The following paragraphs introduce the reader to the period of ethnographic observations of a museum area for school children.

4. The "Discovery" exhibition

The Head of Education department of the museum, her assistant and I discussed what to focus our attention on during our research and they mentioned an area for children that demonstrated criticality since the opening of the museum. The area, named *Discovery* is on the third floor of the MUSE, and it describes and shows children characteristics of the forests in the Alps.

The third floor is divided into four areas: an area that provides information about the flora and the fauna of the Alps through informative panels, representations and videos; another area describes the birds' migration; a third area that is a sort of a labyrinth which simulates the alpine forest with animals, pictures and representative elements; a fourth area, the *Discovery*, is a stylized exemplification of alpine forests (See Figure 1).

Figure 1: the Discovery - MUSE – Italy

Currently, the management of the museum is discussing possible and partial refurbishing of the area, mostly because adults and children alike mistake this area for a playground. Where children lose their self-control and parents sit on the benches relaxing a couple of minutes before proceeding further. The colorful and soft objects organized and exhibited there, recalling a natural science laboratory, are meant to invite children to explore them. The area consists of six main components (See Figure 1): (1) a chest with drawers containing insects, bird feathers and legs and representations of animal skulls and feces (See Figure 2a); three stylized bushes, (2) one of which smells like forest, (3) a component that encourages children to use their tactile sense by guessing the objects linked to the elements in the drawers of the chest and (4) a fourth one has some lenses that magnify the articles in the drawers. In the drawers of a small tower (5) there are representations of wild animal footprints like rate, lynx, wolf, roe and bear. In one of the corners there is also an interactive game (6) that can be used by four people simultaneously.

In the middle of the area there is a representation of a tree that hosts cuddly toys that recall woodland creatures. There is also a table that provides a useful surface for group-guided tour activities.

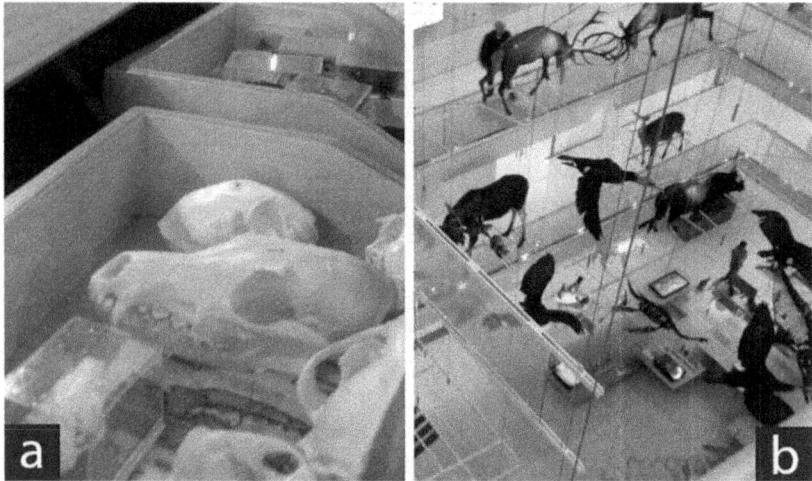

Figure 2: (a) animal skulls in the drawers; (b) suspended animals in the museum "tree".

Since the opening of the museum, in July 2013, the area required small but constant adjustments because of continuous misinterpretation of the space. Very often adults consider the area as a sort of a kindergarten instead of an actual museum-area and allow their children to express themselves regardless the way they do that. In order to contain uncontrolled expressions of vivacity, the museum management has taken several measures. It positioned some silhouettes of plastic bushes on the perimeter to delimit the space. A sign, advising adults to remain with their children has also been placed there. And, finally, it has been decided that one person from the museum staff has to supervise the area at all times.

With some exceptions, due to the overall huge number of visitors during weekends, those measures improved the quality of the visiting experience of the *Discovery*. Firstly, because most of the times children and adults explore the area together; secondly, since the members of staff are professional natural scientists, they provide visitors with continuous, additional information. The third measure taken by the management of the museum had a beneficial effect on visiting this space. As a consequence, some visitors enjoy coming back to the area. My observation is based on two examples. The first one is that of a family that we had the chance to meet three times in the area because parents and children alike enjoyed talking with the staff members. Another family came because the child had visited the area with the school and wished to show and report everything she learned from the staff in that area to her parents.

On one hand, informative panels provide clear information in the perimeter and the friendliness of the environment stimulate children to approach the area; on the other hand, the professionalism, knowledge and skills of the museum staff equally engage children, adults, teenagers and elderly people.

The *Pilots*, as the scientists of the museum are called, are useful for explaining specific elements, which otherwise non-experts would just disregard. One of these elements is animal footprints, for example. Thus, with the support of the Pilots' knowledge visitors can look at the objects in that predetermined space from an innovative perspective (Harty, 2010), since their access to information let them re-configure and redefine the meaning of the space. In this perspective, the environment changes its purpose, and, following a new path, visitors modify their behaviour by interacting with the objects around them and also with other people. As, we will see in detail in the following pages, visitors behave differently if there is an expert around who can provide them with impromptu information about the objects there. Even though their actions might look unpremeditated and confusing in the beginning, they feel at ease among six components.

4.1. What happens in the Woods?

In this sub-paragraph, we describe an everyday experience in the Discovery. With the help of this description we aim to stimulate the readers' interest in infrastructuring process. We talk about our experience during one morning of an ordinary day. We focus on the morning because that is when the events that interest us took place. Our interest here is to underline the kind of dynamics that facilitate understanding the visitors' experience and also that of the museum professionals.

We adopt a diary format interwoven with external explanations in order to express the complexity of the museum environment.

"It is a Wednesday morning, in December. It has been one month now that I have been coming here four times a week after the first period of observations. The museum today will be opened until 10pm. It is five minutes before the opening time and, even if at this time last Sunday there was already a long cue, today there are less people waiting to enter. In order to pass unnoticed I enter from the exit side; I take the elevator wondering who is the Pilot in charge of the Discovery today."

The *Pilot* can be negatively influenced by my observations if she or he considers them inadequate, and may choose to keep me at a distance. Fortunately, very often I perceive a positive feeling from the *Pilots* that facilitate my research. Their know-how is a precious resource for me, even though I prefer looking at the situations without pre-concepts so I do not interview them.

"I look around. Two Pilots are in charge of this floor, one of the entire floor and the other one just of the Discovery. I can work really well with both of them. In fact once the one who is looking after the entire floor spent some of his free time explaining me some basics aspects of the exhibition on this floor. The Pilot in the Discovery area is in charge of this space for a week now and every day I come I find her here. For at least a quarter of an hour we will not see any visitor on this floor since visitors start their visit either from the first or from the fifth floor. Thus, I keep talking with the two Pilots. As it often happens, they start sharing their museum-episodes with me. They usually describe the criticality and the tough situations they have been involved in."

Sometimes the *Pilots* guide schools group tours and they decide how to organize the visit and what to say to the students. They also tell me how they improved their knowledge on the subject in question and how they get new information for their guided tours. For example, they read bro-chures and books, and visit natural parks together with other *Pilots*. Very often they are not aware of how much time they spend training. According to their statements, learning is part of their job description, so they do it willingly. But later on they intermingle this new information with their personal experience and with that obtained *"in the wild"* of the museum of natural science. Having this much information, their help and input become priceless for museum visitors.

> *"Today, the Pilot in charge of the Discovery is telling us about her personal experience with some mice in her house. She is living up in the mountains where they border the forest and she has some difficulties with keeping mice off her property. She is telling us about some methods for capturing mice, which seem to have worked for almost all the mice but one. As she has been telling us, one last mouse got smarter over the past hunting attempts. The other Pilot suggests additional solutions. The ways he suggests to get rid of mice are linked to his professional knowledge of the forest wildlife. The Pilots' enthusiasm stimulates my interest and thirst for knowledge. Every time I have the opportunity to discuss with the Pilots, I learn something new and the wish to deepen my studies grows. Therefore, whenever there is time and the possibility, I do not hesitate to ask them more questions."*

Very often visitors are enthusiastic to receive additional information, too, so they ask *Pilots* for more detailed explanations. That happens mostly in the *Discovery* area, where visitors remain longer, due to its cosiness. Plus, there are fewer people there, usually, no more than twelve, which means three families. The *Pilots* are generally willing to provide additional information, if visitors are really interested in knowing more about wildlife in the forest. Their experience also helps *Pilots to* easily understand if there actually is a real interest behind visitors' questions, mainly when it comes to youngsters or children. This important category of visitors in the *Discovery* area manifests their interest through questions and interacting with authentic objects rather than using the interactive game. (See Figure 1 object n. 6). Teenagers and adults, on the other hand, have a different approach to the exhibit. They manifest their interest by immediately starting investigating with the aid of the interactive game. This game is aimed to teach about eating habits of wild animals. Four players can use interactive game simultaneously. Each one of the participants has to choose an animal-avatar; each animal-avatar eats as many animals as the player can drag and drop from the middle of the screen (See Figure 3).

The interactive game is very lifelike and even though it is useful for putting the teenagers and adult visitors at ease, it stimulates questions like

"Does the hawk eat everything?" or *"How is it possible that the mouse doesn't eat worms?"*

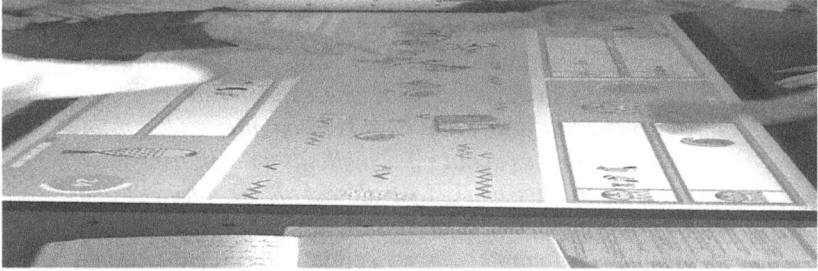

Figure 3: Drag and drop; children and an adult playing with the interactive game

"After talking about techniques for capturing mice, we open a new discussion about eating habits that push some animal species, like owls, to move away from the city centers, where there are no small animals anymore. Afterwards, I ask for clarifications about the interactive game, wondering if it is realistic or if it is just an approximate representation of natural conditions. Both Pilots tell me that the game is actually close to reality, just with some minor simplifications. One of the two scientists, after a brief pause says smiling "... I can see why you'd have trouble understanding it.""

"A first bunch of active, elderly visitors arrives with the group guide. The three of us take our positions as neither Pilots nor I can sit when visitors are around. The Pilot in charge of the floor stands next to the glass-fence. I stand behind the chest of drawers with my red notebook. I am visible enough but without interfering. The other Pilot arranges the informative files in the Discovery. Two men do not appear to be really interested in the guide explanation and stroll around, looking from time to time my way – I am writing down everything that was said earlier in my notebook. The two men walk to a case with two Californian lizards inside and comment while waving in front of the infrared camera installed to look at the temperature of lizards. The case is exactly in front of the Discovery therefore they move away from their group and enter the area. Perhaps because the height of the

*bush for the tactile experience (see Figure 1 object n.3) is also
suitable for adults, or maybe because it is in a good position,
they push the small mushroom on the top of the bush as if
they were pushing some buttons to switch on something. The
Pilot intervenes describing them the space and showing the
more interesting pieces: the skull of a young deer with an ant-
ler and the skull of the buckskin with horns. With this action
she breaks the ice, introduces me and specifies the reasons for
my being there. The two men call two friends of theirs over,
who were still with the group, in order to share with them the
interesting information given by the Pilot. In turn, the four
men ask for additional information related to their own experience in the woods. By sharing each other's memories of
the forest, the Pilot and the men stimulate and activate conditions for mutual learning mediated by the objects in the
chest of drawer. It seems that the Discovery becomes an actual forest: a sensible source for sharing environmental and
natural experience and knowledge."*

The environment, even though designed for children, stimulates multiple categories of visitors to learn and to converse filling the generation
gap. Similar situations occur more often when visitors touch objects rather than when they use visual and audio devices. Hence, dialogues between visitors and with the *Pilots* start spontaneously.

Visitors demonstrate interest in the exhibition itself; therefore the exhibition can be considered a successful one. The design of the exhibition
can stimulate different levels of interest. This doesn't mean that everyone
appreciates all the exhibits; this means that the design of the exhibition
met all needs.

*"After a quarter of an hour the men are still in the Discov-
ery. No one else comes on the third floor today, and while
three of them leave the space, the fourth one asks about a
bush of flowers (see Figure 1 object n.1). The Pilot is called by
a colleague on the walky-talky and has to leave for a couple
of minutes. Thus, it is left to me to explain what the challenge
is, that is he has to recognise what kind of smell each flower
has. The man accepts the challenge and smells. He recognises
the six perfumes after a couple of tries (visitors usually need a*

few suggestions). Seeing my surprise the man explains me that he has worked for years as a chef and says that this job trains people to distinguish different smells. Besides, he really enjoys walking in the woods. Moreover, he shares with me his experiences in the woods while picking up mushrooms and about how he learned the right techniques to do that when he was younger and had to read the signs in the forest. In the meanwhile the Pilot comes back and a girl and her mother are approaching the area. The man thanks for the time spent in the Discovery, says goodbye and leaves. The child and her mother enter. I introduce myself because the Pilot is giving information to another visitor that has just entered at the same time. Ann[14] is three years old and with her mother is exploring the tactile bush (Figure 1 object n. 3) and in the meantime two other children enter the area with their father – Liza is two years old and Mat is five years old. Liza scampers to the direction of the tactile bush and observes carefully Ann's actions before imitating her."

Very often children avoid the tactile bush when no one else is using it. We suppose that it is because they have to put their hand in a hole without knowing what it is in there. This action provokes suspicion and even fear. Another reason for the children feeling uneasy while using the game comes from the fact that they may be afraid of making mistakes while guessing. Very often visitors, both adults and children, pull out the small mushroom on the top of the bush first to watch everything there is inside and then they touch the objects there.

"Ann and Liza explore together the tactile bush, and the parents play with them even though Liza's father moves from time to time to the tower with footprints (Figure 1 object n. 5), where Mat is. Mat is more attracted by them than by touching unknown things. In the meantime, the Pilot is giving the boy useful information about the footprints in the tower. Mat's eyes are glowing with interest and he asks numerous questions that make the Pilot move to the chest of drawers to provide it. Meanwhile Ann and her mother leave

---

[14] In order to preserve participants' anonimity, names are fictitious.

the area to go for lunch; Liza, holding her father's hand, joins Mat who is still talking with the Pilot. The discussion is enriched with their father's memories about their mountain trip taken during summer. The child even starts giving some details he remembers. It is lunchtime and after forty minutes of talking and playing the father and the two children leave the Discovery area. It is empty again so I can take my break. During that morning nobody used the interactive game."

This usually happens when the *Pilot* is available and when there are too few people. The game is a space for sharing knowledge when there are too much visitors, and attraction for teenagers, so they use it as an excuse to enter an area designed for children.

"When I come back a five-year-old girl enters the area with her mother and they are both attracted by the smelly bush (Figure 1 object n. 2). *The space becomes quickly a research environment for the child has a small notebook where she draws the things she observes. Obviously, this is not the first time she comes to visit the area. After having introduced myself, I ask the child for information. The mother smiles when the child tells me that she has been there with her school and she think her daughter might want to become a natural scientist that would work with the museum. The Pilot asks the child about her interest in nature in order to give her some information about that. Therefore, they start talking about the forests in the Alps and about the changes happened there during the past fifty years because of the urbanization of the area. The child doesn't draw anymore and listens carefully to the Pilot as if she had been telling her a fairy tale. After the short dialog about the forest they leave since the child has already seen the elements exposed in the area during her previous visit."*

"A few minutes later, a father with two children enters the Discovery. They look around to decide where to start from, and the elder child, a nine year old boy, chooses to start with the interactive game. The three of them sit and try to comprehend how the game functions. Understanding this game

is quite challenging even though the title "Acchiappa la Pap-pa"[15] gives users a hint. This has been the first time today that somebody uses the interactive game. They play until all of them manage to gather the same amount of food for their animal-avatar. Since they all have chosen animals that have similar diets and they all play to win, they decide to change the animal-avatars with ones with different diets. The reason why they do that is because the food available for each avatar is limited. The two children and their father were playing with the game imitating the actual needs of wild animals. They decided to choose different animal-avatars in order to have the same chances to arrive first and win the game. In-deed, in the forest there are carnivores, herbivores and omni-vores, and the youngest child chose the omnivore avatar (the fox) in order to have more food choices."

5. Technological Infrastructuring: collaborating to design exhibitions

Doing field research in museums is about opening a window to the dynamics of Infrastructuring, and to the continuous design activity and interpretation of a space. It is about looking at possible changes required by the environment itself and by the people who act in it, as well. Indeed, we take into account the interrelation among the environment, humans and non-humans to clarify the meaning of infrastructuring as a process that involves the construction of knowledge through technology. The ways in which museum visitors create knowledge is individual and tacit and it is not necessarily related to the textual elements exposed in the area. It is about TI is a temporary and contextualized experience that has to do with touching, discussing, interpreting and manipulating objects and with understanding them.

As we have written in the beginning of this chapter, Infrastructuring combines materiality and knowledge that give sense to this technology in a specific environment. In fact, we share Montmollin's (1996) opinion on the description of technical activities, who says that the technical activities have meaning when also considered a social process. Thus, we consider "technological aids" like that chest of drawers that hosts footprints and

---

[15] The translation from the Italian title to English would be "*Grab the grub*".

animal skulls, as well as the interactive game. The action of opening the drawers and making their technological feature the source of a discussion, stimulates an interpretation of the environment that moves and follows the present needs.

We can also say that the process of design exhibitions is something that occurs in a limited working period, in a specific context and through and because of technologies. In this view, the design activity of thinking, experiencing and manipulating technologies, and also that of sharing knowledge, takes place in configured environments. There, it acquires new meanings through interrelationships between visitors and technology. As shown in the previous paragraph visitors and *Pilots* look at the environment with fresh eyes every time and design new exhibition every single time. When visitors enter the space and move around in order to decide upon how to interact with the objects, they activate a set of practices and changes that influence the *Pilots'* actions. At the same time the *Pilots'* behaviour affects visitors' actions, as well as the presence or the absence of other visitors.

The design of the environment is previously defined by museum and design professionals, therefore visitors and museum staff have to take it as a given. The process of creating relationships and meaning during the visit adjust the *a priory* design for the immediate requirements of visitors and *Pilots*. While doing so, we all participate in designing knowledge: everyone from her or his point of view and perspective provides something new to the others, which can not only modify but also improve the meaning of that environment. TI is about interpreting the environment and re-designing it for creating knowledge by manipulating technology. In a museum context, where the focus is on creating knowledge, TI means altering the exhibition with everyone's participation and arising new meanings and understanding in an entertaining yet scientific and technological way.

The observations made in the museum of Trento stimulate a reconsideration of the design process as an outcome of contextualized activities that includes and requires technologies to occur. Indeed, the interpretation of technologies and the actions embodied in these technologies suggest an overview of the exhibition as an evolving environment. During our observations, the exhibition environment has been perceived as a blank page, where visitors and *Pilots* have to write on their stories like the above mentioned story of the forests in the Alps. The process of drawing new contents stimulates interpretation and reconfiguration of the objects in connection to previous experience and knowledge of both visitors and

Pilots. Thus, the process of sharing knowledge is a practical and contextualized interaction. For instance, the man who explained the reasons for being able to recognizing smells was extrapolating and decontextualizing that smell so as to recognize it. He was indeed reconfiguring the smells in another context, giving sense to the bush structure. Moreover, reconfiguring and interpreting the exhibition environment is a common process that lets visitors have their own interpretation of the exhibition. For example, the father and the two children identified themselves with some animals in order to win the game. Other visitors played using the same animal-avatar but having in mind different targets like deciding, who is faster in dragging and dropping. Thus, the exhibition design is something that evolves with every participant, whether we take into consideration visitors, museum staff or researchers.

Clearly, describing the visiting process as an infrastructuring process of technology we implicitly consider actions meant for the creation and stimulation of knowledge through the mediation of objects, structures and items. This is not the case for other structured institutions with educational purpose, such as schools. Starting with Mody and Kaiser's (2008) opinion, who describe classrooms as messy place, we look at museum exhibitions in the same way. In fact, studied from different perspectives and for different reasons, museum exhibitions contribute to the construction of knowledge involving experts and non-experts and stimulating different interpretations of specific subjects. In this perspective, TI is about building relationships and connections between contents, information, and the people who act in that context, while giving a meaning to technology. Thus, infrastructuring is a process that takes place *here* and *now*, reconfigures the exhibition environment in the eyes of the participants and has ramifications into the future of both visitors and the museum staff.

The creation of knowledge and looking at the exhibition with fresh eyes is about designing a new exhibition starting from the old one with the help of visitors and the museum staff. Thus, they all contribute to develop something new. The new exhibit is seen as permanent by visitors, who are temporary experiencing the exhibition, and it is seen temporary by the museum staff.

TI provides designers with an interpretation of museum exhibitions and of the devices existing there. This concept highlights the complexity of a museum environment by looking at technologies as if they were a means to interpret and understand that environment. Because of the temporary, contextualized and ongoing effects of interpreting technologies in a museum environment, the introduction of technologies should to take into consideration several aspects like: (1) the meanings of technologies, (2) the reasons for introducing those specific technologies there, (3) the possible effects that these technologies have upon other technologies or upon the environment as a whole and (4) to the relationship with the people who use the space and with previous knowledge.

Additionally, designing a museum environment is about reshaping future and knowledge, embedding everyday actions into a given social context and interweaving professional expertise with the creativity of non-experts. That can be achieved using objects, games, and informative files, visual representations of nature and so on and so forth. Thus, designing an exhibition is a social experience that goes hand in hand with the concept of Infrastructuring. That is valid whether we talk about KI if the emphasis is on the knowledge, or, if the focus is on technology, we can call it TI. Still, Infrastructuring is a much more complex process that includes multiple elements, takes into account the kind of relationships that arise in that given context, and can relate to different targets. In the context of a museum, the moment of sharing knowledge between expert and non-expert creates relationships that connect current contextual conditions, human and non-human to forward a perspective of knowledge change.

The designing process is intrinsically connected to the technological experience of both visitors and the museum staff. Thus, we underline the role of people in the museum to create new understanding through testing and experiencing the space itself. Expert designers have the key role in thinking and creating a space that invites visitors to create their own path of knowledge. Professional designers could argue that there is not intentionality in the process of creating knowledge but we agree with that up to a certain extent. Hence, we rather describe this infrastructuring process one that develops within the context itself.

Conclusion

The evolution of museums as inclusive and open environments, calls into question the museum visiting experience as a practice to create collective knowledge. This chapter talks about the concept of design as a social activity that occurs in museum contexts and through museum objects to make knowledge. Thus, the chapter focuses on the delicate dynamics around sharing and creating knowledge in the context of a museum exhibition professionally designed for children and redesigned through everyday actions and interpretations by visitors and museum staff. Using an ethnographic point of view we introduce the notion of making knowledge in the context of museums, how and when knowledge occurs, through which dynamics people stimulate knowledge and create the conditions to share it. These dynamics and conditions are about reconfiguring the environment through people's perspectives and interpretations that might be different for norms and forms.

The reconfiguration of the space redefines the design process as an infrastructuring activity using techniques that make the exhibition define the visiting experience as a continuous and evolving activity to create knowledge rather than a predefined and structured action. Thus, the concept of IT emphasizes the process of giving meaning, reconfiguring and reshaping the museum environment through technology. TI, the reconfiguration and the reshaping of the environment, the connection between experts and non-experts with the help of technology, memories and previous knowledge and understanding, is about using a personal touch and interpreting the context as a stimulus to create experiences and understanding.

Thus, this chapter shall stimulate further reasoning on the complexity of TEE and about how the dynamics of acting in these environments are actual design processes that look towards a desirable future (Shön, 1983). Being active in a TEE is about participating to everyday actions. IT gives them significance by using objects and techniques to understand them, and stimulates dialogues to reshapes and interprets the space. In this perspective, we consider designing exhibitions an additional process that implies giving meaning to the exhibition, making it clear and tangible instead of creating something from the beginning for both the visitors and museum staff. By now, we should have a clear image of how museum exhibitions operate. Even though they are designed by designer experts and museum professionals they are not just about reconfiguring and creating relationships through people and technologies every day and for everyone. Moreover, we should be looking at the exhibition as an open, blank notebook in which people draw and write their own story. We have to look at the design of an exhibition from a new and open-ended perspective.

Acknowledgements

Firstly, I have to thank professor Vincenzo D'Andrea for his priceless human and professional support. Secondly, I thank the visitors who allowed us to be a part of their visiting experience and the Pilots who shared their knowledge. Last but not least, thanks to the management of the Museum of Science of Trento and, specifically to Samuela Caliari and Rosaria Viola for their involvement in this research.

References

Bennett, T. (1995), *The Birth of the Museum: History, Theory, Politics.* New York & London: Routledge.

Binder, T., De Michelis, G., Ehn, P., Jacucci G., Linde, P. and Wagner, I. (2011), *Design Things. A. Telier.* Cambridge: The MIT Press.

Boud, D. (2006) "Creating the space for reflection at work", in Boud, D., Cressey, P., Docherty, P. (eds.), *Productive Reflection at Work.* New York & London: Routledge.

Bowker, G. C., Star, S. L. (2000), *Sorting Things Out: Classification and Its Consequences.* Cambridge: MIT Press.

Branscomb, L. M. (1995), *Confessions of a Technophile.* Woodbury: AIP Press.

Bruni, A., Pinch, T., Schubert, C. (2013), "Technologically Dense Environments: What For? What Next?", *Italian Journal of Science & Technology Studies,* 4 (2), pp. 51-72.

Clarke, A. E., Star, S. L. (2008), "The Social World Framework: A theory/ Methods Package", in Hackett, E., Amsterdamska, O., Lynch, M., Wajcman, J. (eds.) *The Handbook of Science and Technology Studies.* Cambridge: MIT Press.

Edwards, P. N., Jackson, S. J., Bowker, G. C., Knobel, C. P. (2007). "Understanding Infrastructure: Dynamics, Tensions, and Design". Ann Arbor: Deep Blue. http://hdl.handle.net/2027.42/49353.

Edwards, P. N., Jackson, S. J., Chalmers, M. K., Bowker, G. C., Borgman, C. L., Ribes, D., Burton, M., Calvert, S. (2013), "Knowledge Infrastructures: Intellectual Frameworks and Research Challenges". Ann Arbor: Deep Blue. http://hdl.handle.net/2027.42/97552.

Garfinkel, H. (1967), *Studies in Ethnomethodology.* Cambridge: Polity Press.

Gibson, C. C. (2005), "In Pursuit of Better Policy Outcomes", *Journal of Economic Behavior & Organization,* 57 (2), pp. 227–230.

Oudshoorn, N., Pinch, T. (2008), "User-Technology Relationships: Some Recent Developments", in Hackett, E., Amsterdamska, O., Lynch, M., Wajcman, J. (eds.) *The Handbook of Science and Technology Studies.* Cambridge: The MIT Press.

Hackett, E., Amsterdamska, O., Lynch, M., Wajcman, J. (eds.) (2008), *The Handbook of Science and Technology Studies.* Cambridge: MIT Press.

Harty, C. (2010), "Implementing innovation: designers, users and actor networks", *Technology Analysis & Strategic Management,* 22 (3), pp. 297-315.

Ingold, T. (2001), *Ecologia della Cultura.* Roma: Meltemi.

Kaptelinin, V., Bannon, L. J. (2012), "Interaction Design Beyond the Product: Creating Technology-Enhanced Activity Space", *Human-Computer Interaction,* 27 (3), pp. 277-309.

Karasti, H., Baker, K. S. (2008), "Community Design: Growing One's Own Information Infrastructure", *PDC'08,* Oct 1-4 2008; Bloomington: ACM Press.

Karasti, H., Syrjänen, A-L. (2004), "Artful infrastructuring in two cases of community PD", *PDC'04,* July 27-31 2004; Toronto: ACM Press.

Latour, B. (1996), *Aramis or the love of technology.* Cambridge: Harvard University Press.

Latour, B. (2009), "A Cautious Prometheus? A Few Steps Toward a Philosophy of Design (With Special Attention to Peter Sloterdijk)" in Hackney, F., Glynne, J., Minton, V. (eds.), *Networks of Design. Proceedings of the 2008 Annual International Conference of the Design History Society (UK) University College Falmouth,* 3-6 September. Boca Raton, Universal Publishers, pp. 2-10.

Macdonald, S. (2006), "Expanding museum studies: An introduction", in Macdonald, S. (ed.), *A companion to museum studies.* Oxford: Blackwell Publishing.

MacKenzie, D. (1996), *Knowing machines. Essays on technical change.* Cambridge: MIT Press.

Marttila et al. (2013), "Infrastructuring the Commons?" Extended blog post based on the presentation at Infrastructuring the Commons Seminar, Helsinki, Finland. http://co-p2p.mlog.taik.fi.

Mody, C., Kaiser, D. (2008), "Scientific Training and the creation of scientific knowledge" in Hackett, E., Amsterdamska, O., Lynch, M., Wajcman, J. (eds.) *The Handbook of Science and Technology Studies,* Cambridge: MIT Press.

Montmollin, M. (1996), *L'ergonimie,* Paris: La Découverte.

Nardi, B. (1996), *Context and Consciousness: Activity Theory and Human-Computer Interaction*. Cambridge: MIT Press.

Olsen, P. B., Heaton, L. (2010), "Knowing through design" in Simonsen, J., Bærenholdt, J.O., Büscher, M. and Scheuer, J.D. (eds.), *Design Research Synergies from interdisciplinary perspectives*, New York and London: Routledge.

Pipek, V., Wulf, V. (2009), "Infrastructuring: Toward an Integrated Perspective on the Design and Use of Information Technology", *Journal of the Association for Information Systems*, 10 (5), pp. 306-332.

Shön, D. A. (1983), *The reflective practitioner: How professionals think in action*. New York: Basic Books.

Silverman, D. (2008), *Doing qualitative research: a comprehensive Guide*. Thousand Oaks: Sage.

Silverstone, R. Hirsh, E., Morley, D. (1992), "Information and Communication Technologies and the Moral Economy of the Household" in Silverstone, R. and Hirsh, E. (eds.), *Consuming Technologies: Media and Information Domestic Spaces*. London: Routledge.

Star, S. L., and Ruhleder, K. (1996), "Steps toward an ecology of infrastructure design and access for large information spaces", *Information systems research*, 7 (1), pp. 111-134.

Star, S.L., Griesemer, J.R. (1989), "Institutional Ecology, Translations, and Boundary Objects: Amateurs and Professionals in Berkeley's Museum of Vertebrate Zoology", *Social Studies of Science*, 19, pp. 387–420.

CONTINUOUS RE-CONFIGURING OF INVISIBLE SOCIAL STRUCTURES

Yoko Akama

Introduction

In the context of large scale "wicked problems" (Rittel and Webber, 1973) such as natural disasters, no one entity can tackle this problem alone. Centralized, one-size-fits-all approaches to policy and service delivery are increasingly recognized as being ineffectual due to the diverse character and needs of communities (COAG, 2011; Burns et al., 2006). As such, in the last ten years, design has become increasingly viewed as a means of harnessing latent creativity and enabling social innovation in organizations and communities to address entrenched issues and effect change for the social and public good. These are explored in fields such as design for social innovation, service design and participatory design, to name a few. These fields pursue ways to support designing that are performed by non-design experts that can bring local knowledge and specific competences. People involved in projects can then become collaborative co-designers and co-producers with the ability to draw on their "creativity, organizational capabilities and entrepreneurship, and therefore capable of figuring out, enhancing and managing new solutions" (Manzini and Rizzo, 2011: p. 201). Designing here is seen as a way to enhance the creativity and inventiveness of ordinary people to tackle problems in their daily lives. This chapter presents an example of designing to catalyse a transformative process through unlocking tacit knowledge and revealing hidden relational structures.

Large-scale challenges like natural disasters require collaboration of many stakeholders, including governments, organizations and communities. In this section's theme on emerging methodologies and practices in understanding work, organization and technology, my focus is to foreground social constructs and relations of groups in settings that include, but go beyond bounded formal structures. The site of designing that shifts from bounded contexts to one that is more dynamic and heterogeneous reflects how contemporary participatory design (PD) discourse is also evolving. PD originated in Scandinavian trade union movement in the 70s that pursued ways for workers to have a voice and direct involvement in workplace technology. Since then, the ethical and political concern has been at the forefront for PD to pursue how people such as workers, "users", community or polity participate in the design process to co-create the changes they desire (Simonsen and Robertson, 2013).

More recently, however, PD is shifting the frame of reference from its traditional concern of "democracy at work" with identifiable stakeholders within an organization, towards contexts that are now more "heterogeneous, partly open and public" (Bannon and Ehn, 2014: p.57). As touched on briefly, this reflects our understanding of how large-scale change and impact go beyond organizational and geographical boundaries, facilitated by globalization and digital technology. A growing interest of PD work in communities has prompted DiSalvo and colleagues to notice how community settings are less standardized, less discrete and the practices are more interwoven. They observe the dynamic way in which "needs emerge, design objects change, designers morph and the design process is continuously reconstructed by all interested publics" (DiSalvo et al., 2013: p. 203). Here, we see the strong influence of Actor Network Theory (ANT), Science and Technology Studies (STS) and post-phenomenological discourses in attempting to understand the social world as fluid, emergent, and distributed socio-material assembly of actions. Together with notions of "infrastructuring", which extended Star and Ruhleder's (1996) pioneering ethnographic work to emphasize how relational, organizing socio-material practices are always becoming, these ideas are influencing a conception of PD as a way to continuously align interests through which "matters of concern" are negotiated among participants (Bannon and Ehn, 2014, Latour, 2008). In other words, we see a pronounced awareness that design is not applied to products, services or ICT systems alone. Instead, Bannon and Ehn describe the need for PD to be seen as "long-term relationships through artful integration" (2014: p. 57) and to enable ways in which people can participate in continuous co-creation of socio-material collectives. For PD, this shift is especially important to avoid limiting the ethical and political concern towards designing or implementing ICTs alone to enact or enable change, but to pursue a way to bring people into designing the invisible mediating structures they are enmeshed within (Light and Akama, 2014). This resonates with the growing scholarship and practices in design for social innovation, which are examining diverse and distributed agents to enable co-creation models, peer-to-peer production and community-driven change through grass-roots social networks (Meroni and Sangiorgi, 2011). The relational emphasis then becomes the focus of design to support innovation between people, among personal, professional and community relationships, drawing upon the latent creativity and social capital lying in-between such networks. In this chapter, I explore how design can assist in making such hidden relational structures visible, so it can be re-configured on-goingly in a participatory manner.

This chapter details a participatory approach designed to mutually understand social relations as well as re-make them for fire preparedness. It draws upon a program of research that spans over five years in working with regional communities and emergency agencies in Australia, tracing three key stages of its evolution. The first section begins with the development of a participatory visual methodology using *Playful Triggers* (Akama et al., 2007, Akama and Ivanka, 2010, Loi, 2005) to understand the role of social networks in disaster preparedness. *Playful Triggers* are everyday objects like buttons, beads, matchsticks, toy animals, used in an interactive manner that enabled the participant and researchers to collaboratively explore complex dimensions of people's social networks. Visualizing people's relationships facilitated cursory, tacit knowledge to be made explicit and comprehensive as the conversation unfolded. This assisted the participants to literally "see" their personal networks manifesting as a visual diagram, helping them to understand how and why their connection to others become critical in an emergency. This methodology allowed the researchers to gather a richer and more human-centerd data for analysis, avoid imagined notion of a "community" that can hide social heterogeneity, as well as provide participants with a self-reflective mechanism to heighten their awareness of the broader relational structures they are enmeshed within.

The next phase of the research evolution manifested when this methodology became part of the Australian Emergency Management Institute's (AEMI) training program from 2012 onwards. AEMI embedded this methodology within their *Community in Emergency Management* course to train practitioners from various emergency management (EM) sectors across Australia, enabling them to experience this method first-hand. The discussion here reveals how it helped EM practitioners address their own nebulous idea of a "community" and provide an entry point to understand the variety of people that constitute it. More importantly, this became an opportunity to re-examine their top-down, authority-centerd model of emergency service provision towards a community-centerd engagement strategy. It required a shift from their usual EM practices on imparting information on household safety such as clearing gutters of debris, mowing the lawn, cutting vegetation around the property and fire-readiness supplies (Akama and Ivanka, 2010), and to focus their attention to see the significance of neighborhood relations as equally valuable in strengthening preparedness. Visualizing their own social networks enabled further conversation on re-configuring their social relations to be more connected to the community they work within, and more importantly, how this awareness was catalytic to re-configuring power structures enmeshed in EM culture towards adopting a community-centerd practice.

Ever since the participatory visual methodology was embedded into AEMI's training program, feedback began trickling in from EM practitioners who had continued to incorporate it into their strategies for community engagement and address local relations for preparedness. Briefly, I trace the ways in which two practitioners tailored this approach into two different disaster contexts and "re-designed" their own way of structuring social relations within their local community. This in turn has enabled their local residents to foster and strategize ways of connecting with one another for preparedness to develop a form of community-based resilience. This is beginning to provide glimpses of a gradual restructuring of power-dynamics between these communities and emergency services that challenged over-dependency upon the authorities for instruction. Such signs further indicate how the culture of individualistic self-sufficiency and hazard minimization priorities are gradually shifting to also encourage neighborly, community cooperation.

Here, this five-year study is starting to show tentative signs of how designing, in the absence of designers or researchers, is continuing through people's participation, re-configuring new social structures for preparedness in disasters. This exploration of the role and agency of social relations and "design-after-design" resonates with the work of several scholars in PD. For example, Dinder and Iversen (2014) examined "knotworks" as open, fluid, symbiotic and dispersed assemblies of relationships, and how this dynamically developed and transformed during and after design's implementation. Their research incorporates Ehn's (2008) argument for "design-after-design" in PD to pursue ways for continuous appropriation and re-design; an argument also extended in Light and Akama's (2014) paper that looked at ways for design to structure future social relations. This chapter's discussion owes much to Light and Akama's collaborative work in particular to examine how participation can be on-going in the making of people's futures. The influence from transformation design is also strongly seen in this chapter's argument, to build skills and capacity for on-going change so that people and communities can keep adapting and transforming themselves beyond the instigators departure (Sangiorgi, 2011). The discussion below explores these ideas further through a specific context of disaster preparedness in Australia.

1. Background: bushfires (wildfire) in Australia and the importance of social networks

Bushfires are a continuing and increasing threat in Australia, intensified by global warming and extreme climatic changes. The scale and catastrophe of *Black Saturday* on February 7th 2009, which still stands out as one of the worst natural disasters in the state of Victoria, triggered a government funded Bushfire Cooperative Research Center (CRC) to investigate critical problems that centered on communicating risk to communities. The case study I draw upon here is a component of a five-year research project called *Effective Communication: Communities and Bushfire* (2010-2014), funded by the Bushfire CRC and undertaken by researchers at RMIT University, Australia. The research aimed to develop a robust and analytical understanding of communities and shape communication strategies for mobilizing bushfire preparedness.

Given that communities are complex, dynamic and diverse, our team focused on attempting to understand the role of social networks in mitigating the risk of disasters, including fire. Studies of communities hit by a catastrophe such as landslides or heatwaves demonstrate that people with well-connected social networks are more likely to recover than others where their networks are obliterated or non-existent (Gilchrist, 2009). Based on interviews with residents who experienced bushfires in North East Victoria during 2003-2009, Stelling and colleagues (2011) report that survivors coped more effectively when they were part of "good support networks" that included friends, family and their broader network. This suggested the mounting evidence of the importance of fostering social interactions between family, friends and neighbors before and during fire, also observed by other hazards researchers in the US (see Brenkert-Smith, 2010).

Initial fieldwork by the research team revealed the changing nature of communities driven by socio-economic and amenity-led migration, and that this is creating diverse rural-urban interface communities in fire prone areas in Australia. These rapid changes are presenting a challenge for fire agencies to consider how a diversity of people responds to risk, determined by how they interpret environmental and geographic conditions. Looking at social networks was one way to begin understanding this plurality and complexity that make up a "community of place", which in disasters, tend to be centerd on risks that are site-specific. The first stage of the *Effective Communication: Communities and Bushfires* project comprised an ethnographic-type study of bushfire-prone localities in four states across Australia, including Victoria, Tasmania, Western Australia and New South Wales. This scoping study examined the dimensions of awareness and preparedness for bushfires within these communities. These initial interviews highlighted several residents in southeast Tasmania, an island state of Australia, who are actively using their social networks to increase awareness and preparedness in their communities. A total of ten participants were selected from three localities in Tasmania, based on their willingness to volunteer and participate in this study (see Akama et al., 2014). However, for this chapter's discussion, it focuses on three female residents who participated in the research to co-explore, through *Playful Triggers*, what kinds of people are part of their networks, what kind of knowledge were fostered among it, and what this enabled for the residents. Notions like trust and reciprocity were also explored to understand how this was expressed or demonstrated and why certain members were more relied upon than others. This participatory, ethnomethodological approach also enabled the residents to make sense of learned characteristics of people, contexts and relationships that underlay knowledge seeking and sharing when the fire came to their locality. This, in turn, helped them foreground particular connections between people, whether they are friends, neighbors, acquaintances, colleagues or members of the fire agencies as central in preparing for such disaster.

2. Making sense of social networks through Playful Triggers

The development of a participatory visual methodology began by building on the work of Daria Loi (2005: p. 18) who coined *Playful Triggers* as objects or artifacts that:

> "*generate receptive modes through their tactile, visual, mysterious, playful, tridimensional, poetic, ambiguous and metaphorical qualities. These triggers ask people to challenge taken for granted or conventional ways of doing, seeing and*

articulating things to co-generate shared understandings and collaborative practices".

Inspired by Loi's work, I developed the idea further through my Doctorate study as a visual methodology when it was used in complement to an interview to understand the complex interactions and knowledge embedded within project teams (see further detail in Akama et al., 2007). Here, I discovered that the objects could act as "scaffolds" to access, interpret, visualize, articulate and communicate implicit knowledge through facilitated conversations where learning is generative and supported by the construction of temporary structures (Sanders, 2000; Vygotsky, 1978; Wood, Bruner and Ross, 1976). This ethnomethodological orientation was extended again during the *Effective Communication: Communities and Bushfires* project to understand people's social network (see Fig. 1). An ethnomethodological approach focuses on the ways in which people understand their everyday activities from within and reflexively display their understanding of it (Garfinkel, 1967). In other words, research participants are invited to become active co-creators of knowledge in ways that may benefit their own understanding of themselves and emergent phenomena. The *Playful Triggers* are ethnomethodological by nature because they assist the co-creation of meaning and rarifying the sense-making process in a constructivist way (Akama, 2008). Consequently, ethnomethodology employs a documentarian method to read everyday events as opportunities through which members of the community use their cultural competence and contextual knowledge to make sense of the world and, in turn, how they use that understanding (Button, 2000). When placed in a specific context, the objects take on the meanings placed on them by the participants. These objects involve translation, coordination and alignment between different perspectives in order to enhance the co-creation of shared understanding.

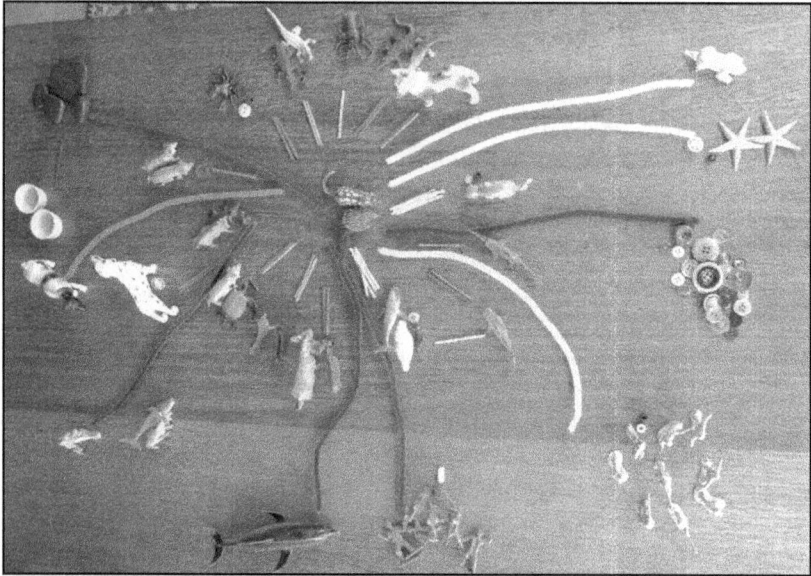

Fig 1. An example of a social network visualized using *Playful Triggers*

Contemporary framings of design and ethnography, or design anthropology, go beyond the objectifying tendencies of ethnographic studies of, or about, persons or phenomena. They instead create a form of practice that departs from the temporality of the ethnographic past, and that engages with design and people as they move into the future (Akama et al., 2015). Artifacts here can be considered as "a language of interaction" (Krippendorff, 2006: p. 46) that can materialise ways to collaboratively explore and "make" emerging worlds, possible alternatives and potential futures (Gunn, et al., 2013). Taking this into disaster preparedness research, the methodology aimed to support ways for participants to understand their social networks by also imagining what "could happen" – interactions that lie in the future, and in an emergency. This revealed various qualities of people and their social capital that are valuable that simply capturing their past or that normative interactions may not reveal. In a scenario of an on-coming fire, "who you trust" or "who you will rely on", inevitably changes according to contextual and contingent factors. Conversations on seeking advice or providing assistance became a focal point, prompting participants to consider other people in their network, for example, the local fire brigade or neighbors with specific knowledge on fire or preparedness. Yet, the visualization exercise also brings forth challenging questions for people to confront, as it can highlight that some plans are ill considered, for example, the person you most rely upon may not be contactable, or live too far away to provide immediate help.

Such future-oriented conversation is a common methodological approach in design anthropology. Future scenarios, fictions and visions has a long history of exploration by design researchers (see Dunne and Raby, 2013, Manzini and Jegou, 2004) to stimulate and heighten emotive-cognition skills, useful for planning strategies and preparedness such as climate change or health-care provisions. For participants who had not experienced a fire in their locality, hypothetical instances of an on-coming fire led to conversations about other people outside of their kinship and regular contacts to others in their networks who they would seek advice, help and support from. This also meant that their mapping of "community of place" became more complex and diverse, extending well beyond their circle of friends, as depicted in figure 1.

As such, whilst retaining a methodological principle to provide "handles" for thick description and interpretation, the objects enables a conversational engagement where both researcher and participants would manipulate them on the table in order to explore the details of the participant's social interactions. The objects provided an accessible interface, performing as an ice-breaker, putting the participants at ease to establish an informal relationship with the researcher. It is undertaken in pairs or as a group where each participant is invited to choose various animals to denote different characteristics of people. For example, one person chose a starfish to represent one of her friends "... because she's pretty well out there and has got tentacles and things everywhere. She's a pretty good star." This enabled an enriched and personal understanding of the kinds of people that the participant were connected to. The objects also aided in recalling which animal was who when the network mapping became more complex. The participant also nominated how to distinguish the frequency of contact with someone, selecting different colored matchsticks or pipe cleaners. In highlighting who they would see as being trustworthy in an emergency, they could place another object alongside the animals, like a button, bead or stone. There was no right or wrong way to create the visualization as it was not governed by rules set by the researcher. These conversations often evolved where questions, curiosity and intrigue of personal relations triggered a memory or past interaction, prompting the participant to note and visualize various qualities of a person or relationship. These ephemeral assemblies of objects enabled an accessible, fluid and temporal scaffold to build upon and to delve deeply into the participants' social world. The participants could also change their mind about someone as the conversation continued, especially on the topics of seeking advice, trustworthiness and reciprocity in the context of an emergency. Once a visual network manifests, many participants are often surprised with the outcome and what it meant to them. For example, one woman remarked, "it looks impressive when you do it like that", and indeed, her network displayed the critical role that people played in assisting her in a recent fire. The approach used here can be seen as Action Research that can also help practitioners develop reflective practice skills and assist organization members develop a culture of enquiry as part of their work life (Cherry, 1999; Reason, 2001). As such, the methodological capacity to assist emergency management staff to engage with their communities will be discussed in the latter section of this paper.

3. Visualizing resilience

Fire, often being a sudden, stressful, event-based occurrence can change the dynamics of a network. It can "test" normative relationships and create situations where people's roles are emergent, especially when there are no formal or organizational boundaries. In our study of ten residents in Tasmania, closeness or frequency of contact with friends in people's networks was not a constant factor in determining who was sought out in an emergency. Instead, other contingent factors became more relevant, such as knowing that the other person were close-by and available, or the location of their house providing a vantage point to see the smoke or direction of the fire. In an on-coming fire, the actions taken by people are mobilized within a complex system of inter-relationships. The network analysis of the three females shows a collective phenomenon where different people have assisted them in different ways.

Female A and W were selected for our study because they could be typically labeled as "vulnerable" residents given that female W was more than 70 years old and female A lived alone at the time of research. Notions of assumed vulnerability is problematic in disempowering and placing limitations on what people can achieve, yet it commonly appears in disaster literature, ranging from those who are elderly; have physical/mental health issues; those with children; those who are living on their own; those living in remote areas; those without means of transport; those living in "unsound buildings"; those in denial of the risks they face and recently arrived residents, and more (Fothergill and Peek, 2004, Stelling et al., 2011). In fact, as the discussion below attests, this study revealed how the women's relational knowledge, communication and support networks became central to their preparedness, demonstrating their adaptive capacity towards future disasters.

Female A and W both visualized female N as being trustworthy, reliable and a source of information, by adding a bead next to the animal that represented her. Indeed, Female N's network was highly connected to various members of the community and she explains, "I probably actively work at my network", valuing the support that she provides to others, as well as the support she receives from her network. Despite not having a local, close kin, all three females identified many number of people in their community, who they had turned to in an emergency, and those who had contacted them to offer assistance. Availability of mutual assistance and having sources of informal help has been indicated as important in a support network (Wenger, 1995).

In terms of sudden fire that can "test" normative relationships, Female A was shocked by her immediate neighbour who did not assist her in the fire:

> "*[M]y immediate neighbour, for instance, could see the fires behind my place, didn't even come over to see if I was all right. ... I was gobsmacked, yes. ... Knew I was on my own, so that was just sheer thoughtlessness on his part, absolute thoughtlessness. ... So the person who did actually ring me up was in fact [Female N], to make sure that I was okay ... I think [my immediate neighbour] was more worried about getting his hay out.*"

Such tension and differences in agendas – the neighbour who was more concerned about protecting his hay than the welfare of his immediate neighbour – were common stories told by participants, thereby manifesting the complexity of relational dynamics that are part of the community fabric. Since discovering this, Female A, now knows not to rely on her immediate neighbour in an emergency and visualized her trust and reliance with other members in her network, particularly on Female N who assisted her. Female N was critical to A and W's preparation and risk mitigation. She helped them clear out the gutters and putting tennis balls in them and filling it up with water. Female W said: "I apparently got a gold star [from the fire authority] for being so prepared".

Links to the fire agency is critical in ensuring that communication re-inforces the knowledge-flow that takes place amongst the network, limiting the risks of ill-informed communication taking place. Such linking networks performed by the local fire brigade were important for the three female residents, and they all visualized their relationship and trust of individuals who belonged to the fire brigade. Both female A and W explained that the local brigade had kept an eye out for them, regularly maintaining contact to assure their safety when the fire was approaching. The two females' prior attendance at a fire preparation talk had alerted the authority staff to their needs. This example demonstrates the remarkable social and collective preparedness towards bushfire, built upon layers of knowledge, engagement and trust, which means that these residents are in a less vulnerable situation than conventional demographic identification may imply. The story shared by female A reminds us how dynamics can change drastically in an emergency, and anticipating changes - as well as building dialogue earlier with others - can assist in being better prepared. By stepping through such conversations, local residents were able to see the significance of resilience built by a mesh-work of people. Discussing these aspects is a first step to acknowledging these truths in a way that builds strategy rather than hope.

These tangible network descriptions are beginning to clarify notions of community, an understanding that is still lacking in bushfire research, and this lack is also evident in how emergency agencies are engaging communities. What this study had begun to demonstrate is a potential for building resilience through enabling a reflexive understanding of social relations among residents for survival. Resilience of communities is dependent on social interaction and collective action based on networks of relationships, reciprocity, trust, and social norms (McAslan, 2011). The study of the network of three women summarized above shows their adaptive capacity in building resilience collectively and their proactiveness towards preparedness. The participatory visual approach had assisted in revealing, reflecting upon and communicating this insight to address knowledge gaps in how social network could catalyze resilience and the well-being of individuals and communities.

4. Addressing entrenched practices in the emergency management sector

Disaster and emergency service agencies are beginning to realise that conventional, agency-driven "command and control" structure reinforces the power-dynamics between the "expert" fire authorities and the "non-expert" community, entrenching further dependency and disempowerment by the community (Akama et al., 2012). A climate-change report by the Resilient Futures Strategy Forum in Western Australia (Platt, 2008) highlights obstacles regarding siloed agencies, tension between collaboration and competition, and a lack of connectivity and awareness of critical networks required to come together to appropriately address the problems holistically. The *Black Saturday* tragedy had made this issue more visible and acute. Despite policy changes outlined in the National Strategy for Disaster Resilience that states that building resilience is a shared responsibility between households, businesses, communities and governments (COAG, 2011), agencies are still struggling to change their culture and practices in working with the community and catalyze their preparedness, compounded by a lack of understanding what a "community" is. Past research indicates mixed views on how the community perceives the role and effectiveness of fire authorities. Akama and Ivanka (2010) report that there are strong emotions held by some members of the community caused by "meeting fatigue" and mistrust that presenters were simply "towing the company line". The fire authorities' speakers who undertake community talks are required to adhere to a management-approved script to avoid any potential litigation (Goodman et al., 2009), disabling them from offering personal opinions to questions that are locally specific and situated. This impression of impenetrable bureaucracy, so unappealing to the locals, is another factor that distances the fire authorities from the communities they want to engage with. Non-local agency representatives with little in-depth knowledge of the local area are unable to build the necessary trust with the community or provide information that is relevant to their specific contexts.

Exacerbating this problem is the abundance of information and communication channels dedicated to household preparation, which are providing a false perception that effective communication is taking place between the authorities and the community. This can be critiqued, however, that transmission and distribution of information is taking place, together with perpetual reinforcements of control through such transmissions (Carey, 1998), reflecting the top-down culture that pervades the emergency management sector. A stronger belief in the fire agencies' ability to manage the threat of bushfire can also reduce levels of personal bushfire mitigation (Paton, 2006). It can be argued that the transmission and control of communication diminishes empowerment, participation and capacity-building for change by the community. To further evidence this view, the researchers have observed complacency for preparedness and dependency on the fire services to "tell them what to do" in many other communities that were studied. The changing demographic of these areas also compounds issues of dependency and false-expectations. Urban dwellers that are used to service delivery are moving into rural settings where self-reliance and locally-based initiatives become more important.

Australian Emergency Management Institute (AEMI) is the government's Center of Excellence for knowledge and capability development in the national emergency management (EM) sector. I was approached by AEMI to incorporate my research and the participatory visual methodology I developed into their *Community in Emergency Management*, to train various EM practitioners from local government, community development, fire services, State Emergency Services, police, ambulance and councils from all parts of Australia. The course is an intense, four-day program that takes the EM practitioners through a learning process on community engagement in urban and rural settings, with culturally and linguistically diverse communities, and engenders a culture of responsibility in agencies and communities towards collective resilience. Within this program, I facilitate a two-hour workshop to assist EM practitioners experience a hands-on learning process of using the objects to visualize their own social network of the community they live or work with. This has two purposes, firstly to explore, examine and reflect upon their relational connection to others (Fig. 2) and secondly, to teach them how to use this method in the communities they work with. The activity often catalyses revelations of how the community is diverse and resourceful because of its networks and provokes thinking on ways they can harness its latent capacity in an emergency. Discussion on trust, reciprocity, advice and emotional support takes place, enabling the staff to see that their own relationships with people are important in fostering and building social capital.

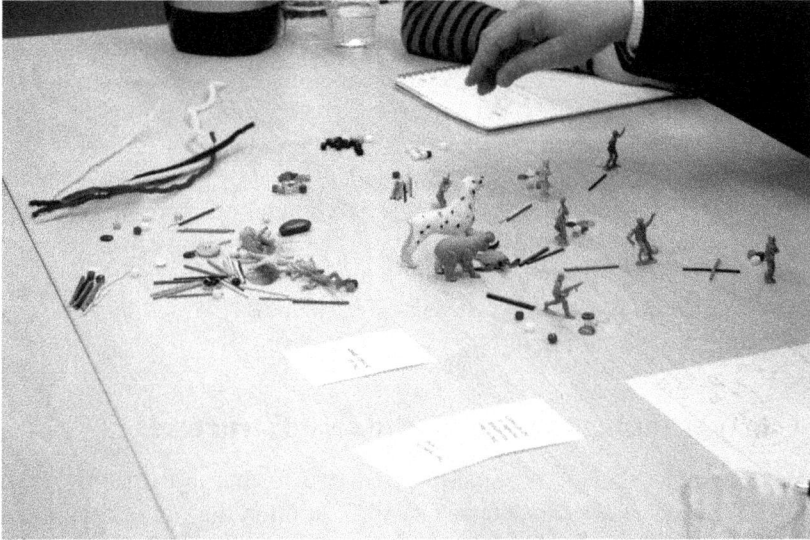

Figure 2: AEMI training course for EM practitioners, learning how to use the participatory visual methodology

The workshop is open-ended, scaffolded in a way to enable the conversation to take its natural course. Visualizing each person's understanding catalyzed numerous location-specific, fire related conversations, driven and shared amongst the EM practitioners. What was most striking to observe is how motivated and willing all practitioners were in taking part in the activities, due to the informal quality of the artifacts and the approach. In participating in this workshop, they were experiencing, firsthand, the enjoyment and effectiveness of engaging in a generative, bottom-up process of community-centerd process, which is in stark contrast to their accustomed agency-centerd management practices. The evaluation sheets consistently demonstrate that most practitioners learn how to engage the community through a participatory process, assisting them to adapt this to their own roles and work practices.

By the end of four days of intense learning and experiencing, firsthand, the challenges and potential of being engaged in a dialogic, generative and bottom-up process for disaster mitigation, the feedback suggests how many begin to understand the need to change their top-down management practices, question their assumptions they might have had about communities, or curb their over-reliance on ICTs as the main vehicle to communicate with residents. In other words, with the aid of tools like the participatory visual methodology through this educative framework, they have absorbed, like osmosis, each other's every day experiences and knowledge practices, to create a shared experience of the changing organizational cultures to which they belong, and also more importantly, begin to manifest how they might practice this differently. This educative process is indicating ways to foreground hidden social constructs in EM practices, so each person can potentially re-configure and re-make it ongoingly. The next section briefly follows the manner in which two EM practitioners continued to re-configuring they practices and examines how they appropriated and evolved the participatory visual methodology in their local communities.

5. Continuing to re-configure social structures

Two EM practitioners, who were introduced to the participatory visual methodology, were curious to see its application in the context and communities they worked within. M works for a local council located in a peri-urban suburb of Sydney in New South Wales, bordering three large National Parks. The risk of fire is significant for the residents, but being so close to the city, many have a false sense of security for service provision and assistance in an emergency. M was tasked to lead a pilot strategy on reducing risks and impacts from climate extreme, such as heat stress, bushfires, storm and droughts. Before commencing the pilot, M shares how she "felt quite open to make [the methodology] what we wanted and how it would work for our local area ... there's lots to play with here ... I would definitely be experimenting with what seems to works best, not only in engaging people but really helping people to get their thinking to a level where they haven't gone to before...". She viewed the application of this methodology as key to develop a sense of shared responsibility amongst the local community, strengthen communication networks and enhance neighborhood resilience.

M facilitated a series of three workshops. The feedback and follow up after six months attests its effective outcome. One resident voiced how they discovered the "importance of interaction with neighbors", whilst another said the value was in "realizing that some people have no communication network", observed in the visualization exercise. It motivated many to complete a bushfire survival plan for the first time or follow up conversations with their family and neighbors about being prepared. Remarkably, one resident was so concerned for his neighbors who missed M's workshop that he sent a personal invitation to everyone on his street and hosted a gathering at his home. He organized the local fire emergency staff to come and relay the information he had gained.

There are also indications in which M considered the role of other materials, such as CDs containing information and resources, not merely as reminders of the workshop but as a strategy to build further connections in the community. Multiple copies of these CDs were taken at every workshop, and the feedback from residents indicated that they were passed on to neighbors. M called these "a gift" that can lubricate a tricky dialogue between unfamiliar residents, of "impinging on your space wanting to have this conversation with you [about bushfires by saying] ... "I've got something to offer you" ... a step into that conversation that makes it much easier". These resources have more value by coming through a neighbor, rather than receiving it cold and impersonally in the letterbox, especially when accompanied with personal stories. M intended such materials to become a bridge that can help make a difficult conversation easier with the potential of lowering the social barriers in this urban neighborhood – "I know you missed the workshop and I thought you might find it helpful to know". Here, we begin to see how M's embodiment of the participatory methodology grows and evolve in ways that are knitting collective actions, experiences and concerns of the residents through the workshops, and beyond it, becoming woven into people's everyday realities and creating new relational bonds between neighbours. In other words, her practice is continually re-configuring by entangling with the complex dimensions of risk, mitigation and encounters with the community, and in turn, facilitating new ways for people's social configuring in strengthening resilience.

In another remote town in Queensland, Australia, an Aboriginal and Torres Strait Islander community had experienced a succession of devastating floods, resulting in widespread infrastructure damage. The state government instructed the local council to implement a Disaster Management Plan, again, reflecting the legacy of "top-down" governance in emergency management. The authority's intervention is a familiar story but more wretched in this community context, echoing the town's historical, colonial treatment of Aboriginal and Torres Strait Islander people, assuming them as vulnerable, needing control and protection because they were perceived as being unable to make their own decisions (Blake, 2001). Committed to building the fundamentals of a trusting and respectful relationship, J was keen to integrate the participatory visual methodology into a disaster awareness weekend in partnership with the community, emergency services, local council and Aboriginal elders as a way to establish ownership and find a way forward for disaster planning. She was confident in introducing this approach, explaining how:

> *"the methodology was perfect for discussions and worked well with literacy levels. The Aboriginal and Torres Strait Islander community particularly enjoy yarning about their community [and] connections ... this is important as many people go ... and talk at them rather than with them ... This method allowed great interactions and learnings about their community ... placed locals at the center of their own solutions."*

In particular, J describes the effective visual nature of the methodology in mapping their networks – it enabled the residents to see the extent to which their kinship and friendship ties were inter-woven, manifesting tangible evidence of their tightknit community. It was an eye-opener for the participants who may have tacitly assumed their connection to one another. One participant in J's workshop commented that, "the [social network exercise] was very good ... for the simple reason that you think of your groups, but when you sit down and think who you're involved with, it's a big network that I'm involved with ... it's good to be able to refer people to other organisations [when you're helping others]." For this resident, her priority lay in helping others, especially her grandchildren. Furthermore, the visualization enabled her to see ways in which many others were connected to her, leading to a realization that she, too, can also be assisted. Knowing this, and that she could call on others for help, eased her anxiety in circumstances where she may not be able to provide assistance to those that needed her help. Many residents voiced how empowered they felt in both self-recognizing and collectively acknowledging the strong bonds between people in this community.

As a further demonstration of J's participatory practice, J facilitated a group discussion with the residents where she encouraged them to nominated two tasks they could undertake as a strategy of moving forward. This ensured that preparation was connected to their lives and those around them. Most volunteered to take on roles in their own street, such as the assistance they could provide to others and identifying information that they could pass on. This group discussion enabled all to know what each other were going to do, ensuring that any one person was not overburdened. Gradually, through such dialogue, this group recognized that they didn't need to be totally dependent upon the emergency agencies, nor did they have to be totally self-sufficient and do everything alone. Such stories of work practices, told through M and J's experiences, are beginning to indicate incremental shifts towards re-configuring power-dynamics between these communities and EM agencies as well as people's re-configuring of their social relations towards strengthening resilience.

Conclusion: on designing as a living, evolving process

When designing is considered and pursued as "long-term relationship through artful integration" (Bannon and Ehn, 2014: p. 57), it can enable ways in which people can participate in the continuous co-creation of socio-material collectives. Designing here is a "living" change process (Meroni and Sangiorgi, 2011) that can continue to evolve, coming to life through life, transforming the very people who are participating in its process. Visualizing social networks is not a literal process of revealing or capturing hidden dimensions that already exist to understand sociological patterns of interactions. This is a fundamental difference between Social Network Analysis and the participatory design approach discussed here. Giving social relations a static visual form might seem like pinning down butterflies, killing the very essence of living, yet, I am reminded of the cyclical nature of doing – designing, making, visualizing, materializing – whereby materials are also participating in our becoming and "people and materials meet, align and make each other act" (Eriksen, 2012: p.24). In this socio-material view, non-human objects can act upon us, just as visualizing one's social relations acts upon oneself in a reflexive manner. In other words, visualizing social structures for someone has the possibility of bringing forth a heightened awareness and curiosity to explore what their relationships might mean to them, specifically in an emergency. This is because when social relations – which is possibly more felt than seen, remain hidden than being explicit, often emergent than neatly assembled – are made tangible, it has the potential to catalyze new understandings, altering trajectories of change. In this view, our becoming is always relational and heterogeneous – the singular "I" does not precede the relation of "we" (Nancy, 2000) – we are continuously becoming among relational ecologies of being and non-beings (Akama, 2012). As argued elsewhere in PD, it is not meaningful to separate the method from the practitioner but to see it as a configuration where impact is mediated by performance, embodiment and contingency of the moment that is highly contextual

(Light and Akama, 2012). This understanding helps us from isolating the visual methodology alone as being causal to enabling change, and to acknowledge more generally that such methods, embodied and enacted through practice, provide glimpses in which changes are being influenced centrally through people's participation. More importantly, the participatory approach discussed here does not prescribe the kinds of social relations that people ought to have with one another, but can provide an opportunity to give it focus and a method for careful consideration.

The residents and emergency management (EM) practitioners who took part in this five-year research program perhaps anticipated or even desired change towards preparedness without knowing the specifics of how. This uncertainty was also my research question. The participants' intrigue, concern and open-ness to co-explore such questions together has possibly invited them to design their own unique approaches towards building and strengthening resilience. This change towards preparedness is seen when the three female residents in Tasmania realized that their resilience lay in their trust, reciprocity and willingness to help to one another. It is reported by EM practitioners, who discovered that their own relationships with members of the community mattered in fostering and building social capital. It is heard in a variety of stories that persuaded people to overcome awkward social barriers to introduce themselves to their neighbours. It is witnessed in residents who became less individually prepared to collectively prepared and now knowing more about one another to ensure survival. Such shared experiences catalyses into something real with meaning and connection to their lives, absorbed within people's practices, enacted in their own ways of continuing the processes of actualization and transformation.

Attempting to understand or intervene in contingencies of everyday action can be harder when boundaries are less formal and defined, such as the contexts encountered by this research. By foregrounding the social constructs and relations of groups in communities and emergency management sector, and enabling ways for hidden structures to be made visible through participation, it has explored various ways in which participants were able to reflect on and make sense of their social relations as well as encourage its on-going re-configuration to build and strengthen resilience for disasters. The participatory visual methodology embodies and manifests complex socio-material practices, coming to life through people's engagement, ownership and adaptation of it. This can be seen as a form of every-day designing, not driven or undertaken by designers or researchers, but by ordinary people in open and serendipitous ways, harnessing their experiences, knowledge, relationships and social capital and inviting inventiveness to tackle seemingly insurmountable problems together. This resonates with Herbert Simon's (1968) infamous definition of design; "Everyone designs who devises courses of action aimed at changing existing situations into preferred ones", undertaken by ordinary citizens in a manner and direction they wish to pursue. This kind of designing is a deliberative ethical and political act, foregrounded in participatory design, where designers or researchers do not determine what the outcomes "ought to be", but rather, act as "custodians of care " (Light and Akama, 2014) to open up diverse ways for people to learn, debate, reflect, make mistakes and continue creating the kinds of environments, social relations and futures they might wish to participate in.

Acknowledgments

This paper is based on a five-year research funded by the Bushfire Co-Operative Research Center. I would like to thank my research team in *Effective Communication: Communities and Bushfires*, and all the participants in AEMI and the editors of this book.

References

Akama, Y. (2008), *The tao of communication design practice: manifesting implicit values through human-centerd design*, PhD Thesis, School of Applied Communication, RMIT University, Melbourne, Australia.

Akama, Y. (2012), "A 'way of being': Zen and the art of being a human-centerd practitioner", *Design Philosophy Papers*, 1, pp. 1-10.

Akama, Y, Chaplin, S., Fairbrother, P. (2014), "Role of social networks in community preparedness for bushfire", *International Journal of Disaster Resilience in the Built Environment*, 5 (3), pp. 277-291.

Akama, Y., Cooper, R., Vaughan, L., Viller, S., Simpson, M., Yuille, J. (2007), "Show and tell: Accessing and communicating implicit knowledge through artifacts", *Artifact*, 1 (3), pp. 172-181.

Akama, Y., Ivanka, T. (2010). "What community? Facilitating awareness of 'community' through Playful Triggers" in Bodker, K., Bratteig, T. , Loi D., Robinson, T. (eds.), *Proceedings from The Conference on Participatory Design 2010, Sydney, Australia.* ACM Digital Library, pp. 11-20.

Akama, Y., Pink, S., Fergusson, A. (2015), "Design + Ethnography + Futures: Surrendering in Uncertainty", paper presented to *CHI '15*, Seoul, Republic of Korea, pp. 531-542.

Bannon, L. J., Ehn, P. (2013), "Design: design matters in Participatory Design", in Simonsen, J., Robertson, T. (eds.), *Routledge International Handbook of Participatory Design*, London and New York: Routledge, pp. 37-63.

Blake, T. (2001), *A dumping ground: a history of the Cherbourg Settlement.* St Lucia, Queensland: University of Queensland Press.

Brenkert-Smith, H. (2010), "Building bridges to fight fire: the role of informal social interactions in six Colorado wildland-urban interface communities", *International Journal of Wildland Fire*, 19, pp. 689-697.

Burns, C., Cottam, H., Vanstone, C., Winhall, J. (2006), *RED paper 02: Transformation design*, London: The Design Council.

Button, G. (2000), "The ethnographic tradition in design", *Design Studies*, 21 (4), pp. 319-332.

Carey, J. (1998), *Communication as culture: essays on media and society.* London: Routledge.

Cherry, N. (1999), *Action research: a pathway to action, knowledge and learning.* Melbourne: RMIT Publishing.

Council of Australian Governments (2011), National Strategy for Disaster Resilience, Commonwealth of Australia Feb 2011, retrieved 12th December 2012 from http://www.em.gov.au/Documents/1National%20Strategy%20for%20 Disaster%20Resilience%20-%20pdf.PDF

Dindler, C., Iversen, O. S. (2014), "Relational Expertise in Participatory Design", *Participatory Design Conference 2014*, Windhoek, Namibia, ACM Digital Library pp. 41-50.

DiSalvo, C., Clement, A., Pipek, V. (2013), "Communities: Participatory Design for, with and by communities", in Simonsen J., Robertson T. (eds.), *Routledge International Handbook of Participatory Design.* London and New York: Routledge, pp. 182-209.

Dunne, A., Raby, F. (2013), *Speculative Everything: Design, Fiction, and Social Dreaming.* Cambridge: The MIT Press.

Eriksen, M. A. (2012), "Material matters in co-designing: formatting & staging with participating materials in co-design projects", Malmö University, PhD Thesis.

Fothergill, A., Peek, L. A. (2004), "Poverty and Disasters in the United States: A Review of Recent Sociological findings", *Natural Hazards*, 32, pp. 89-110.

Garfinkel, H. (1967), *Studies in Ethnomethodology.* Englewood Cliffs: Prentice-Hall.

Gilchrist, A. (2009), *The well-connected community: A networking approach to community development.* Bristol: Policy Press.

Goodman, H., Stevens, K., Rowe, C. (2009), *Mt Bold Case Study:* Bushfire. CRC report for the Country Fire Service Community Education Unit, RMIT University

Gunn, W., Otto, T., Charlotte-Smith, R. (eds.) (2013), *Design Anthropology: Theory and Practice.* London and New York: Bloomsbury.

Krippendorff, K. (2006), *The Semantic Turn: A New Foundation for Design.* Boca Raton: Taylor & Francis.

Latour, B. (2008), "Powers of the Facsimile: A Turing Test on Science and Literature", in Burn S. J., Dempsey P. (eds.), *Intersections: Essays on Richard Powers*, Urbana-Champaign, IL: Archive Press, pp. 263-292.

Light, A., Akama, Y. (2014), "Structuring Future Social Relations: The Politics of Care in Participatory Practice", *Proceedings from The Conference on Participatory Design 2014*. ACM Digital Library, pp. 151-160

Light, A., Akama, Y. (2012), "The human touch: from method to participatory practice in facilitating design with communities", *Proceedings from The Conference on Participatory Design 2010, Sydney, Australia.* ACM Digital Library, pp. 61-70.

Loi, D. (2005). *The Book of Probes. Lavoretti Per Bimbi: Playful Triggers as key to foster collaborative practices and workspaces where people learn, Wonder and play.* PhD Thesis, RMIT University, Melbourne, Australia.

Manzini, E., Jegou, F. (2004), "Sustainable Everyday: Scenarios of Urban Life", Retrieved 27 October, 2007, from http://sustainable-everyday.net/scenarios/?page_id=28

Manzini, E., Rizzo, F. (2011), "Small Projects/Large Changes: Participatory Design as an Open Participated Process", *Co:Design: International Journal of CoCreation in Design and the Arts*, 7 (3-4), pp. 199-215.

McAslan, A. (2011), *Community resilience: understanding the concept and its application*, from Torrens Resilience Institute, Adelaide, Australia. Website: www.torrensresilience.org

Meroni, A., Sangiorgi, D. (2011), *Design for services.* Farnham: Gower.

Nancy, J.-L. (2000), *Being Singular Plural.* Translated by R. D. Richardson and A. E. O'Byrne. Stanford: Stanford University Press.

Paton, D., Kelly, G., Burgelt, P., Doherty, M. (2006), "Preparing for bushfires: understanding intentions", *Disaster Prevention and Management*, 15 (4), pp. 566-575.

Platt, D. (2008), *Planning for growth, climate change & water shortages.* Resilient Futures Network.

Reason, P. (2001), *Learning and Change through Action Research.* London: Sage.

Rittel, H., Webber, M. (1973), "Dilemmas in a general theory of planning", *Policy Sciences*, 4 (2), pp. 155-169.

Sangiorgi, D. (2011), "Transformative Services and Transformation Design", *International Journal of Design*, 5 (2), pp. 29-40.

Sanders, E. (2000), "Generative Tools for CoDesigning", in Scrivener, S., Ball, L., Woodcock, A. (eds.), *Collaborative Design: Proceedings of CoDesigning 2000*. London: Springer-Verlag. pp. 3-12.

Simon, H. A. (1968), *The sciences of the artificial*. Cambridge: MIT Press.

Simonsen, J., Robertson, T. (eds.) (2013), *Routledge International Handbook of Participatory Design*, New York: Routledge.

Star, S. L., Ruhlder, K. (1996), "Steps Toward an Ecology of Infrastructure: Design and Access for Large Information Spaces", *Information Systems Research*, 7 (1), pp. 111-34.

Stelling, A., Millar, J., Boon, H., Cottrell, A., King, D., Stevenson, B. (2011), *Recovery from natural disasters: Community experiences of bushfires in North East Victoria from 2003-2009*: Institute for Land, Water and Society, report no. 65.

Vygotsky, L. S. (1978), *Mind in society: The development of higher psychological processes*, Cambridge, Massachusetts: Harvard University Press.

Wenger, G. C. (1995), "A comparison of urban and rural support networks", *Ageing and Society*, 15, pp. 59-81.

Wood, D., Bruner, J., Ross, G. (1976), "The Role of Tutoring in Problem Solving", *Journal of Child Psychology and Psychiatry*, 17, pp. 89-100.

SECTION 3

Issues of Technology, Work and Organization in Design Settings

DISTRIBUTED DESIGN TRAJECTORIES
THE GLOBAL MANUFACTURE OF TECHNOLOGIES AND ORGANIZATIONS

Cornelius Schubert

Introduction

Design is often thought of in the singular – one technology or artifact conceived by a single designer – but it rarely happens in the singular. Complex technologies are created in teams spanning technical as well as organizational boundaries; design is not confined to studios or laboratories, but transcends individual organizations and sites as well as the divide between designers and users. In short, technologies and organizations are designed, and design also must be organized in distributed settings of humans and artifacts. By asking how design is organized, the following chapter does not emphasize design as a distinct social practice of a specialized group of actors who create new artifacts. The aim, instead, is to shed light upon design processes in which technical artifacts and social organization are mutually shaped.

Two aspects of design make it an interesting concept for understanding the interrelations of work, technology and organization. First, it is a *deliberate engagement with the future*, either in terms of opening up new possibilities and potential or in new ways of ensuring that things stay the same, whereas the former is more often associated with design than the latter. Design, in a nutshell, is creative action. We typically think of new products such as cars, computers or kitchen appliances as being – more or less well – designed. In this sense, design is not only creative, but hopefully aesthetically pleasing and elegant in use. Such positive aesthetic connotations are often fused into common understandings of design, extending to national characteristics ascribed to "Scandinavian" or "Italian" design, for example. These aesthetic connotations, however, tend to overshadow the basic idea that something new is created, irrespective of its aesthetic value. I will stick to the basic idea of mindfully created novelty, with the addition that design also includes some purpose that can be aesthetic, functional, or both. Second, design is hardly a process of ad hoc creation.

Rather, it is a *controlled process of turning ideas into objects*. This resembles the move from theory to practice in an academic perspective. Plans are made and turned into tangible things. The process of design can, again, be based on aesthetic criteria, as in designing a vase, or rational criteria, as in designing a start-up company. In both cases, ideas are turned into reality and in settings like industrial design or the Bauhaus movement, aesthetics and rationality are not considered opposites, but two sides of the same coin. Design would thus seem to follow a one-way route – from head to hands to artifact. "Head" in this case is a stand-in for the individual designer or design team that authors a new product.

A general cognitive formulation of design can provide a valuable contribution to organization studies, because it refers to a central tenet in organizational research, namely analyzing the deliberate planning processes that originate in ideas and that are subsequently put into practice. At the same time, this entails the pitfall that design might become merely a more fashionable (sic!) label for the otherwise mundane terms of management or engineering. In contrast, the notion of distributed design puts the focus on the ways in which work, technology and organization are interrelated in processes of design, how past and present are mindfully coordinated and how specific solutions emerge from contingent design practices. It does not take the designer's or design team's ideas as a starting point, but focuses on the material settings in which design ideas are born out of the creative manipulation of existing objects.

The argument put forth is thus concerned with processes of change and increasing stabilization. It draws on ideas from organization studies as well as science and technology studies and is closely related to issues of innovation and institutionalization. It therefore transcends the micro level of concrete design work and focusses on the organizational dynamics of designing across time and space. The complexities of distributed design will be illustrated by drawing on an empirical study of developing novel manufacturing technologies in the semiconductor industry. These elaborate systems technologies are developed in globally coordinated ventures over 15 to 20 years. They include the design of diverse technological components and the tailoring of multiplex organizational arrangements. They are extremely expensive and highly uncertain. As design processes go, it is certainly an extreme case. But I will use it here to contrast notions involving single artifacts and individual designers and to illustrate how a design process may be distributed over time, space, actors and artifacts.

1. Approaching a notion of distributed design

Conceiving design as an inherently distributed practice allows us to look more closely into the intricate relations of technologies and organizations. In a special issue of *Organization Science* on the management of technology, Wanda Orlikowski (1992) once noted that there is a gap in the organizational literature between studies of *design* and studies of *use*. Studies of design contexts typically highlight the *social construction* and *interpretative flexibility* of technologies (Pinch and Bijker 1984), whereas studies of use contexts typically emphasize the impact of technologies on human actions – even though this impact is often more an issue of appropriation and domestication rather than simple determination (Silverstone and Hirsch 1992; Oudshoorn and Pinch 2003). Orlikowski criticizes the fundamental distinction between design and use situations and instead advocates a distinction between a *design mode* and a *use mode* of technology, to be drawn solely for the purpose of analytical convenience (1992, p. 408). She uses this analytical distinction to argue for the "duality of technology", which – in line with Giddens' (1984) idea of the duality of structure – serves to conceive technology both as a medium and result of human action: technology structures just as well as it is structured. Orlikowski thus already hints at the manifold relations in which design and use as well as technologies and organizations are intertwined. Neither should be reduced to an isolated or purified form. Rather, they should be treated as constitutive parts of a larger, more complex and distributed process.

More recently, the relations of technologies and organizations have received increased attention by focusing on issues of materiality in organization studies (Orlikowski 2010; Leonardi et al. 2012; Carlile et al. 2013; Jarzabkowski and Pinch 2013). By drawing on insights from science and technology studies, the mutual constitution of the social and material (i.e. organizational and technical) became more apparent and the distributed nature of human actions and institutions (and design) moved into the spotlight (Bruni 2005; Oudshoorn et al. 2005). Distributed design then considers human agency to be distributed (Rammert 2012) through technology and organization. Designers use a number of technical means in order to accomplish their task, which is more often than not a specific part in a larger sequence of coordinated activities.

Similarly, the relations of design and use have been spelled out in greater detail. There is no longer a grand divide between the two aspects; they are increasingly seen as distinct steps in an ongoing shaping of actors and artifacts. Recent design theories are indeed starting to conceptualize use as a distinct form of design itself (Bredies 2014), thus transgressing the boundaries between experts and laypersons, design labs and everyday practice. Extending design perspectives into use situations follows the theoretical leads of appropriation and domestication by enhancing the role users play in the re-definition and stabilization of technical artifacts (Kline and Pinch 1996). The notion of distributed design then does not stop with the work of the designers, but follows the design process as it is co-created by different users over time.[16]

This notion of distributed design thus carries a material and a temporal dimension. The *material dimension* concerns the entities engaged in the design process. It conceives design work not only as a collaborative venture connecting various designers, but as one that freely associates humans and non-humans alike (Callon 1986, p. 200). For design, this can be specified in two ways. First, design work itself resembles what Hutchins called "distributed cognition" (Hutchins 1995). Hutchins argues that cognition is rarely confined to a single human mind. He uses the examples of marine and air navigation to show how this work is inherently socially and technically distributed. Whether at sea or in flight, navigators align their tasks using a multitude of instruments and media that together comprise the task of modern navigation.[17] Second, in view of its product, the design process can be understood as a form of "heterogeneous engineering" (Law 1987, see also Plontke in this volume). Similar to Law's example of Portuguese colonial expansion and the design of the caravel, designers seek to anticipate possible adverse forces in the use situation and counter them already in their design. Design then consist of incorporating the projected socio-material use network into the respective artifacts. This example already points to the *temporal dimension* of distributed design. Put bluntly, distributed design is always in the making. Never finished, it is not concerned with ready-made artifacts, but with the dynamic processes of design and use in action. This perspective conceives artifacts (technologies and organizations, for that matter) as inherently indeterminate. They may

---

[16] Unfortunately, my own empirical case of semiconductor manufacturing does not cover the actual implementation of the technology. It does, however, trace the impact of powerful technology users (companies like Intel and Samsung) in all phases of the design process.

[17] Not surprisingly, the idea of distributed cognition has already found its way into design concepts for information and communication technologies, especially human–computer interaction (HCI) and computer-supported cooperative work (CSCW).

still achieve temporary closure (Pinch and Bijker 1984) or irreversibility (Callon 1991), if they are embedded in well aligned associations. How durable those phases of closure and irreversibility become depends on the degree, in which they are able to incorporate conflicting interests, actors and material arrangements.

My version of distributed design clearly resonates with concepts found in science and technology studies, such as the "social construction of technological systems" (Bijker et al. 1987), the "sociology of translation" (Callon 1986), "situated action" (Suchman 2007) or "social worlds" (Clarke and Star 2008). It tries to open up the black box of design and to reconstruct the materiality, meaning, fluidity and stabilization of design processes.

Even though it has a strong connection to micro-sociological approaches, it should also be possible to scale it to more global and historical techno-organizational dimensions along the lines of Noble's (1977) "America by Design". Distributed design thus outlines a general creative and productive engagement with the material and the social world (Popitz 2000 [1997]). It entails purpose, novelty, and control as well as unintended consequences, stability, and emergence. And as I stated in the introduction, it comprises a deliberate engagement with the future and the turning of ideas into objects. What it does not entail is normative statements about the "good" or "bad" design of single technological artifacts (Norman 1988; Tenner 1996).

The analysis of distributed design processes therefore resembles what (Garfinkel et al. 1981) referred to as the "potter's object" versus the "coroner's problem". By studying how a team of astronomers go about discovering a pulsar using optical methods, their portrayal of a scientific discovery is not a gradual reconstruction of a fact, similar to the chain of events that leads to a coroner's verdict in a murder case. Rather, they show how the scientific fact emerges out of the interaction of instruments and scientists over an extended period of time. In this sense, it is far more similar to a potter who forms a distinct bowl out of a lump of clay on the pottery wheel. Like pottery, distributed design is an open-ended process, but not a random one. Borrowing from the work of Anselm Strauss and his colleagues, I view this process as a design "trajectory" (Glaser and Strauss 1965; Wiener et al. 1979). According to Strauss, a trajectory "refers to a course of action but also embraces the interaction of multiple actors and contingencies that may be unanticipated and not entirely manageable" (Strauss 1993, p. 53). He emphasizes the emergent unfolding of a trajecto-

ry over time as well as the activities that contribute to this gradual evolution. In contrast to Strauss's broad notion of trajectory, which may refer to
such diverse processes as "an engineering project, chronic illness, dying, a
social revolution, or national problems attending mass or 'uncontrollable'
immigration" (ibid.), a design trajectory would start with a novel idea or a
goal, born out of the concrete engagement with a practical problem,
which is then pursued through the interactive design process until a more
or less final artifact is created. Of course and as stated above, the design
trajectory does not stop with the making of a product but continues on
into the creative adoption by users. It does, however, carry the notion of
the increasing and mutual stabilization of technical and organizational
features, thereby demonstrating a sensitivity to the concrete processes in
which the products of design take shape.

The concept of a design trajectory complements the overall notion of
distributed design in two ways. First, it emphasizes the interrelatedness of
the material and temporal dimensions of distributed design. The temporal
order of the trajectory entails that the distributed elements of design are
not simply dispersed, but that they are integrated in a flow of events and
interactions in which they are connected not only in the present, but also
in the past and future. Design happens in what G.H. Mead called a "spacious present" (1938, p. 220), where both past and future are created from
the present (Mead 1932). Design makes a break with routine approaches
and reflects on how they might be re-arranged. It therefore builds upon
and re-interprets the past while trying to create the future at the same
time. A design trajectory represents an ordered, yet mutable sequence of
events that interrelates the heterogeneous elements of distributed design.
Both technology and organization then account for some of the stabilities
as well as some of the changes in design trajectories. The second point
builds upon the first. If we understand a design trajectory as a continuously evolving process, it becomes difficult to clearly distinguish between the
means and ends. The novel idea used somewhat casually to lead into my
discussion of the design trajectory in the previous paragraph should not
be misunderstood as the a priori formulation of a definite end or purpose
determining the design process. Like in case of the potter's object, the
eventual form emerges out of the manufacturing process itself. In a trajectory in the Straussian sense, ideas and goals are continuously reconfigured
in ongoing series of interactions. Strauss draws on Mead and Dewey in
order to elaborate the transformation of ends in what he calls "trajectory
projection" (Strauss 1993, p. 55). Ends should be thought of as "ends-in-

view" (Dewey 1939, pp. 40), ends which are shaped by the means employed.

This point is important for analyzing distributed design processes, because it underscores how the means of distributed design shape the design outcome as well as the initial goals. Dosi (1982) suggested that technological developments follow "technological trajectories" which are circumscribed by a supporting "technological paradigm". While such a notion lacks the openness of Strauss's trajectory concept, it neatly illustrates how the given technical and organizational features contribute to the future design of technologies. The idea of the design trajectory privileges neither change nor stability, but rather looks for mediating interactions and how they are balanced in concrete design processes.

I will leave my conceptual discussion at this point and hope that the basic outlook of my argument has become clear. In a few words, the notion of distributed design is aimed at understanding the mutual shaping of technologies and organizations in design processes. Even though it draws upon many micro-sociological insights, it can also be used to transcend distinct design situations so as to address the formation of socio-material orders on a larger scale. In the following empirical section of this paper, I will take up the points mentioned above and relate them to global design processes in the semiconductor industry.

2. Designing technologies and organizations in semiconductor manufacturing

The interrelated design trajectories that go into making modern computer chips are, for all practical intents and purposes, virtually innumerable. This form of manufacturing is a costly and sophisticated systems technology in which each component has to perform according to highly demanding specifications. The process may take 15 to 20 years from the initial idea to its implementation on the factory floor. The research presented here was conducted in the interdisciplinary project "Path Creating Networks. Innovating Next Generation Lithography in Germany and the U.S." and I will draw on some ideas that were developed by the project team (cf. Windeler and Schubert 2007; Sydow et al. 2012; Schubert et al. 2013).[18]

---

[18] Principal investigators were Jörg Sydow and Arnold Windeler. The researchers included Knut Lange, Uli Meyer, Guido Möllering, and Gordon Müller-Seitz.

In order to exemplify how the distributed design of semiconductor manufacturing technologies is organized, it is necessary to go into some detail about the technology and how it is related to organizational structures in the semiconductor industry. One characteristic of these production technologies is that the users are often closely engaged with the designers. There is no strict separation between customers and producers. Large semiconductor manufacturing companies like Intel and Samsung, the so-called device makers, are not simply buyers of a ready-made technology but figure as prominent (and dominant) commissioners who initiate and organize the distributed design process as a whole. The tool makers who then manufacture the production technology, companies like ASML, Canon, and Nikon, collaborate with the device makers in numerous research and development endeavors. Both device makers and tool makers also coordinate several supply chains that need to be aligned for creating and using the manufacturing technology. Device makers directly fund certain companies in the tool maker supply chains, for instance, in order to increase their control of the overall process. This collective organization of distributed design is a far cry from classic linear models where design and use are parceled off to distinct groups of actors. A second characteristic is that the design of the manufacturing technology is closely related to computer chip design and vice versa. Designing integrated circuits (ICs) thus depends to a large degree on the underlying manufacturing technology. Lithography, the current manufacturing technology, creates chip patterns by selectively exposing a photosensitive polymer, or photoresist, to a specific wavelength of light, removing the parts of the substrate not protected by the photoresist and then removing the applied layer to reveal the intended structures. Lithography today is a highly sophisticated process that must be lined up with extreme precision on the nanometer scale. Circuit patterns are ultimately manufactured through the repeated application and exposure of photoresist layers. Consequently, certain structures are easier to create than others. These demands led to the implementation of "lithography-friendly design", i.e. rules concerning the chip's architecture based on the fundamental principles of its underlying manufacturing technology. Again we see that the notion of distributed design necessarily includes multiple and complex alignments and the interference of several separate design trajectories.

Two further contributing factors for distributed design in the semiconductor industry are the immense financial resources and the inherent uncertainty as to whether a technology can successfully transition from a laboratory proof of principle to the shop floor of a high-volume manufacturing environment. No single company today is willing or even able to provide both the technical know-how and the financial backing for the design of a novel manufacturing technology. This and the transformation from hierarchical in-house R&D to global inter-organizational networks since the mid-1980s has contributed heavily to an increase in collaborative and distributed design.

Given these circumstances, I would like to use the history of increasingly distributed design trajectories in the semiconductor industry to show how the organization of manufacturing technology design has changed over the last half century. My focus will be on the last 30 years and the increase of distributed design though networked R&D, but a summary glance at the previous alignments of technologies and organizations in the field is helpful for an understanding of the current developments (see Langlois and Steinmueller 1999).[19]

3. From in-house to networked research and development

The transistor developed at AT&T's Bell Labs in 1947 and the integrated circuit in 1958 at Texas Instruments were seminal innovations accomplished by the in-house laboratories of large and vertically integrated electrical companies. Whereas AT&T decided to make the design and manufacturing process of transistors publicly available through broad licensing models, most technological advancements of ICs in the U.S. in the 1960s were made by smaller companies that relied on secrecy and rapid innovation cycles framed by tight anti-trust laws and near exclusive military or state funding. At the time, innovations to semiconductors were mainly driven by innovations in the manufacturing technologies. Contact lithography and the associated chemical processes were taken up in 1962. From then on lithography became the prime method for transferring the chip design onto the silicon wafers and many of the advancements came from enhancing the basic manufacturing principle and thereby gaining an advantage over competitors. Chip design and chip manufacturing were thus all but inseparable in the start-up companies of this era. They were also part of more or less integrated supply chains. The first start-up companies

---

[19] The case at hand also speaks to the literature on innovation networks (Powell et al. 1996; Sydow et al. 2012 and Parolin in this volume), but I will concentrate on the notion of distributed design for the following analysis.

grew as the industry matured and even though semiconductor manufacturing is a science-based field, advancements mainly originated from engineers in the company labs rather than from basic research by university scientists.

Maintaining a close in-house link between chip design and manufacturing was the hallmark of progress in semiconductor manufacturing up until the 1980s, as large companies like IBM coordinated the transition from one generation of technology to the next. But as early as the 1970s, the industry's equipment suppliers began to create integrated manufacturing solutions such as the wafer stepper introduced by CGA in 1978. These machines are at the heart of modern-day lithography and combine all required steps for IC manufacturing. They are also a main driver in the mass production of inexpensive computer chips. This resulted in a dual dynamic within the industry: on the one hand, specialized and increasingly complex equipment was made available for semiconductor manufacturing; on the other hand, this equipment standardized the cheap production of computer chips through high-volume manufacturing (HVM) for global markets.

Since then, the design trajectories of computer chips and their manufacturing equipment have become increasingly distributed on a global scale (Chuma 2006; Malerba et al. 2008). This development occurs in a field characterized by fierce competition among the various companies. Device makers like Intel, AMD and Samsung compete over IC design for processor and memory architectures. They also compete over the concrete manufacturing processes in their own manufacturing plants ("fabs") and made-to-order production facilities at so-called semiconductor foundries like TSMC in Taiwan. Indeed, some classic device maker companies like AMD have completely outsourced their production and become "fabless" manufacturers, shifting their focus more to the chip design than the manufacturing technology. This is important to note, because distributed design in the semiconductor industry is not uniformly consensual, but a highly conflict-laden process of "heterogeneous cooperation" (Star & Griesemer 1989) or "heterogeneous engineering" (Law 1987).

4. Organizing distributed design trajectories

The design of new semiconductor manufacturing technologies is highly competitive, expensive, uncertain, and time-consuming. It also requires a high level of coordination among the participating organizations. This is especially true since the rapid succession of new IC generations is directly linked to advancements in the manufacturing technology. Living by the fast-paced innovation credo of Moore's Law (Moore 1965), the semiconductor industry has extended the technical limits of optical lithography far beyond expectation (Henderson 1995) and still relies on this basic process, though meanwhile transfigured by numerous technical advancements. Potential alternatives therefore always compete with the established technology and despite all of the industry's efforts to introduce a next-generation lithography (NGL) technique, no alternative has been able to succeed the reigning and ever improved solution of optical lithography (Sydow et al. 2012). This essentially comes down to the issue that the semiconductor industry coordinates at least three interrelated design trajectories: first, that of the chips themselves, second, that of improving the existing manufacturing technology and, third, that of innovating an alternative technological option. Over the next pages, I will concentrate on the third trajectory, because it presents an extreme case of distributed design.

5. Setting up collaborative ventures

The search for an alternative solution to replace optical lithography is nearly as old as optical lithography itself. IBM, for instance, already started working on X-ray lithography, which uses X-rays instead of ultraviolet light, in the late 1960s. This new contender makes for an interesting case, because the whole design trajectory from the initial ideas and experimental set-ups to possible applications in semiconductor fabs is likely to take 15 to 20 years. Organizing the design trajectory involves nearly all industry actors, from the device makers to tool manufacturers and component suppliers within different supply chains. It transgresses industry boundaries and connects companies with university research labs and government funding agencies. What interests me in this case and in this chapter, is how such prolonged and distributed design trajectories can be sustained over time. So I will continue with the story of collaborative research and development within the semiconductor industry.

Pushing the envelope of nanoscale innovation is the self-imposed industry-wide standard of technological progress. It brings together diverse developments, which are all measured in relation to their capacity for extending the credo of Moore's Law. This way, it serves as a collective compass that introduces stability into the field by laying out a shared pathway for progress, while at the same time spurring immense efforts in R&D to reach this end. This orientation is supplemented by the industry's tendency to focus on one single technological solution for HVM of computer chips. This trend started in the early 1970s as U.S. equipment suppliers initiated a standards organization called the Semiconductor Equipment and Materials International (SEMI) to counteract the highly individual demands of the device makers.

The design and use of semiconductor manufacturing technologies is closely mirrored by the continuous re-staging of organizational and inter-organizational relations. Especially the collaborative venture of singling out one promising technology for the whole industry has the effect of assembling powerful actors behind competing distributed design trajectories. The organizational changes required to accommodate these collaborative undertakings started in the 1970s, but grew much more pronounced in the 1980s. At that time, U.S. device manufacturers came under strong pressure from Japanese competitors; the Reagan administration, in response, began to relax its strict anti-trust laws to help U.S. manufacturers and their suppliers retain their edge.

The biggest step towards collectively organizing distributed design trajectories in semiconductor manufacturing was taken with the establishment of the Semiconductor Manufacturing Technology Consortium (SE-MATECH) in 1987. The consortium's aim was to strengthen the U.S. supplier base, pool resources and provide for future domestic and international consumer and defense needs (Browning & Shetler 2000). SE-MATECH brought together 14 device makers (among them AT&T, IBM, Intel, and Hewlett-Packard) and was initially funded through equal shares by the companies and the U.S. Department of Defense (each with USD 100 million annually). SEMATECH's history is intriguing, because it shows how the consortium had to be adjusted in its early years to fit the heterogeneous interests of stakeholders – amounting to nothing less than a major re-design of the way U.S. semiconductor manufacturing technology was developed (Grindley et al. 1994). SEMATECH subsequently became the central hub for coordinating the distributed design trajectories to advance semiconductor manufacturing technologies.

5.1. Designing technologies and organizations

The intermingling of technical and organizational aspects becomes more apparent once we look at the ways in which different component supply chains become entangled in the technological architecture.

This requires to look at the basic lithographic process in greater detail. Inside the wafer stepper, the silicon wafers are coated with a photosensitive *resist*, which is then exposed to the circuit's pattern by projecting a specific wavelength, e.g. 193 nm, of ultraviolet (UV) light. The UV light is emitted from a light source, usually a laser. The IC pattern is created by the UV light travelling through a *mask* carrying the chip design template, which is then projected through a series of lenses (*optics*) onto the *wafer*. The wafer is moved on a wafer stage, step by step – hence the name "wafer stepper" – under the optical array in order to expose every single field (die) on the wafer. Behind each component – stepper, resist, mask, optics, wafer – lie different networks of material and subcomponent suppliers. Stepper manufacturers ASML, Nikon, and Canon, for instance, have to integrate the light source from highly specialized suppliers with equally specialized optics, masks and resists that are supplied by yet other companies. Today, mask manufacturers, resist suppliers and stepper producers work at the respective boundaries of physics, chemistry and mechanics, employing a broad range of tricks and tweaks to produce state-of-the-art microchips by proudly outsmarting textbook physics. Since about 2000, the circuit's patterns have been smaller than the wavelength of light used for lithography itself, to name just one example.

This leads to the situation that the eventual buyers of the systems technology, i.e. the device makers, have to coordinate the individual supply chains on site in the factories for successful manufacturing. They have to closely monitor all the incremental enhancements and evaluate their progress, thus exerting a high degree of control along the supply chains. At the same time, the supplier companies are the major drivers behind these incremental enhancements, trying to sell their advanced equipment to the chip manufacturers while being in fierce competition with other suppliers. Because of the high level of technological expertise, which literally defines the leading edge of high-volume manufacturing, nearly all stakeholders need to take part in collaborative technology development to engage in later market transactions. The technological specifications therefore help shape the possible constellations of actors who are willing and able to enter and maintain the distributed design trajectory.

As the technology becomes more and more complex, we can also see an increasing interrelation between the supplier companies themselves. First, because they produce highly interrelated technologies, the companies might, to some extent, be able to compensate for the shortcomings of one component by increasing the performance their own product. For instance, a lag in resist development may be countered by improved source performance, thus securing a larger proportion of the technology's overall value for the source supplier. Second, and on the flipside of the first point, all components must fulfil the highest quality standards for mass production, e.g. if the resist for a new lithography generation does not meet the required demands, the whole technology will not turn out to be profitable. This is one of the reasons why the semiconductor industry prefers the conservative extension of its current technology over a more radical shift to a new alternative. Novel solutions always come with greater technical and economic uncertainty.

Specific R&D practices in the semiconductor manufacturing industry have special relevance for organizing distributed design trajectories, since they are the legitimate and accepted forms of developing and driving technological change. Because collaborative R&D is central for distributed design, I will especially concentrate on practices surrounding this issue. In the case at hand, these are primarily practices of mutually monitoring the progress of others, aligning one's company's activities with the activities of others, and signaling the company's interests to others. I will focus on a bundle of practices that involve specific mutual monitoring activities in organizing distributed design trajectories, namely orientation practices, negotiation practices, and coordination practices (cf. Schubert et al. 2013).

5.2. Organizing orientation

Organizing distributed design trajectories is primarily a question of mobilizing companies to partake in a costly and uncertain collective venture with their competitors and customers. It is also a question of timing these efforts so that the technologies become available when needed. The most prominent example of collectively engaging with the future in the semiconductor industry is the International Technology Roadmap for Semiconductors (ITRS). The ITRS combines the industry's expectations for manufacturing technologies 15 years into the future. Simply put, the ITRS is the material manifestation of Moore's Law, created by aggregating the industry's perception of how to best fulfil its predictions by targeting the manufacturing technology. This is accomplished by globally distributed technology working groups (TWG) which assess the progress of each technology, on the basis of which they then compile the ITRS at six-month intervals. The ITRS thus provides a relevant collective orientation and helps to allocate resources for a specific technological option. If a technology is thought likely to fulfil expectations and thus assumes a prominent position on the ITRS, it may attract more attention from interested companies. Furthermore, the ITRS reduces uncertainties related to timing that are prevalent in the field (Linden et al. 2000: 96), since it not only states which technology is deemed successful for a given technology node, but also when the industry expects the technology to be used for manufacturing. This information is absolutely crucial and any delay can lead to bankruptcy, primarily in cases where companies have invested heavily according to the roadmap but the actual manufacturing is postponed for one or two years, and with it their return on investment. Such timing problems contributed to the demise of the stepper manufacturer SVG, which was bought by ASML after 193 nm lithography was pushed back and customers withdrew in the late 1990s.

Even though technology roadmapping hardly provides an accurate forecast of the future, the techno-economic framing of expectations concerning systems technologies under development is an essential part of organizing distributed design trajectories. It is precisely the collaborative and consensual nature of these technologies that makes their results difficult to dispute. This allows roadmaps to serve as somewhat objectified devices for technology assessment. Companies with enough technological and financial resources to support multiple alternatives can use the ITRS to assess the expectations of others, attempting to get a feel for the industry's general commitment to any given manufacturing technology and maneuver strategically based on their findings. The ITRS then becomes a mediating model (Morgan and Morrison 1999), which relates the anticipations about the future with past and present techno-economic structures. In sum, it becomes clear that in order to coordinate a distributed design trajectory in semiconductor manufacturing, managing its techno-economic framing is crucial. Especially when a technology is in its early stages, positive ITRS evaluations can help to increase support by drawing in more relevant actors.

In short, practices of orientation help semiconductor companies to render their self-made dynamic R&D environment meaningful, which is a fundamental condition for managing distributed design trajectories. These practices are so important that they actually materialize in institutionalized means of orientation like the ITRS, as a specific form of institutional practice that integrates diverse assessment activities and casts them into a regulative framework – consisting of an international roadmap committee, regional and international technology working groups, and the management office at SEMATECH. Such practices of orientation create a shared perception of the course of technological development in two ways. First, companies may attend conferences, read the roadmap and closely follow the collaborative activities of others; second, they may use well-prepared press releases or plenary talks at major conferences as signaling events to communicate opinions to others. Companies and their representatives need to competently interpret these signals and skilfully account for their own plans and actions.

In the semiconductor manufacturing industry, such practices may quickly become institutionalized. At a 2004 conference organized by SEMATECH called the Litho Forum, attendees from around the world were asked to participate in an opinion survey on the development status of various lithography options. Results were made publicly available on the SEMATECH website and due to the success of the first conference, a follow-up event was held in 2006, where the participants expressed their interest in yet another conference in 2007 or 2008. As a key aspect of the conference, gaining orientation is underlined in a SEMATECH press release[20] that quotes organizer Walt Trybula: "The Forum is not about picking winners. That will be done by end users ordering tools"; and Betsy Weitzman, SEMATECH's chief operating officer for advanced technology pointed out: "We came to the Litho Forum as an industry to gather data, not to determine strategies". Whether such events can actually be "strategy-free" remains to be determined, but it is interesting to note that the organizers were very outspoken on the issue and actively frame the conference as a "mere" information-gathering locale, i.e. a place to gain orientation. It also remains to be seen how much the results of the orientation practices are then used to influence strategic decision-making in the corporations.

5.3. Organizing negotiation

The second set of practices are negotiation practices. They are related to the orientation practices and many negotiations may also take place at or around conferences. Once the actors have oriented themselves in the field, they must negotiate possible alliances and technological solutions. Negotiations are held on many different levels and in different locales. Rather institutionalized negotiation practices are to be found in the formal steering committees of R&D consortia like SEMATECH, where the member companies strategically decide on program funding. Informal negotia-

---

[20] http://www.sematech.org/corporate/news/releases/20040130.htm

tion is practiced at the numerous talks surrounding conferences. All our industry sources point to the significance of such "off the record" conversations with colleagues, where possibilities are discussed which are then negotiated within the individual corporations. At a more inter-corporate level, tool suppliers like ASML invite their customers and suppliers for small workshops at which technological options are first discussed openly before the representatives of the corporations engage in secret bilateral negotiations on the mutual alignment of the product roadmaps and strategic research agendas of individual companies. During all negotiations, the companies are faced with the problem of disclosing sensitive information. They need to disclose enough information for their partners or customers to reach realistic conclusions, but they should not disclose too much, especially when engaged in networked R&D ventures with more than one partner. Like the practices of orientation, negotiation practices are based on previous experience, especially the history of past negotiations and their outcomes.

Organizing distributed design trajectories can be understood mainly as the skilful negotiation of strategic interests within actor collectives and, of course, forging the alliances that constitute the basis for these negotiations in the first place. Because of the multitude, the importance and sometimes the secrecy of negotiation practices, I cannot give a comprehensive picture here. It is necessary, however, to point out the pivotal role such practices play on many levels and in numerous locales within the distributed design contexts of developing semiconductor manufacturing technology.

5.4. Organizing coordination

Last but not least, once the actors have sufficiently pursued activities of orientation and negotiation in order to form a coherent assemblage, they use practices of coordination to implement their collaborative efforts. In the semiconductor manufacturing industry, coordination usually takes place under the auspices of the aforementioned collaborative ventures, that is, corporate R&D consortia like SEMATECH, government-funded programs like MEDEA+ in Europe or university-affiliated test facilities like IMEC in Belgium. The networked character of these practices has become taken for granted, though not unproblematic, in the industry since the mid-1990s. Increasingly, the R&D networks have transcended national boundaries, making semiconductor manufacturing technology a truly global arrangement. The multitude of institutionalized coordination practices, fixed in diverse collaborative R&D industry ventures and public-private partnerships has taken on such an extent that practically all our industry sources stressed the need for a better calibration of various parallel efforts happening all over the world.

Meta-organizations are sometimes created for this purpose, like the IEUVI in 2003, an international initiative which pursues the development of Extreme Ultraviolet Lithography (EUVL), then the most promising NGL candidate. IEUVI is a network of consortia in the U.S. (SEMATECH, SRC, INVENT), Europe (MEDEA+, LETI, IMEC), and Asia (ASET, EUVA, MIRAI, SELETE). According to its website, the IEUVI's mission is to a) align R&D activities with the ITRS, b) coordinate collaborative R&D activities among consortia and c) manage knowledge of EUVL IP.[21] Coordination practices are therefore ongoing activities which need to be constantly monitored and evaluated by the participants. Consortia initiate or participate in series of workshops, usually dedicated to one technological option, where all the global actors come together. From the analysis of the semiconductor manufacturing industry, we can see that it is impossible to think of distributed design without referring to inter-organizational networks and their taken-for-granted practices of coordination. The social practices of coordination can, however, not be reduced to simplistic explanations involving technological or economic determination, which would argue that they increase certainty and abate financial worries in the development of sophisticated systems technologies by sharing risks and costs, because networked R&D introduces new risks and costs itself.

One main issue of this is intellectual property. Whereas anti-trust laws, national protectionist regulations and military funding played a significant role in the past, their influence on the global R&D processes for current HVM has since decreased. Also, ethical topics and associated government regulations, relevant in fields such as biotechnology, are usually not an issue in the semiconductor industry. Patents, on the other hand, are a key element of collaborative corporative R&D and thus constitute a central focus of distributed design trajectories. The early history of SEMATECH vividly illustrates the problems of having competitors join in collaborative R&D (Carayannis and Alexander 2004). Concerns about collaboration are not equally distributed within the industry. Chip manufacturers usually see fewer problems because lithography is merely a tool they employ to produce chips. Their competition with other manufactur-

---

[21] http://www.ieuvi.org/IEUVI_obj.htm

ers is based on chip design. Equipment suppliers, on the other end, are engaged in a direct competition focused on the production technology, making lithography tool development the central source of rivalry and the struggle for market shares.

The chip manufacturers usually use patents to protect an option that could result in a broad variety of technological alternatives and minimize interference in key technologies from other companies. If the latter does apply, they often grant exclusive rights to equipment manufacturers for jointly developed products. For IP generated in an R&D consortium, contracts often entail the right of first refusal for the participating companies. This way, the manufacturers co-create IP which may be only peripheral to them but highly sensitive for the supplier company, thereby stilling their concerns over supplier loyalties. The closer the technology gets to eventual HVM, the tighter the contractual arrangements usually become, often taking the form of strictly bilateral projects. Consortia like SEMACTECH are a central locus for coordinating such sensitive issues by keeping records and evaluations of previous collaborative endeavors to be used for tailoring the contracts for future projects.

The practices for organizing distributed design trajectories described above are hardly unique to the semiconductor manufacturing industry and we should assume that similar activities of mutual monitoring and strategic alignment of actor constellations and technological options will be found in other fields. Also, the distinction between practices of orientation, negotiation and coordination is primarily an analytical taxonomy used for framing the diverse practices and their related activities. In the real world of designing semiconductor manufacturing technology, all three aspects are inseparably interwoven.

Conclusion

To sum up my discussion of the long-term, globally distributed design trajectories in the semiconductor industry, I would like to recapitulate the key points. The main thrust of my argument was to situate large-scale design processes as distributed endeavors that assemble diverse actors, technologies and organizations over extended periods of time. The case of the semiconductor manufacturing industry was employed to illustrate the increasingly distributed nature of designing complex systems technologies. It also served to show how technological and organizational design become intertwined in distributed design trajectories and through the organized practices of orientation, negotiation, and cooperation. In addition, the case made clear that distributed design should be understood as a process of socio-material and temporal emergence that essentially cuts across the domains of design and use.

The empirical case was reconstructed using concepts from science and technology studies and organizations studies, especially drawing on pragmatist philosophy and interactionist sociology. This perspective allows us to understand design as processes of creativity and change – not just an aesthetic reformulation of a given artifact. Design is at once esoteric and mundane; it creates something new by drawing on countless existing entities. It is not *creatio ex nihilo*, but a problem-centerd process of inquiry that follows from a problematic situation and seeks closure by adjusting and combining the old with the new.

My take on design consists of two characteristic features of design work: design is the open-ended and future-oriented practice of turning ideas into artifacts. This, I admit, is no ground-breaking statement. What makes design or engineering an interesting issue to study from a sociological perspective is that it allows us to analyze "society in the making" (Callon 1987). Socio-technical change becomes accessible at a level of practice, of concrete construction. For our analysis, we are then directed towards the means of design work (see Janda in this volume). In the case of semiconductor manufacturing, these means consisted of organized practices of orientation, negotiation and coordination. We could characterize them as infrastructures of design work, because they have evolved into institutionalized, nearly taken-for-granted ways of "going on". This essentially turns our attention away from the finished product and towards the contingent processes that may or may not lead to a finished product.

Relating back to Strauss, distributed design trajectories consist not only of functionally differentiated tasks that are seamlessly integrated through increasingly networked types of coordination, but also of manifold "articulations" (Strauss 1988) through which unexpected developments are managed. The mutual shaping of organizations and technologies in the course of innovating next-generation lithography then appears as an open-ended process in which interests, inter-organizational relations, even the past and the future of semiconductor manufacturing are "mangled in practice" (Pickering 1993). This perspective also highlights that ideas cannot be simply materialized into functioning technologies, but rather that technological and organizational obstacles must be overcome through a concerted effort within the industry.

My notion of distributed design then is quite mundane. Like other projects and trajectories, design evolves in interaction, it may change course as powerful actors seek to gain influence or as technological breakthroughs do not happen as predicted. The closely interrelated developments of technological and organizational features as well as the nearly inseparable ties between design and use are typical for high-tech design, but the basic interdependencies should be observable in other cases as well.

That most design trajectories today, especially if they involve organized design processes, should be understood in terms of distributed design does not need any further explanation. The pragmatist-interactionist framework I have laid out in the beginning of this chapter highlights this point neatly. But even more so, it emphasizes the fact that whatever is being distributed must at the same time be re-integrated and articulated in concrete practices. By adopting a material and temporal perspective on design, we are then able to trace the ways in which ideas take shape through interactions over time. However, the final outcome at the end of the trajectory cannot be fully anticipated or controlled. Comparing distributed design trajectories in diverse fields would then enable us to sketch out the similarities and differences of design as a social process that essentially produces novel material and organizational arrangements.

References

Bijker, W.E., Hughes, T.P., Pinch, T. J. (eds.) (1987), *The social construction of technological systems*. Cambridge, MIT Press.

Bredies, K. (2014), *Gebrauch als Design. Über eine unterschätzte Form der Gestaltung*. Bielefeld: Transcript.

Browning, L.D., Shetler, J.C. (2000), *SEMATECH. Saving the U.S. semiconductor industry*. College Station: Texas A&M University Press.

Bruni, A. (2005), "Shadowing software and clinical records. On the ethnography of non-humans and heterogeneous contexts", *Organization*, 12 (3), pp. 357-378.

Callon, M. (1986), "Some elements of a sociology of translation. Domestication of the scallops and the fishermen of Saint Brieuc bay", in Law, J. (ed.), *Power, action and belief: a new sociology of knowledge?* London: Routledge, pp. 196-233.

Callon, M. (1991), "Techno-economic networks and irreversibility", in Law, J.(ed.) *A sociology of monsters? Essays on power, technology and domination*. London: Routledge, pp. 132–161.

Carlile, P.R., Nicolini, D., Langley, A., Tsoukas, H. (eds.) (2013), *How Matter Matters. Objects, Artifacts, and Materiality in Organization Studies*. Oxford: Oxford University Press.

Chuma, H. (2006), "Increasing complexity and limits of organization in the microlithography industry. Implications for science-based industries", *Research Policy*, 35 (3), pp. 394–411.

Clarke, A.E., Star, S.L. (2008), "The Social Worlds Framework. A Theory/Methods Package", in Hackett, E. J., Amsterdamska, O., Lynch, M., Wajcman, J. (eds.), *The Handbook of Science and Technology Studies*. Cambridge: MIT Press, pp. 113-137.

Dewey, J. (1939), "Theory of valuation", *International Encyclopedia of Unified Science*, 2 (4), pp. 1-67.

Dosi, G. (1982), "Technological paradigms and technological trajectories", *Research Policy*, 11 (3), pp. 147-162.

Garfinkel, H., Lynch, M., Livingston, E. (1981), "The work of a discovering science construed with materials from the optically discovered pulsar", *Philosophy of the Social Sciences*, 11 (2), pp. 131-158.

Giddens, A. (1984), *The constitution of society. Outline of the theory of structuration.* Berkeley: University of California Press.

Glaser, B.G., Strauss, A.L. (1965), *Awareness of dying.* Chicago: Aldine Pub. Co.

Grindley, P., Mowery, D.C., Silverman, B. (1994), "SEMATECH and collaborative research. Lessons in the design of high-technology consortia", *Journal of Policy Analysis and Management*, 13 (4), pp. 723-758.

Henderson, R. (1995), "Of life cycles real and imaginary. The unexpected long old age of optical lithography", *Research Policy*, 24 (4), pp. 631-643.

Hutchins, E. (1995), *Cognition in the wild.*, Cambridge: MIT Press.

Jarzabkowski, P., Pinch, T.J. (2013), "Sociomateriality is 'the New Black'. Accomplishing repurposing, reinscripting and repairing in contex", *M@n@gement*, 16 (5), pp. 579-592.

Kline, R., Pinch, T.J. (1996), "Users as agents of technological change. The social construction of the automobile in the rural United States", *Technology and Culture*, 37 (4), pp. 763-795

Langlois, R. N., Steinmueller, W. E. (1999), "The evolution of competitive advantage in the worldwide semiconductor industry, 1947-199", in Mowery, D.C., Nelson, R.R. (eds), *The sources of industrial leadership.* Cambridge: Cambridge University Press, pp. 19-78.

Law, J. (1987), "Technology and heterogeneous engineering. The case of portuguese expansion", in Bijker, W. E., Hughes, T. P., Pinch, T. J. (eds.), *The social construction of technological systems.* Cambridge: MIT Press, pp. 111-135.

Leonardi, P.M., Nardi, Bonnie A., Kallinikos, J. (eds) (2012), *Materiality and Organizing. Social Interaction in a Technological World.* Oxford: Oxford University Press.

Linden, G., Mowery, D.C., Ham Ziedonis, R.(2000), "National technology policy in global markets: Developing Next-Generation Lithography in the semiconductor industry", *Business and Politics*, 2 (2), pp. 93-113.

Malerba, F., Nelson, R.R., Orsenigo, L., Winter, S. (2008), "Vertical integration and disintegration of computer firms. A history-friendly model of the coevolution of the computer and semiconductor industries", *Industrial and Corporate Change*, 17 (2), pp. 197–231.

Mead, G. H. (1932), *The philosophy of the present*. London: Open Court.

Mead, G. H. (1938), *The philosophy of the act*. Chicago: University of Chicago Press.

Moore, G.E. (1965), "Cramming more components onto integrated circuits", *Electronics*, 38 (8), pp. 114–117.

Morgan, M. S. and Morrison, M. (1999), "Models as mediating instruments", in Morrison, M., Morgan, M.S. (eds.), *Models as mediators. Perspectives on natural and social science*. Cambridge: Cambridge University Press, pp. 10-37.

Noble, David F. (1977), *America by design. Science, technology, and the rise of corporate capitalism*. New York: Knopf.

Norman, D.A. (1988), *The design of everyday things*. New York, Basic Books.

Orlikowski, W.J. (1992), "The duality of technology. Rethinking the concept of technology in organizations", *Organization Science*, 3 (3), pp. 398-427.

Orlikowski, W.J. (2010), "The sociomateriality of organisational life. Considering technology in management research", *Cambridge Journal of Economics*, 34 (1), pp. 125-141.

Oudshoorn, N., Brouns, M., van Oost, E. (2005), "Diversity and distributed agency in the design and use of medical video communication technologies.", in Harbers, H. (ed.), *Inside the politics of technology. Agency and normativity in the co-production of technology and society*, Amsterdam: Amsterdam University Press, pp. 85-105.

Oudshoorn, N., Pinch, T.J. (eds.) (2003), *How users matter. The co-construction of users and technology*. Cambridge: MIT Press.

Pickering, A. (1993), "The mangle of practice. Agency and emergence in the sociology of science", *American Journal of Sociology*, 99 (3), pp. 559-589.

Pinch, T. J., Bijker, W.E. (1984), "The social construction of facts and artifacts. Or how the sociology of science and the sociology of technology might benefit each other", *Social Studies of Science*, 14 (3), pp. 399-441.

Popitz, H. (2000) [1997], *Wege der Kreativität*. Tübingen: Mohr Siebeck.

Powell, W. W., Koput, K. W., Smith-Doerr, L. (1996), "Interorganizational collaboration and the locus of innovation: Networks of learning in biotechnology", *Administrative Science Quarterly*, 41 (1), pp. 116-145.

Rammert, W. (2012), "Distributed agency and advanced technology. Or: How to analyze constellations of collective inter-agency", in Passoth, J.-H., Peuker, B., Schillmeier, M. (eds.), *Agency without actors? New approaches to collective action*. London: Routledge, pp. 89-112.

Schubert, C., Sydow, J., Windeler, A. (2013), "The means of managing momentum. Bridging technological paths and organisational fields", *Research Policy*, 42 (8), pp. 1389-1405.

Silverstone, R., Hirsch, E. (eds.) (1992), *Consuming technologies. Media and information in domestic spaces*. London, Routledge.

Star, S.L., Griesemer, J.R. (1989), "Institutional ecology, 'translations' and boundary objects. Amateurs and professionals in Berkeley's Museum of Vertebrate Zoology, 1907-39", *Social Studies of Science*, 19 (3), pp. 387-420.

Strauss, A.L. (1988), "The Articulation of Project Work. An Organizational Process", *The Sociological Quarterly*, 29 (2), pp. 163-178.

Strauss, A.L. (1993), *Continual Permutations of Action*. New York: de Gruyter.

Suchman, L. A. (2007), *Human-machine reconfigurations. Plans and situated actions*. Cambridge: Cambridge University Press.

Sydow, J., Windeler, A., Schubert, C., Möllering, G. (2012), "Organizing R&D consortia for path creation and extension. The case of semiconductor manufacturing technologies", *Organization Studies*, 33 (7), pp. 907-936.

Tenner, E. (1996), *Why things bite back. Technology and the revenge effect*. London: Fourth Estate.

Wiener, C., Strauss, A.L., Fagerhaugh, S., Suczek, B. (1979), "Trajectories, biographies and the evolving medical technology scene. Labor and delivery and the intensive care nursery", *Sociology of Health and Illness*, 1 (3), pp. 261-283.

Windeler, A., Schubert, C. (2007), "Technologieentwicklung und
    Marktkonstitution" in Beckert, J., Diaz-Bone, R., Ganßmann, H. (eds.),
    Märkte als soziale Strukturen. Frankfurt/M., Campus, pp. 217-233.

THE MEANS OF DESIGN WORK
MODELS, SKETCHES, AND RELATED OBJECTS IN THE CREATION OF NEW TECHNOLOGIES

Valentin Janda

Introduction: reversing the perspective on work and design

This article addresses the thematic issues of this book: design, work, technology, and organizations. But, unlike most studies on organizational practices, it concentrates less on the incessant shaping and design of workplaces and entire organizations through practices of work. Instead, the primary thematic focus lies in examining how design professionals employ different means of work to anticipate future useful functions and objects in the development of new technological artifacts and the organization of this process. Work in design projects[22] is characterised by a remarkably low division of labour. In their daily routines, designers perform tasks such as crafting, programming, inventing use scenarios, debugging electric circuits and much more. They create analogies, search for images online, "mash up" different ideas in sketches, or create various types of models. The low division of labour offers the rare chance to study the same actors working on very different problems, with entirely different means of work within the same project. This allows to compare their work practices and the means employed, as personal style, organizational setting, and financial background, along with other intervening factors, are kept stable over the course of the project.

My thesis is that design work can only be done in immediate interaction with arrangements of different materials and symbols that I refer to as *means of design*. Means always consist of both symbolic and material properties which enable and constrain the anticipation and construction of new technological artifacts. Designers need to solve abstract problems, in the case studied here how to "help groups navigate in foreign cities", by

---

[22] This notion of design derives from my experiences as an ethnographic researcher; nevertheless, design work in general seems to be less divided than in production, for example.

constructing objects and procedures. Their project goals harbour uncertainties which first need to be created and are subsequently reduced over time as the design process continues. As this study emphasises, means of design vary in character as they hold different enabling and constraining features (what Gibson 1986 calls "affordances"). Designers must therefore organise their projects and tasks in such a way that uncertainties can be addressed and possibilities activated by interacting with and through means that successively enable them to advance towards new designs.

In the first part of this paper, I discuss concepts and theoretical approaches to develop a sociological perspective on design work. In the second part, these ideas are then used to analyze three exemplary cases of design work. I start in section 2 by referring to John Dewey and his notion of work as a primal and enduring pursuit of creating certainty. Design – as any social action – is therefore understood as an ongoing and practical "quest for certainty" following John Dewey's terminology. The interplay of indeterminacy and anticipation permits an understanding of interaction with the environment in general and, more specifically, interaction in design work. To move from the basic interactional level to organised activity in the design process, Anselm Strauss's concept of an "arc of work" is used to highlight the interweaving of countless interaction sequences in the process of designing. This concept provides a vehicle for understanding the designer's work activities as an organised arc of work driven by anticipations and valuations of future objects. Complex and multi-layered work concerning interaction with others and actions directed towards objects, material and technology is best reflected in the notions of anticipation and object formulated by George H. Mead. In section 3, I provide a brief methodological commentary on the difficulty of finding constraints that derive from means of work while leaving intertwined social constraints aside. Section 4 presents three short empirical cases: the identification of related objects (1), the disassembly of well-known technologies to create new ones from their bits and pieces (2), and the construction of models (3). These cases all involve prototypical sequences of interaction, where words, visuals and models become means of design. I will analyze how the interactions with different means of design and their properties need to be orchestrated in order to finish the given design project. Controversial types and means of interaction in design then illustrate that different means address different types of tasks and problems in design. I conclude this study by postulating that the character of different means of design must be taken seriously in order to understand the different logics of social processes such as design work.

1. Accounting for socio-material work

My argument is based on the premise that the iteration of action and sensemaking is ubiquitous in all social processes and, therefore, in design work, too. Like any other process of action or work, design is composed of interactions that employ symbolic and material entities – most commonly: words, gestures, texts, sketches, models and others. Deviating from a purely social constructivist stance toward technology, I argue that the means of design are not only "intermediaries" but relevant "mediators" in the process of work (Latour, 2000: p. 18). This perspective is in keeping with one of Bruno Latour's central criticisms of social theory:

> *"Soft humans and weak moralities are all sociologists can get. The society they try to recompose with bodies and norms constantly crumbles. Something is missing."* (Latour, 1992: p. 227)

Latour thus encounters a fundamental problem of mainstream social theory and offers his own solution. Though actor-network theory proposes a seemingly radical departure in promising to do away with the ontological differences between humans and the physical world, this break derives from a semiotic principle (Callon, 1986: p. 82 fn4) and, lamentably, does not manage to leave the realm of semiotics. Concepts such as delegation (Latour, 1992: pp. 248-254) or Latour's four forms of technical mediation (Latour, 2002: pp. 216-232) do mediate between symbolic and material properties of actors, but they primarily stress their significance for social action. Inherent properties of symbolic, visual, or material actants are secondary. Taking semiotic symmetry as starting point, however, ultimately erases decades of insightful and capable social theory that offers us numerous concepts for understanding and exploring socio-material situations. Pragmatism has a longstanding tradition of micro-level interaction analysis, especially in contexts of work. Drawing on the ideas of John Dewey, Anselm Strauss, and George H. Mead, I would like to develop a pragmatist/interactionist perspective on the affordances of the means – in this case of design work –, without abandoning the valuable sociological insights which actor-network theory sacrifices in the name of semiotic symmetry. This pragmatist views holds a second benefit: unlike the lens offered by actor-network theory, emerging technologies (Callon, 1986; Latour, 1983; Latour, 1996) can be conceptualised in the same notions and vocabulary as technologies in use (Latour, 1992; Latour, 2000).

1.1. Dewey: working out uncertainty

Design work, as any social action, is conducted to minimise the perils of existence by actively engaging with the environment and creating certainty out of indeterminate situations. Formulated by the American philosopher John Dewey in 1929, this basic assumption remains as striking today as it was then, because it has the potential to help us understand design work by fixing its relevant coordinates. In *"The Quest for Certainty"*, Dewey starts his argument by criticising his fellow philosophers, and their ancient Greek predecessors, for dividing knowledge into a sublime realm of philosophy and an inferior realm of knowledge about practical action and material artifacts. Dewey is doubtful about the existence of a purely philosophical, theoretical realm of knowledge. More fundamentally, he doubts the validity of a basic divide between practical and theoretical knowledge.

> *"Philosophy in maintaining its claim to be a superior form of knowledge was compelled to take an invidious and so to say malicious attitude toward the conclusions of natural science."* (Dewey, 1929: p. 28).

Dewey's rigorous line of argumentation cuts across the established but artificial division that claims the superiority of theory and the lesser value of practical knowledge. He concludes that pure knowledge cannot exist by itself because every act, including an act of knowing, is always found in some practical context and situation. In this assumption lies the core of his argument for a single, united form of knowledge.

> *"And it is a strict truism that no one would care about any exclusively theoretical uncertainty or certainty."* (Dewey, 1929: p. 38).

Dewey argues at length that, in the constant quest for certainty, only one form of practice and knowledge exists.[23] Hence the philosopher's

---

[23] One can find parallels between Dewey's efforts for a whole and unified understanding of acting and knowing and Bruno Latour's attempts, six decades later, to unlearn the difference between material and social logics as described in *"We Have Never Been Modern"* (Latour, 1993).

elaborate and enduring efforts for "pure", or theoretical, certainty are condemned to failure. As this argumentation cannot be elaborated here in detail for the design cases presented and discussed below, we must be satisfied with adopting this central assumption: uncertainty, along with its perils and risks, forms the bedrock of the work of social actors, conceptualised as an active and practical engagement with their environment. Every attempt to face uncertainty is rooted in practical action – the only way to overcome uncertain situations. Whether applied to the uncertainties of everyday life or to the uncertainties of scientific endeavours, this assumption leaves no room for differences between theoretical and practical knowledge. Dewey's line of argumentation unifies the notion of work into one condensed effort with a purely practical character at all times. This does not, of course, mean that work as a basic form of action does not find manifold ways and methods to actively face uncertainty, for example, in the development of new technologies.

> "*In the absence of that organic guidance given by their structure to other animals, man had to find out what he was about, and he could find out only by studying the environment which constituted the means, obstacles and results of his behaviour. The desire for intellectual or cognitive understanding had no meaning except as a means of obtaining greater security as to the issues of action.*" (Dewey, 1929: p. 38)

With an increasing security as to one's own and other actors' actions and their consequences, the relation between action and object becomes more predictable. Greater predictability, then, is the premise for planned and methodical action, for example in the context of work.

> "*Henceforth the quest for certainty becomes the search for methods of control; that is, regulation of conditions of change with respect to their consequences.*" (Dewey, 1929: p. 128)

Design work is also called on, as every form of action, to deal with uncertainty. Transforming uncertainty into a unified whole, as Dewey would have it, can be understood as advancing the design process insofar that the very open and vague situation that characterises early project stages gradually acquires shape over time. This is typical for any work situation in Dewey's sense.

> *"Inquiry is the controlled or directed transformation of an indeterminate situation into one that is so determinate in its constituent distinctions and relations as to convert the elements of the original situation into a unified whole."* (Dewey, 1938: pp. 104)

The quote is striking for the efforts of designers described in the empirical part of this paper. At the very beginning of the six-month design process, none of the designers has a clue about what will result from their work. During the process, multiple certainties and uncertainties will be created, sorted, and perhaps even disappear completely. Later project conditions are more determinate insofar as relations between its elements become clearer and more unified, in other words: more certain. Up until this point, Dewey's conceptual framework fits perfectly for the case of a textile orientation device developed by two designers. I would like to note however that Dewey's concept of uncertainty can be extended by distinguishing two basic forms: intended and unintended uncertainties, in design these two forms are highly visible as uncertainty is an essential resource for the designers work. Both forms will be discussed in further detail below. Reversing Dewey's relation between work and certainty, it becomes obvious that the designers who challenge themselves to create certainty thrive on uncertainty as the raw material for their job: no uncertainty, no work. As will be shown, designers draw from a repertoire of methods to generate uncertainty, the aspects of which they resolve later in the process. Uncertainty thus becomes a resource for their work; it is actively and repeatedly increased and decreased over time. Especially in the early stages of design processes, the designers in my cases created their own uncertainties – a finding which goes beyond Dewey's conceptualizations as he mainly took uncertainty as given problem.

In the empirical study outlined on these pages, the designers aimed to create a meaningful and functional technology to help tourists navigate foreign cities. Their work therefore consisted of efforts to inquire into uncertain situations and explore promising uncertainties which, in turn, held the potential to be transformed into interesting solutions. An understanding of these processes of design work requires piecing together many different types of action, as work needs to be organised from countless interactions which actively modulate – increase and decrease – certainty. Start-ing with Dewey's insightful premise of work as practical problem solving, in the next step a notion of organised work is crucial to move from the basic level of general interactions to a more concrete notion of means and coordination in design.

1.2. Strauss: aligning the designer's efforts

Anselm Strauss, who advanced many ideas of the Chicago School and who co-founded the method of grounded theory, also imported central in-sights from pragmatist philosophy into interactionist sociology. Besides his well-known and essential contributions to the field of methods, the logic of pragmatism can also be seen in the implementation of these methods in his own research on diverse kinds of work (Strauss, 1959; Gla-ser, Strauss, 1965). In his studies on the work of medical practitioners (Becker, Geer, Hughes, Strauss, 1961; Glaser, Strauss, 1965), Strauss devel-oped a concept of work that bundles the countless interactions involved in medicine. His pragmatist notion of work is therefore almost as basic as action itself.[24]

> "Implicit in the Pragmatist theoretical action scheme is the idea of work – imagining, trying out, assessing actions or lines of actions involves "working things out," to use a com-mon phrase. Work is entailed in the process of unblocking the blocked action, and moving along into the future."
> (Strauss, 1993: p. 52)

The previous assumption of reducing uncertainty in design work thus perfectly matches Strauss's notion of work. Both notions define work as something that actively addresses the social and material world to in-

---

[24] In a rather innovative perspective in his day, Strauss set forth an understanding of organisation that viewed work – and not hierarchy or other elements of structure – as a major explanatory element of organisation: "The division of work among classes of persons may therefore be different during different phases of the project or trajectory, each successive one perhaps necessitating new classes with particular skills or relying on different skills of the same workers. It is the skills and actions which are the essential elements then, not simply the class of worker as such" (Strauss, 1985: pp. 4).

crease the predictability of situations (Dewey) or "unblock" blocked actions (Strauss). Both notions, moreover, emphasise a chronological perspective, which is important to gain insight into the gradual evolution of design processes. Nevertheless, comparing the many similarities of the concepts is not the objective here, as it is their differences that hold interesting benefits for the present analysis: Dewey's instructive and exceedingly crucial understanding of work is rather too short-lived for the present context. In design projects, work needs to be organised; individual endeavours that seek and abate uncertainty must be interrelated with regard to project goals (e.g. creating new interactive navigation tools and furthering design knowledge) and project constraints (e.g. project schedules, financial constraints). Inherent similarities in these two concepts of work allow us to embed Dewey's philosophical notion of work in Strauss's sociological concepts of work and organising. According to Strauss, work is organised with reference to two organizational constraints: the permanent progression of time and activities that aim to unblock action. These two constraints will be outlined as an analytical frame for analysing design work in the empirical chapter. To summarise: Strauss defines work as a mode of organised interaction; the boundaries between work and other types of interactions such as play or fantasy are fuzzy (Strauss, 1993: p. 95). In order to expand this understanding of work and organising, his notions of *arc of work* and *line of work* are very helpful.

> "*An arc for any given trajectory – or project – consists of
> the totality of tasks arrayed both sequentially and simultane-
> ously along the course of the trajectory or project.*" (Strauss,
> 1985: p. 4)

In the present study on design work, the design of a wearable computing device shall be understood as such an arc of work. This concept permits us to bundle the countless interactions that increase and decrease certainty in the process of designing this wearable navigation device. Strauss's broad notion of arcs in which work is organised with regard to time and socio-material constraints and opportunities allows us to go well beyond the basic interactionist perspective that insightfully describes the relation between action and certainty. With Strauss, Dewey's basic idea of work as a process of resolving (and creating) uncertainty can be extended by the notion of an *arc of design*.

Strauss's line of work then, on a higher level, relates several arcs of design (Strauss, 1993: p. 14) to grasp wider work contexts such as multiple projects or an entire organization. For this study, arcs of work are a crucial entity to combine an interactionist analysis of design activities with the effects of these interactions on the overall process of developing a new technology. To sum up, all actions and interactions pursue the objective of creating certainty – which, at times, also requires uncertainty. To understand multiple different actions and interactions in the context of design work, the notion of arc of design must stand up to in-depth scrutiny. Before going into the empirical details of the design process, a detailed understanding of means of design must also be elaborated, because work is not only organised around but also mediated by manifold semantic and material devices. In the next section, I will discuss the difference between object and symbol, as well as between anticipation and concreteness.

1.3. Mead: objects and anticipations of work

Many interactions in design work are readily apparent to the empirical observer: discussion, enquiry, scribbling, comparing, building models, testing, debating, and so forth. In consequence, the means of this work are words, sketches, drawings or pictures, and objects. These means are created in the work situation itself or co-opted from other situations. They can be combined or divided, explored, made durable or scrapped, since these are the same means that are processed in the arc of design. For the purposes of this article, all of these entities intertwined in design-related interactions are referred to as means of design. They populate every arc of design in diverse forms such as anticipations, symbols, or tangible and malleable material objects. They derive from the designers' actions and shape them at the same time. Design thus draws from diverse means occurring in manifold forms. To find a common thread in this empirical complexity, I will elaborate the conceptual framework of "means" in the following.

Referring to Mead, objects (like palpable things) and symbols (like words) are matters of interaction. In most actions, objects and symbols are only dealt within an anticipatory sense. Anticipation can be understood as calling forth the properties of objects in one's mind while the objects themselves are distant or absent. At a distance, properties are anticipated[25] and, regardless of their accuracy, these anticipations form the basis for action as William I. Thomas and Dorothy S. Thomas have convincingly argued (Thomas, 1928: p. 527). Every competent actor anticipates the meaning of a verbal symbol as he anticipates the properties of a wooden bridge before setting out to cross it, step by step. Anticipated properties can turn out to be correct, but it is here that the differences between symbolic and material entities become apparent. While symbols often belong to a realm of common knowledge, the material properties of objects can be verified through common or systematic investigation. In most everyday situations, meanings and properties are anticipated accurately and the differences between objects and symbols do not come to bear; for the process of design, however, where both meaning and material functions are still in the making, these differences do matter. Like symbols, objects are mostly referenced from a generalised perspective through thought or anticipation. Unlike symbols, material entities refer to something that Mead calls the "physical object". Similar to Latour (2006: p. 39), referring to a material world is a condition for every interaction with an object.[26]

> "*The physical object is found to be that object to which there is no social response which calls out again a social response in the individual. The objects with which we cannot carry on social intercourse are the physical objects of the world.*" (Mead, 1934: p.184 fn)

For an analysis of design work, these different notions of objects must be sorted out: Building on physical objects, objects in general are mostly

---

[25] Mead employs the notion of "anticipation" for assumptions regarding the material world, whereas his well-known concept of 'role taking' holds the same idea, but applies it to the social sphere (Joas, 1980: p. 152f.; Lüdtke, 2011: p. 246). Mead developed the notion of "taking the role of the other" for this same social mechanism in interactions involving a stronger degree of contingency. Insightful critic on Mead's a priori division between human actors and everything else can be found in Lüdtke (2011: p. 249f.). Lüdtke stresses that the ability to interact must be conceptualised as an attribute of actors and not based on a simple categorical (person, animal, robot etc.) ascription.

[26] Latour then stresses that with no exception materialities are to be found in contexts of action.

dealt with as "distant objects" (Mead, 1932: p. 128f.). This means that, for example, when crossing a street, actors anticipate the resistance of the ground with every step, the height of the curb, the speed and relative distance of an approaching car, and so forth. The meaning of an approaching car, our resulting caution, and the significance of a possible crash is, in most cases, only anticipative, as most of us have never been involved in a pedestrian collision. Anticipation creates properties of objects at a distance (distant objects), these properties lead to action, no matter their accuracy. According to Mead, every action is based on anticipation and experience, as actors continuously "design" their relevant conditions for action. In contrast to symbols, distant objects relate to further notions of an object; most objects can become "contact reality" (Mead, 1932: p. 131) through direct interaction, i.e. physical touch and observation.

> "The surface we call smooth calls out a tendency to stroke it, but that one may not do this until he has reached it and got hold of it means that the actual appearance of smoothness or pleasantness awaits the manipulatory resistance of the physical thing." (Mead, 1932: p. 131)

The object is felt and seen in the very same moment, therefore enriching the actor's experience. Mead's notion of objects – despite most interaction taking place in the realm of anticipation – is squarely planted in a physical world. An object's meaning – in contrast to a symbol – is not entirely the product of the social construction of reality. Objects and their physicality exist and these properties are relevant for human-object interactions.[27] Mead's notion of objects and symbols comes together in the space that defines their shared and social meaning. This meaning is the motor that drives most actions involving objects and symbols. But contrary to symbols, objects do have a material side that can be accessed through physical contact and referenced repeatedly in interactions, e.g. in cutting with a knife or phone calls by wire. In the arc of design, symbols,

---

[27] Mead's pragmatist notion of objects depicted here can be easily related to Gibson's 'affordances' of objects, as the latter enable and constrain actors as well (Gibson, 1986). Due to this similarity, Gibson is a good reference point, but Mead's understanding of objects allows to conceptualise constraining or enabling properties not as depending on the objects alone, but as features of action. Objects then become constituent features of social processes instead of external entities.

"distant objects" and "objects in contact reality" are crucial entities, be-cause they make up the means of design for the designers' work.[28]

By way of a brief summary before continuing to the empirical case: de-sign work consists, as any social action, of relations between actors and objects. These relations are processed by discussions, texts, pictures, sketches, and models that I have termed the means of design. Employing means allows the designers to tackle (i.e. to create and reduce) the uncer-tainties of design work. Like any work, design work is characterised by unblocking of blocked actions and, from time to time, intentionally setting up "roadblocks", in other words, manufacturing uncertainty, that can lead to creative problem solving. The means, however, are not simply em-ployed to process uncertainties; they may also raise – whether intentional-ly or not – uncertainties, too, as every means has its own format. An em-pirical analysis reveals that the anticipation of objects does not always correspond to their actual properties or that the meaning of symbols or objects can vary among different individuals or sequences of action. De-sign work therefore does not usually go according to plan. In design, as in other forms of social action, meanings as well as material properties are created, validated, and proceeded upon. As this study shows, objects and symbols bring with them different formats that can, at turns, accelerate or decelerate the ongoing arc of design. Considering the data, it will be in-sightful to question whether the share of rather anticipatory means (words, pictures, usage scenarios) prevalent at the beginning of the pro-cess tends to shift towards more physical means (sketches, models, proto-types) near the end.

2. Some thoughts on methods to focus on means of de-sign

To a sociologist it comes as no surprise that work in general implies count-less social and organizational constraints which enable, impede, and therefore shape actions. Designers make many decisions; they have lim-ited budgets, time, and manpower. As individuals they bring a unique socialization and set of experiences, but they are also part of a hierarchical setting, faced with micro-political situations in an organizational context,

---

[28] All means of design are symbolic and material at the same time. In some cases, the designers tend to refer more to the physical side (e.g. in using scissors); in other cases, the symbolic properties are more important (e.g. in speaking).

and so forth. Work presents countless aspects and research questions for a sociologist when enquiring into the world of designers. For this study, however, the main focus lies in the constraints and possibilities that result from applying different means of design – all other sociological questions have to be left aside.

As Kalthoff stresses, qualitative research is about certain social phenomena and relations; a strictly technical approach and application of methods does not lead to a comprehensive understanding of social phenomena (Kalthoff, 2010: p. 353). Because my interest lies in understanding how individuals do what they do and how their social and material situation evokes various interactions, an ethnographic perspective presented a promising possibility for my research questions (Kalthoff, 2010: p. 358). Due to the multi-faceted work setting of the designers I observed, I decided to collect different types of data. Field notes, for example, helped me sketch out the broader arc of the process, but also record very detailed descriptions. I took photographs to clearly record all items and actors in certain situations and therefore facilitate the reconstruction of a certain situation. In addition, based on a few short videos, I could follow action sequences and discussions in great detail. "Technography", a method developed by Werner Rammert and Cornelius Schubert, combines ethnography with a special interest for technology, it aims: "not to repeat the great tales of technology, but to tell the small exemplary technographies of diverse situations in detail" (Rammert and Schubert, 2006: p. 12; transl. by author). Independent from the method or the specific data collected, my interest was consistently devoted to the progressive development of uncertainty.

The following sequences from a six-month design project will not provide an understanding of the process as a whole, but will instead shed light on the details of design work or, more precisely, on how the initial design problem[29] becomes more or less determinate, at turns, through interactions with different means of design. Dewey's quest for certainty is implied as the goal of design work. Different means of design enable or constrain this goal in interaction. This study focuses on interactive work situations in detail, not on the overall design process.

---

[29] Wolfgang Jonas (2001) asserts that, in contrast to my depiction, the design process does begin with the explicit statement of a design problem.

3. Objects and symbols become means of design

Within the course of this study, I investigate the work of one professional designer (K.) and her student assistant designer (N.). Employed at the Universität der Künste Berlin (Berlin University of the Arts).[30] K. considers her work as "research by/through design"[31]. Work in this lab currently involves creating new technological devices for interaction and developing methods of design, for instance in PhD theses and projects on design methods. K., a designer whom I accompanied over several projects, earned a PhD in design in 2014 and is specialised in interactive textile wearables that are sometimes embedded in familiar clothing or accessories such as scarves, beanies, or pullovers, or also contain new technologies in new forms. The latter might be inventions like textile globes or coin belts. As mentioned above the six-month project started with the problem of navigating in a new city for tourists, but the process of defining this initial problem is not covered here. I consider the invention and construction of one particular wearable device to be an *arc of design* (Strauss, 1985: p. 4); the DRL's efforts to create new forms and objects of interaction constitute the broader *line of work* that cannot be examined here. In this exemplary case, K.'s student assistant works part time at the DRL alongside her Bachelor studies in fashion design. Both designers had parallel work obligations during the six-month project. In the following, I will describe the relation between waxing and waning (un)certainty in interactions by studying the details of three typical work sequences in one arc of design: brainstorming (1), sketching (2), and testing (3).

3.1. Brainstorming touristic affairs

The first excerpt from the design process is a brainstorming technique which is used as a means of design. The aim of this brainstorming approach is to find objects related to an initial design problem, to sort these

---

[30] I am very obliged and thankful for all the open doors and minds I found at the Design Research Lab at the Berlin University of the Arts, in particular I want to thank Dr. Katharina Bredies and her anonymous assistant for giving me insights into their pioneering work in the field of textile interfaces.

[31] Jonas (2007) provides a depiction of the interesting debate on the differences between 'research into/about design', 'research for design', and 'research through/by design'. For a broader view on the question of who designs design see Mareis, Held, and Joost (2013).

ideas, and to make them relevant to the design problem at hand. The design problem that marked the start of this arc of work was in place before my investigation began. Because the DRL in Berlin is concerned with textile interfaces and wearable devices as a broader line of work, the problem of navigating with a wearable interface fits within this line. In the following, a brief narration will shed light on the brainstorming process and afterwards a conceptualization follows.

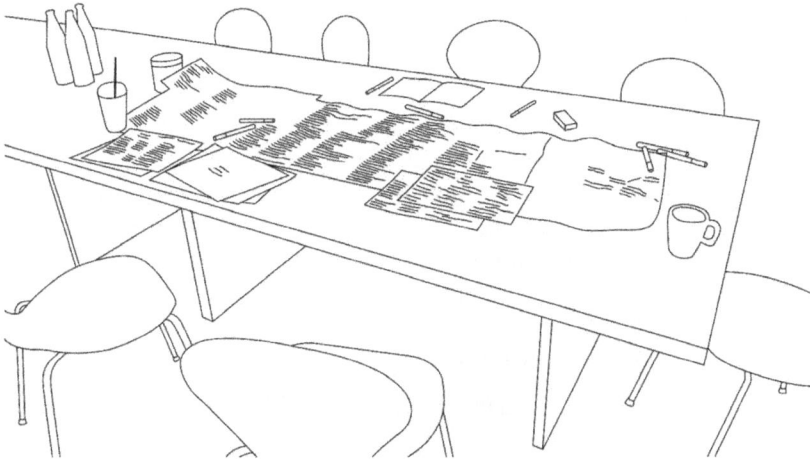

Figure 1: The wordy work of finding analogies

At my second visit, the two designers performed a brainstorming method that appeared very familiar to K. As a participant observer, I sat at the table with K. and N. All three of us were holding black markers. K. explained the method while she unrolled a large sheet of white paper. At first we discussed anything which is typical for tourists, as the potential user groups for the navigation device. During and after the discussion, K. wrote down most of our ideas in keywords. A list of about 16 characteristics of tourists took shape. According to our vocalised perceptions, they included: being outdoors all day, seeing a lot, not speaking the local language, taking many pictures, carrying lots of equipment, showing up in groups, having to do everything on the move, and so forth. In the next step, K. chose seven of these characteristics and we began to seek other entities that share them. Again, we had many ideas; most of them were listed by K.

who, unlike N. and me, constantly used her marker for writing. The second list of analogies covered people who spend a good deal of time outdoors: e.g. Eskimos, athletes, people in the Mediterranean region, and many more. Over the next two hours, seven lists emerged from our ideas and anecdotes – every single keyword in the list was related to one of the properties of tourists. Afterwards, we all chose about 25 of the conceived types of people from the seven lists as particularly promising. The chosen 25 were each written in the center of extra sheets of paper. As a last common task, typical things and features of these chosen entities were noted. Sailors, for example, deal with containers, rum, knives, knots, compasses, and so forth. The afternoon's tasks ended with these various and somewhat curious collections of equipment and features. Following K.'s brainstorming method, we produced long lists of things that broadly relates to the properties of tourists.

During the brainstorming process, all three of us spoke about many different situations, while K. decided whether to list a point or not. As this paper deals with the means of design, and not with decision making in projects or organizations, the decision-making process that occurred while brainstorming will not be addressed here. Instead, when working with uncertainty, the arc of design as a coordinating element composed of interactions and the means of design as the objects of interactions must be identified and related to one another.

At this very early point in the design process, there are still no sketches, models, or materials. Indeed, there is not much for the designers to work with except the initial problem as a reference point. Listing related objects is understood as an endeavour to generate and sort a field of related objects and users. By asking how these objects are used in what related practices, their uncertain relations become clearer. This helps the designer to comprehend a state of affairs. In other words, the designers tackle the uncertainty of an emerging field of objects and practices by sorting many existing examples that they relate to their problem. This is one segment in the arc of design; its actions address the uncertain relations between the recently generated collection of objects and make them more certain by linking them in different ways. The results of this session serve as a reference point later in the arc of design. Even more interesting is another question: what types of interaction are typical for this segment of the arc of design? Discussing, writing, and ordering are generally performed in the realm of symbols, because spoken and written words, lists, and connecting lines are all symbolic entities. Written on paper with markers, these concrete trappings give the symbols form over time. As this session is one of the first of a larger process, it is fair to say that design in this context starts by predominantly working with symbolic means.

With regard to the means of design, the designers stayed in realm of symbols (written and spoken) to tackle uncertainties occurring at this point of the arc. As everyone was familiar with the function and meaning of these everyday objects, there was no need to test the physical properties of rum, containers, compasses, or other common objects. More precisely, the question of analogy here is about an analogy of meaning: which stuff makes sense for different but related people? The analogy does not concern analogies in design. Using symbolic entities is an advantage for the designers, because the exclusion of physical and material characteristics makes sorting and relating quicker and easier – technical details can be left aside. Subsequent tasks in this arc of design like the construction of models, as we will see later, are based on exploring physical properties. For spoken and written symbols as a means of design, we can sum up that symbols allow a quick and easy anticipation of all kind of objects and practices, no matter their material, construction, or technical function. This property of means is due to their symbolic character and does not come as a surprise, since symbols, by definition, are based on a common understanding that enables communication. Using primarily symbolic means frees the designers from the material constraints of the discussed objects. Written and spoken words make it possible for them to freely relate different meanings with relative ease. It is obvious, however, that K. needs to work with a pen and paper to organise all emerging relations. The uncertainty that is part of the navigation question is addressed by all the contributions, thus forming a short span in this arc of design; new elective affinities arose and therefore the question of how to navigate became a little bit less vague.

Facing this uncertainty is the major part in this segment of the designers' work. Uncertainty is also the starting point for their work, however, and at many occasions it becomes obvious that uncertainty is a product of their work, too. Questioning "taken-for-granted" aspects of navigation is a necessary prerequisite to initiate and advance this and any other process of design. Without the ability to question normal functions and the resulting user and object relations, designing is impossible.

3.2. Sketching out future use scenarios

On entering the DRL some days later, I found the two designers in a seminar room. All tables had been placed in the middle of the room and covered with numerous photos. K. and N. were obviously enjoying their work
of melting ideas from the pictured old objects into new concepts. The task
of the day was to "transfer the aspects of the pictured objects into navigation", as K. explained. Because this task brings up many questions for me
as a researcher, I carefully observe the two designers at work.

Figure 2: Disassembling and reassembling situations of use

All sheets of paper on the table show one of 50 objects selected in the
previously depicted brainstorming process. Besides each photo showing
the objects, like sippy cups[32], bumper cars, rifles, dog whistles, and tents in
situations of use, a brief list gives an overview of the individual object's
properties, materials, design, users, and goals. K. and N. push the sheets
around and sort them on the table. From time to time they scribble down
a comic-like scene on paper in which a technology they just dreamt up is
shown in use. While scribbling, they chat uninterruptedly about the pic-

---

[32] A sippy cup or sprout cup helps young children to drink, as the cup's cover is
moulded into a short, thick drinking straw.

tured scenes and their own experiences with those objects. Again, everyone chimes in with amusing anecdotes about themselves or friends and
families using – and sometimes cursing – the pictured items. These anecdotes seem trivial, but they are the raw material for the ongoing invention
of new scenarios of use[33]. Unlike pictures, stories give insight into the details of practices intertwined with objects: as I start to chat with K. about a
sippy cup shown in a picture and the interesting fact that infants always
manage to keep the right side up with the opening pointing towards their
mouth, she casually starts a new drawing: an infant holding a cup-like
object in both hands is shown with the Berlin subway in the background.
An arrow and a question mark symbolise the quest for orientation; K. describes the new object as leading visitors through the city, especially when
decisions are necessary, for example, after finding the right subway line
but accidentally taking the train going in the wrong direction. Or finding
the right road but not knowing which way to turn. To sum up, the feature
of orientation was extracted from the situation of drinking from a baby
cup, magnified, re-contextualised, and then graphically visualised in a
new situation, a situation where orientation is demanded, at once a reference to the initial design problem. By isolating features of well-known
objects and reassembling them in new ways, about 25 sketches for navigation devices were created. All these ideas emerged through different stories and situations of use. Stories, personal anecdotes, and experiences
breathe life into these ideas but, more importantly, such stories contain
the practices, including the intentions, problems, and benefits, that go
with the use of every object. With regard to the initial design problem and
its inherent uncertainty, it is obvious that the new situation of use is beginning to take form.

Visualizations in photos and later in sketches enable K. and N. to develop scenarios of use. If K. does not understand one of N.'s sketches,
more words, stories, and pen strokes are mobilised to create a shared understanding or, as Mead would have it, a significant symbol which holds a
shared meaning. Again, various interactions counteract the uncertainty
that stems from the initial design problem, though types of interaction
vary. This segment of the arc of design is filled with different means of
design, as the objects of interaction are not only spoken and written

---

[33] In my research, the question of what was being designed or invented here was
harder to answer than expected. In this case, one could say use scenarios are
invented, while in the brainstorming session, relations and analogies were
developed.

words, but also the photos and sketches used to illustrate scenes of future use. From now on, these sketches can be referred to again at any point in this and other arcs of design.

Like in the first sequence, the designers work with symbolic means to deconstruct pictures and assemble new sketches. Compared to the brainstorming session, however, these graphics and visuals allow the designers to go into the details of practices of use. How an infant holds a cup is expressed precisely in a sketch but difficult to describe in words (that is, without gestures). The means of design used here are somewhat less abstract and anticipative because they relate more to the material form and properties than the spoken and written words from the first exemplary sequence. Referring to Mead's notion of objects, words as well as pictures are significant objects; the design work discussed here makes it possible to further differentiate significant symbols according to their properties.

While the pictures shown here are accompanied by countless words and descriptions, unlike words, they capture a complex situation in a brief, quick and accessible manner and are essential in research in general (Lynch, 1988: p. 202). The observer understands the future use scenario created by K. and N. more quickly than any text-based description would allow. Because this notable property of visual means of design contrasts words and visuals, we can find that these two means share a different property: like in the first example, K. and N. are free of any material or functional constraints[34]. In this segment of the arc of work, the core activity is designing meaning for a future use by reassembling bits of old objects to form new ones. There is an important difference between symbols and objects or, as Mead would stress, distant objects and contact reality: a flying carpet or a T-shirt that changes its color is easily drawn and its meaning understood, but realising contact reality, or a tangible product, is an entirely different task – often more elaborate than realising a draft. Far from adopting an easy approach by using pictures and sketches, working with means (here: different symbols) that permit creativity and meaningful and promising drafts seems to be an effective strategy for tackling un-

---

[34] Besides the constraints of pen and paper that can become highly relevant at times as Christian Kiesow pointed out for practices of visualisations in mathematics: "The visualization of an infinite number of real figures will always consist of a finite number of colored points, as every point takes a certain room. The inherent logics of mathematical structures cannot be materialised" (Kiesow, 2013: p. 256, transl. by author).

certainty. Visual means therefore enable the designers to pursue the meaning of their drafts before having to deal with their material and functional properties. In my case, the designers tended to organise their work based on its meaning before moving on to technical design aspects.

3.3. From anticipation to testing

After further elaborating the ideas in the sketches, several were selected for further work; most efforts were directed at the idea of a color-changing fabric as an indicator for orientation. Several weeks later, K. and N. had constructed two lines of functional models. The models were all variations of two basic technical solutions. The first electrical conductors and the second applied heat to induce a color change. This color change is intended to indicate an individual's position in relation to his or her group for example to create awareness of not getting lost on a sightseeing tour. The models differ in the electrical resistance of their circuits and in the chemical composition of the textile colors used for the models. For the draft discussed here, the designers anticipated the social meaning of a color-changing sweatshirt on a sightseeing trip in detail and deemed it promising. Its technical implementation was discussed, drawn, and then even released to create an initial model. The actual sweatshirt that is created is based on experiences of the senior designer, on information from books and the internet, as well as on discussions with colleagues. In the sophisticated modelling process, anticipation (of distant objects) is the starting point for every action, but contact reality with materials while working on the models complements this process and cannot be neglected. Colors, surfaces, and prints are not only anticipated, but of course seen and felt as the crafting process progresses. Hence, anticipation of distant objects and contact reality with different entities generally go hand in hand in the modelling phase. At this point in the arc of design, all components and technical links had been worked out, but the vital electrical function, the condition for the desired social meaning, had only been anticipated. In Mead's words, the circuits for color-change remained a distant object existing only in anticipation – nevertheless the designers' work was organised with regard to the anticipation. The functional model is expected now to transfer this draft from an uncertain and anticipated reality to a concrete reality. A successful physical construction of these assumptions would reduce uncertainty significantly, as a new technology for navigation would take on a specific form. By looking in detail at a small segment of the arc of design here, I want to examine how N. and K. work to move their idea into the realm of concrete reality:

Figure 3: Approving anticipations

After several days of working in a silkscreen workshop, N., the assistant designer, returned to the DRL with about 20 technical models for the color-change concept and minor electrical functions. Both designers immediately started to touch, feel, sort, and discuss the models. Interactions between the designers and the objects remained free of any structured approach until K. took one of the models, placed it in front of them (Fig. 3), and began to measure the electrical resistance. For the measurements, she pressed the two contacts of a multimeter onto the textile while looking at the device display, changing the position of the contacts repeatedly before finally concluding that nothing was happening and that the electrical resistance was infinite. In other words: the circuit was non-functional; it had no electrical conductivity. These brief interactions in the form of measurements disproved the designers' assumptions about the model's electrical properties even though, as depicted above, this specific set of assumptions or anticipations of the models properties were discussed for two weeks and led to all the work of planning and producing the technical models. While the idea of electrical color changes reduced the uncertainty related to wearables and navigation and endured numerous anticipations, the measurements and contact reality finally determined the quality of models. In this case, the arc of design came to an unexpected dead-end. The experiment clearly indicates that this effort to eliminate uncertainty does not work. K. and N. are confronted with an unexpected glitch in their arc of work; they have to find another solution, since it became very clear that this line of drafts was not heading in a fruitful direction.

Even though it seemed that a solution for the initial design problem was just around the corner, the designers' specific quest to increase certainty wound up doing the opposite. In the end, another type of navigation device was finally constructed after many hours of work. To understand design, it is essential to understand that the quest for certainty creates certainty *and* uncertainty, both intentional and unintentional. Many parts of this arc of design that aimed to create a navigation prototype ultimately served to uncover different sources of uncertainty instead of producing shared certainty that could withstand rigorous inspection. New uncertainty triggered the need for new plans and ideas to be worked out in the arc of design.

Conclusion: how to interact with right means at the right time

This study emphasises a particular perspective on design work and on work in general. Classical sociological literature identifies the structures, sometimes even "iron cages", in which work is done. Organizations, then, are made of powerful structures (Weber, 1978) or have to arrange themselves in structured fields of organizations (Hoffman, 1999). Either way, powerful social constraints shape organizations and work. Newer studies, often based on rich ethnographic material, show that knowledge, coordination, and the flow of work are composed of situated actions and therefore kept running in action (Luff, Hindmarsch, Heath, 2000; Suchman et al., 1999). This perspective is different as it views actions as situational and based on knowledge and meaning instead of social structures. Nevertheless, both concepts correspond in one elementary assumption: the social entities in question (organization and work) are made purely of other social entities. Cause and consequence are entirely social. My intent in studying design work is to highlight other causes and means that are relevant in the social action of work.

The conceptual underpinnings of this study are formed by a simple assemblage of three pragmatist notions: work, organization, and objects.

Dewey's concept of ongoing practical endeavours to increase certainty forms the core of a notion of work in general and in design. Strauss's broad interactionist understanding of organising is useful to specify Dewey's universal assumptions with an organizational perspective. For Strauss, the countless interactions that make up work can be bundled into arcs of work; the specific efforts the designers take in the presented case are to be understood as arc of design. All project-based efforts to create a new object come together to form such an arc. Strauss helps us to understand that all of these actions in design are coordinated and organised towards achieving a common project goal. A third conceptual idea about objects formulated by Mead helps to understand and diversify the object of work. Like any social action, design relies on anticipating and experiencing social and material entities. In differentiating the material and symbolic properties of these entities, Meads notion allows a differentiated perspective, dividing interaction into an anticipative realm and a concrete realm which both contain the means that the designers use for their work.

This conception makes up the framework for a sociological understanding of design work. Implementing this framework may prove helpful to test and refine it. Considering the initial question of how to characterise work beyond the classical social constraints, the ethnographic data shows that design work is clustered around certain means. These means mark different types of interactions and are therefore highly relevant over the entire arc of design due to their benefits in the production of certainty. In the first example, the verbal and written analogies in their symbolic and anticipative form made it possible to create a web of similarities between various objects. Highly diverse objects and their users became relatives without ever having any one of them at hand. The criteria for these analogies were not made explicit. Spoken and written words as means of design provided enough certainty to elaborate lists and genealogical relationships. What is equally important: they also provided enough uncertainty to find quick and promising analogies without spending too much time or too many resources in debating the details. The second example also contained symbolic means of design, but in this case they were much more visual in their character. These visual means of design were processed in greater detail than the lists. While the lists from the first interaction sequence were used to record and sort well-known objects, with the pictures the designers could assemble new socio-technical situations from the stock gathered in the lists. In other words, as another means of design the visuals allowed a far more detailed approach than the words in the first sequence. The designers were thus able to create something entirely new using this means. The second sequence shoes how the visualised objects were disassembled while highlighting some of their features, for example the orientation of the sippy cup. With pen and paper these objects could be disassembled and reassembled in new ways. Material and technical details were left aside, but the sketches and use scenarios helped work out various details of using the new designs. New ways to navigate the city became more certain. The third and last example examined the construction of several models whereas it became clear that models as means address different uncertainties in design work than visualizations. Various anticipations and visualizations of a color-changeable textile materialised into technical models. Conductivity and other indispensable presuppositions were modelled in these new designs. After measuring these features and determined a lack of conductivity, this draft was scrapped. It did not make good on its promise. As means of design, the technical model helped to address and to work with this uncertainty.

Three short sequences cannot grasp design work as a social process in great detail, but the initial question of means of design and their capabilities can be answered. Words, visuals, and models addressed very different aspects of the overall uncertainty of design work. In this example, words as means allowed the boundaries of the field to be set. Visual means were capable of defining inter-subjective perspectives on promising ideas. The models then, built to create certainty as to the crucial future product function, finally increased uncertainty again.[35]

This study does not permit a detailed picture of the social complexity of a design process as a whole. Quite the opposite, the social process of design work was reduced to the question of how different means were crucial for meeting different challenges in the course of the project. Aside from this, applying concepts enables a researcher to reflect on these cognitive tools: I briefly referenced Latour because his critique of a sociology that excludes questions of materiality (Latour, 1992) is both very striking and very well-known. His "missing masses" do not just condense the morals of a society in a physical form (Latour, 1992: p. 227); they also demand that materials and other means be enacted and accounted for. In contrast to actor-network theory, interactionist social theory is equipped with established notions and concepts to delve into the details of all forms of interaction. Yet my simple framework that interweaves Dewey, Strauss, and

---

[35] One could point out that one option less gives more certainty, but I would stress that an infinite number of options minus one option still is infinite.

Mead exhibited some shortcomings, too. Dewey can help us understand how actors grapple with uncertainty. Its crucial role in work, however, and attempts to use uncertainty as a resource seem to be common in design, but not in Dewey's concept. Mead's notions of anticipative and physical objects hold many insights for such an object-orientated field as design. Nevertheless, his central notion of significant symbols would be even more helpful if different varieties of these symbols could be made more distinct. In my case, the difference between words and visuals should be reflected on in greater detail. Various activities that involve the rapid electronic processing and manipulation of words and visuals would also generally benefit from a differentiated understanding of symbols.

References

Becker, H.S., Geer, B., Hughes, E.C., Strauss, A.L. (1961), *Boys in white. Student culture in medical school.* New Brunswick, NJ: Transaction Books.

Callon, M. (1986), "Some elements of a sociology of translation: domestication of the scallops and the fishermen of St. Brieuc Bay", in Law, J. (ed.), *Power, action, and belief. A new sociology of knowledge?* London, Boston: Routledge & Kegan Paul, pp. 196-223.

Dewey, J. (1929), *The quest for certainty.* New York: Minton, Balch & Company.

Dewey, J. (1938), *Logic. The theory of inquiry.* New York: Henry Holt and Company, Inc.

Gibson, J.J. (1986), *The ecological approach to visual perception.* Hillsdale, NJ: Lawrence Erlbaum Associates.

Glaser, B.G., Strauss, A.L. (1965), *Awareness of dying.* Chicago: Aldine Publishing Company.

Hoffman, A. (1999), "Institutional evolution and change: Environmentalism and the U.S. chemical industry", *Academy of Management Journal,* 42 (4), pp. 351-371.

Joas, H. (1980), *Praktische Intersubjektivität. Die Entwicklung des Werkes von George Herbert Mead.* Frankfurt am Main: Suhrkamp Verlag.

Jonas, W. (2001), "A scenario for design", *Design Issues,* 17 (2), pp. 64-80.

Jonas, W. (2007), "Design research and its meaning to the methodological development of the discipline", in Michel, R. (ed.), *Design research now. Essays and selected projects.* Basel: Birkhäuser Verlag AG, pp. 187-206.

Kalthoff, H. (2010), "Beobachtung und Komplexität. Überlegungen zum Problem der Triangulation", *Sozialer Sinn,* 11 (2), pp. 353-365.

Kiesow, C. (2013), "Visualität in der Mathematik", in Lucht, P., Schmidt, L.M., Tuma, R. (ed.), *Visuelles Wissen und Bilder des Sozialen. Aktuelle Entwicklungen in der visuellen Soziologie.* Wiesbaden: Springer VS, pp. 249-263.

Latour, B. (1983), "Give me a laboratory and I will raise the world", in Knorr Cetina, K., Mulkay, M.J. (eds.), *Science observed. Perspectives on the social study of science.* London, Beverly Hills: Sage Publications, pp. 141-170.

Latour, B. (1992), "Where are the missing masses? The sociology of a few mundane artifacts", in Bijker, W.E., Law, J. (eds.), *Shaping technology/building society. Studies in sociotechnical change.* Cambridge, MA: MIT Press.

Latour, B. (1993), *We have never been modern.* Cambridge, MA: Harvard University Press.

Latour, B. (1996), *Aramis or the love of technology.* Cambridge, MA: Harvard University Press.

Latour, B. (2000), "The Berlin Key or how to do words with things", in Graves-Brown, P.M. (ed.), *Matter, Materiality and Modern Culture.* New York: Routledge, pp. 11-21.

Latour, B. (2002), *Die Hoffnung der Pandora.* Frankfurt am Main: Suhrkamp Verlag.

Latour, B. (2006), "Ethnografie einer Hochtechnologie: Das Pariser Projekt "Aramis" eines automatischen U-Bahn-Systems", in Rammert, W., Schubert, C. (ed.), *Technografie. Zur Mikrosoziologie der Technik.* Frankfurt am Main: Campus-Verlag, pp. 25-60.

Luff, P., Hindmarsh, J., Heath, C. (2000), *Workplace studies. Recovering work practice and informing system design.* New York: Cambridge University Press.

Lüdtke, N. (2011), "Die konstitutiven Bedingungen von Personalität und Sozialität – Konzeptuelle Antworten von George Herbert Mead und Helmut Plessner", in Lüdtke, N., Matsuzaki, H. (ed.), *Akteur – Individuum – Subjekt. Fragen zu 'Personalität' und 'Sozialität'.* Wiesbaden: Springer VS, pp. 239-274.

Lynch, M. (1988), "The externalized retina: Selection and mathematization in the visual documentation of objects in the life sciences", *Human Studies*, 11 (2-3), pp. 201-234.

Mareis, C., Held, M., Joost, G. (2013), *Wer gestaltet die Gestaltung? Praxis, Theorie und Geschichte des partizipatorischen Designs.* Bielefeld: Transcript Verlag.

Mead, G.H. (1932), *The philosophy of the present.* LaSalle, IL: The Open Court Company.

Mead, G.H. (1934), *Mind, self, and society: From the standpoint of a social behaviorist.* Chicago: The University of Chicago Press.

Rammert, W., Schubert, C. (eds.) (2006), *Technografie. Zur Mikrosoziologie der Technik.* Frankfurt am Main: Campus-Verlag.

Strauss, A.L. (1959), *Mirrors and Masks: The search for identity.* Glencoe: The Free Press.

Strauss, A.L. (1985), "Work and the division of labor", *Sociological Quarterly*, 26 (1), pp. 1-19.

Strauss, A.L. (1993), *Continual permutations of action.* New York: Walter de Gruyter Inc.

Suchman, L., Blomberg, J., Orr, J.E., Trigg, R. (1999), "Reconstructing technologies as social practice", *American Behavioral Scientist*, Vol. 43 (3), pp. 392-408.

Thomas, W.I., Thomas, D.S. (1928), *The Child in America. Behavior Problems and Programs.* New York: A.A. Knopf.

Weber, M. (1978), *Economy and society: An outline of interpretative sociology.* Berkeley: University of California Press.

HOW THINGS ARE DESIGNED AND HOW THEY DESIGN

Sandra Plontke

Introduction

"Design" is a multi-faceted concept that is used across a wide range of areas and therefore is conceptualized in different ways.[36] "Design" can describe the form of an artifact and thus refer to the specific shape of an object or product. Words like "artifact" and "product" already indicate that design is something made, framed, patterned, molded, etc., closely linked to certain practices and goal oriented actions. For example, usually we would not talk about the design of a tree but rather about the design of a chair which may be made of wood taken from that tree. In addition, while talking about the design of chairs or other artifacts, we have an idea of how it was made; sometimes we might even puzzle how it was made. Reflecting and talking about design normally involves the more or less articulated design process, the practice of designing.

In so-called humanistic traditions of thought, it is the human who imposes his aesthetic vision and will on the material. In this unilateral and hylomorphic model which goes back to Aristotle, the human brings a specific order into the chaos and is conceptualized as the central principle of differentiation:

---

[36] While in science, people often talk about "research design", in the industry and in management, people more frequently talk about product design, fashion design, corporate design, brand design, organizational design, service design, urban design, interaction design, etc. For the discussion of the ambiguity of the term "design" see Walker, John A. (1989): "Design History and the History of Design" (especially chapter two "Defining the Object of Study" where Walker discusses different definitions of design). For another perspective see Bruno Latour (2008) "A Cautious Prometheus? A Few Steps Towards a Philosophy of Design (with special attention to Peter Sloterdijk)". Here, Latour talks about "the spread in comprehension and extension of the term design" (Latour, 2008, p. 2) and argues for "five advantages of the concept of 'design'" (Latour, 2008, p. 3).

"Form came to be seen as imposed, by an agent with a particular end or goal in mind, while matter – thus rendered passive and inert – was that which was imposed upon." (Ingold, 2010, p. 2)

Design practice, however, can also be seen and analyzed as an interactional process, an interaction between humans and non-humans, between humans and material, between humans, materials, and environment. In this view, design can be conceptualized as a socio-material practice in which humans, material, and environment are seen as interdependent parts within a network of heterogeneous relationships.

In this analytical perspective, the focus is on the human's interaction with matter and with an infrastructure provided by various tools, specific technology, institutional settings, certain collaborators, etc. Applying such a perspective, we pay more attention to the role of non-human agents within that infrastructure. For example, we take greater account of certain materials along with their properties, their possible uses, their resistance, and on the compatibility of different materials with the broader interactional network. All of these aspects can be considered constitutive for design practices as well as for the design objects.[37] In addition, design practices always include the examination of the functionality of the designed artifact and thus also need to reflect on the relationship and interaction between users and artifacts. This is one of the reasons why design practic-

---

[37] Latour emphasizes that the term thing is ethymologically rooted in "assembly" (Latour & Weibel, 2005, p. 22f.; Latour, 2004). Thus, things can be seen as assemblages, i.e., as a conglomerate of relations. Things are constituted through these various relations (to humans, other things, interests, opinions, and ideas), which turn a "matter of fact" into a "matter of concern". In another article Latour applies this idea to a design object. Here, he writes: "The more objects are turned into things – that is, the more matters of facts are turned into matters of concern – the more they are rendered into objects of design through and through" (Latour, 2008, p. 2). By using the term "design object", the Latourian ideas will resonate in this chapter. The design object I am focusing on – the trading card motif – can be seen as a thing, resp. as a "matter of concern" which assembles different references, interests, ideas, requirements, etc.

es are also purpose-oriented, typically towards multiple purposes.[38] In the same line, design practice is also characterized by the need to correspond with the needs and interests as well as the psychological and physical conditions and requirements of the user. That is why design practice always includes some kind of knowledge about possible users and their worlds. The anticipated user of the design object must therefore be envisaged as an additional structuring and order generating quantity within the design process. As such, the anticipated user is inscribed into the design object itself (cf. Akrich, 1992).

Against the background of these introductory remarks, it becomes apparent that the authorship of design cannot be attributed to an independent and isolated human subject but must be understood as a heterogeneous interaction of different elements – including the human agent – within a complex design network. In design research, this perspective of "heterogeneous engineering" (Law, 1989) which also brings the object to the fore has been receiving increasing attention (cf. Mareis, 2010, p. 12).

In the following presentation of observations that I made in the field of video game development, I will adopt some key aspects of this perspective which is also known as Actor-Network Theory (ANT).[39] Since Actor-Network Theory can itself be seen as "a disparate family of material-semiotic tools, sensibilities, and methods of analysis" (Law, 2007, p. 141) and thus bears some family resemblances with semiotic approaches suggested by Charles S. Peirce, Max Weber, Clifford Geertz and others, I will only borrow those aspects that help to convey the perspective described above. I will especially focus on a perspective based on the principle of free association (Callon, 1986; see for example Callon and Law, 1997; Latour, 1999), a perspective which places "the human not above materials (as the creator or user) but among materials" (Sørensen, 2009, p. 2).

---

[38] This purpose-orientation frequently serves as justification for the generally accepted differentiation between design and art. However, especially from an empirical perspective that emphasizes the situatedness of design practices, this differentiation becomes shaky. Taking the example of designers and design practices within computer game development, it can be shown how under certain conditions and in certain situations designers perform themselves as artists and conceive of the design object as a piece of art.

[39] For an ANT perspective on design, exemplified in the field of architectural design, see especially Yaneva (2009).

A concrete example from the field of graphic design in video game development will help illustrate some key characteristics of socio-material assemblages and the decisive role that interactions between human and non-human actors play in their creation. Thus, the attention will not be on the classical Aristotelian and humanistic assumption of stable ontologies but on "patterns of relation" (Sørensen, 2009). This corresponds to the idea of ANT that "treat(s) everything in the social and natural worlds as a continuously generated effect of the webs of relations within which they are located. It assumes that nothing has reality or form outside the enactment of those relations. Its studies explore and characterize the webs and the practices that carry them" (Law, 2007, p. 141).

By applying this perspective in a close study of a design object in its becoming, I want to bring its inextricable links to work, workplace, workers, organization, materiality, and the use of technology respectively technological tools to the fore. Thus, the aim of this contribution is to help opening the black-box of design and design processes and to shed light on the socio-material foundations of design practices and the complexity of the relations between a design object and the links just mentioned. My aim is to investigate how they bring each other into being, how they become defined, and how they define and co-constitute the wider environment they are part of.

1. Theoretical and methodological framework: heterogeneous engineering

In an often quoted essay on heterogeneous engineering[40], John Law raises two central questions: "How do objects, artifacts, and technical practices come to be stabilized? And why do they take the shape or form that they do?" (Law, 1989, p. 111). To answer these questions, he uses the example of Portugal's commercial and naval dominance on the Indian Ocean in the 15th/16th century which he portraits as a process of heterogeneous combination of diverse social and material components. Analyzing the "conditions and the tactics of system building" (Law, 1989, p. 113) he describes, among other things, how the Portuguese ships were built in a way

---

[40] In short, the concept of heterogeneous engineering can be understood as "a framework [...] urgently needed to help researchers identify the specific actions through which an object is made to take shape." (Engeström & Blackler, 2005, p. 313).

that responded to the needs in a hostile environment: In order to traverse the seaway to India safely, the ships had to withstand the raging waters of the Atlantic Ocean, Cape Bojador, the African littoral and hostile Muslim traders. Law emphasizes that he does not want to over-determine the social, like social constructivism does, i.e., he does not want "to add the social as an explanatory afterthought" but rather understand it as "a purely contingent matter" (Law, 1989, p. 113). Accordingly there are numerous other factors which are relevant within the process of system building resp. design processes that have been frequently overlooked and underestimated so far.

"The argument is that those who build artifacts do not concern themselves with artifacts alone but must also consider the way in which the artifacts relate to social, economic, political, and scientific factors. All these factors are interrelated, and all are potentially malleable. The argument, in other words, is that innovators are best seen as system builders: they juggle a wide range of variables as they attempt to relate the variables in an enduring whole." (Law, 1989, p. 112)

In my description and analysis of the design of specific graphics for a computer game, I will employ Law's key expositions when asking how a design object or graphical artifact for a computer game is being stabilized, how it takes shape and how it ends up having the appearance it finally has. Therefore, I will take a closer look at how material and social components are being enrolled in design practice and what kind of resources, "viscourses" (a concept coined by Knorr Cetina, 1999) and other decision guiding factors developers of computer game graphics must relate to when engaging in the process of game development.

By focusing on the design object and practices of work as well as on the environment (the social, economic, political, and scientific factors that Law is looking at), the awareness for the relations among these factors will increase. This perspective, i.e., the question of the object and the significance of focusing on the object in order to gain insights into work and organizations has already been emphasized in the study of organization and design (Engeström and Blackler, p. 2005; Ewenstein and Whyte, 2010).[41]

---

[41] Engeström & Blackler (2005, p. 326): "the notion of object is of particular significance for organization studies. It focuses attention on the organization's work, uncovers practices rather than beliefs, and draws attention to transitions and possibilities."

By drawing upon this perspective, I will describe how in design practice different components are trimmed and shaped in a way that allows them to become part of a stable association with other elements, an association of otherwise disparate parts. In the same vein, I will pay attention to the question in how far the becoming of an artifact, e.g. a graphical design, is exposed to so-called "trials of strength" (Law, 1989) that will or might influence their final appearance and that are also co-constitutive for the design of work and workplaces.

2. Graphic design as heterogeneous engineering

The following ethnographic descriptions are mainly based on participant observations I conducted in the field of video game development. In this paper I will concentrate on observations and converzations regarding a very specific practice within this complex field: the graphic design. In particular I will refer to observations on the development of playing card designs for a mobile game, more precisely a military Trading Card Game (TCG) or Collectible Card Game (CCG). In addition to these observations I will refer to some of the observed graphic designer's comments that he made during his work. At one point I will also refer to a passage of a so called "art book" which documents the "making of" of a certain video game. It will help me to illustrate how the practices of graphic design and artistic work in game development can be influenced by expectations and assumptions about the future, especially about new technologies and tools that the future might bring.

Of course, it is impossible to provide a complete picture of a graphical artifact's genesis and to unfold all of its heterogeneous relations. I will, however, try to convey at least an insight into the relations and interplay of some important aspects and practices that constitute some of the subplots of the larger story of the becoming of a design object. Thus, I hope to contribute to a better understanding of the logics and dynamics in the practices of digital image production, including the joint action of human and non-human actors and factors.

2.1. The interplay of socio-material components in Trading Card Motifs (TCM)

What is a digital trading card? Here is a brief answer: Equivalent to traditional paper-made collectible card games (e.g., Magic: The Gathering,

Pokémon or Yu-Gi-Oh!), digital cards can also be bought, collected, exchanged, traded, evolved, upgraded, won or lost in playful competitions on the internet between millions of gamers resp. smart phone users. A graphical artifact like a single collectible card is therefore connected to a broad infrastructure of socio-economic interests and activities that create and foster new socio-material relations and connect a growing number of different actors and factors. It is precisely this kind of interplay that creates the game with its market, the buyers, winners, losers, etc. Thus, the TCG is quite similar to Law's galley, "an *emergent phenomenon*; that is, it has attributes possessed by none of its individual components" (Law, 1989, p. 115). But let us take a step back and turn towards one of the games protagonists and central (con-)figures: the trading card motif (TC motif) itself. These digital images are even more than a conglomerate of pixels which get together to a specific form, or forms that are organized to particular compositions. Which different entities interweave to let the TC motif emerge?

A first look at the different materials shows, that besides rendered 3D models which the game developer buys from professional providers and amateur tinkerers on the internet, it is especially photo elements found or bought on the internet as well as self-recorded and digitally drawn elements that find their way into the card motif. Moreover, preparatory sketches that become viscourses (Knorr Cetina, 1999) as well as economical, technical and factors concerning time are involved. I will illustrate how these components come together and which additional elements they associate with in the practice of digital image design. To this end, I will tell a sub-story about the creation of realism in the TC motif.

3. Realizing a TCM: the creation of "real world effects" as socio-material association

On the day of observation, the graphic designer works from home[42] and I have the opportunity to observe him for a few hours. I am sitting on a sofa behind him, my notebook by my side. A video camera which will record the activities of the next few hours is placed at an angle behind the designer and his desk. In addition, a screen-capture program records the individual work steps as they appear on the left of two screens in front of the graphic designer. On the left screen, Photoshop – one of the software programs the graphic designer works with – is opened. On this screen the main figurations of the TC motif become visualized and thus observable.[43] This screen is connected to the other screen by an infrared interface. This right screen is the image viewer which he continuously engages with during his work. It provides components which are relevant for the TC motifs, in particular photographs, 3D models, textures, tryouts, private photographs that might once be helpful, and footage from previous research on the designer's current project. The materials stored in the files of the image viewer also contain visual artifacts like tables, charts, slides and sketches that were partially produced in cooperation with colleagues and help planning and communicating certain steps that need to be taken within a project. Many of these items might carry viscourses (Knorr Cetina, 1999).

---

[42] The workplace of video game developers and graphic designers is not locally fixed. They switch workplaces and sometimes rotate between the development studio they are working for and their private "laboratories" – that is how some of the game developers I met call their home offices. Some game developers solely work from home as freelancers. But even when they work from private places they are connected to the rest of the developmental team by technological systems like Skype, e-mail and chat, which carry the social interaction and thus are a constitutive part of it.

[43] Here, I cannot go into a detailed analysis of methodological issues, but I want to point out that the technology I used for my observations contributes to the ways how my data is being designed itself while I am observing how someone else is designing his work and his design object.

3.1. What has been happening before: the search for a realistic style and the development of a viscourse

The preparatory work on the TC designs, for example the process of finding a consensus regarding a certain realistic style, as well as the gross composition of the card designs have largely taken place in an earlier phase, the stage of so-called concept art. The term "concept art" describes a phase within computer game development in which certain concepts, moods and ideas – e.g., on how the game contents should look like and what distinguishing style to use – are visually translated. Thus, core elements of the overall plan are made communicable to the members of the development team as well as to other organizational units like, for example, the publisher, before some of these visualized ideas inscribe their distinctive mark into the end product. The concept art phases were inaccessible to me. There were only a few visual artifacts that the graphic artist referred to during my observation. They document some aspects of these earlier processes and interactions. One of these two artifacts was a composition sketch (Figure 1, below) which outlines the rough inner structure of the motif and also illustrates the work-sharing arrangement between the two designers who were collaborating in this project.

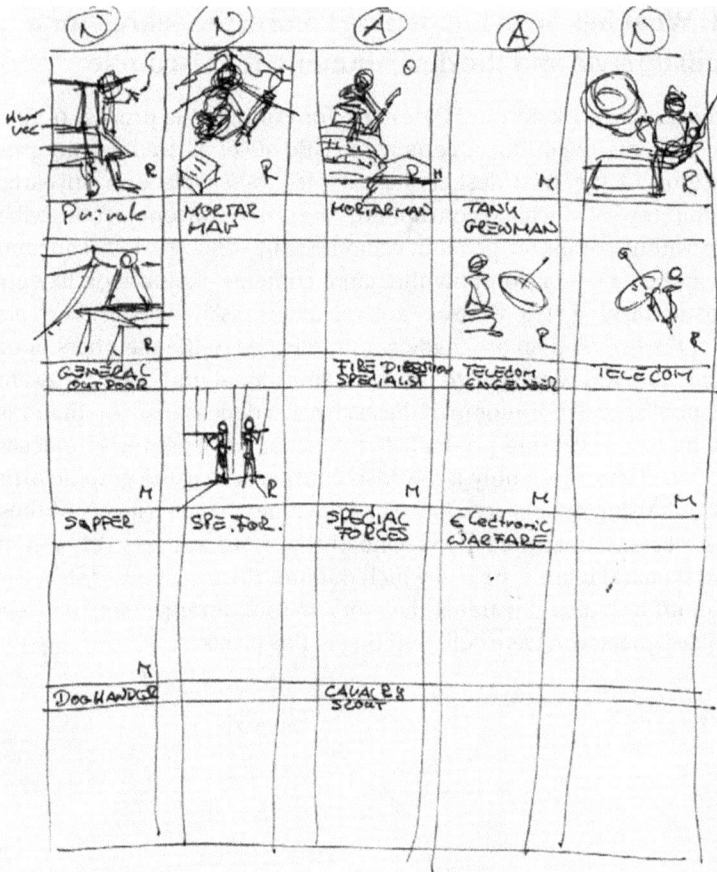

Figure 1: Composition Sketch

In addition, the designer showed me a different kind of preliminary graphics that were also produced together with the other designer. These artifacts were used as trial balloons that served the exploration for a certain style:[44]

> G.D.: *"You also have to make individual graphic designers work cooperatively towards a common style. And in the beginning we actually worked together on the motifs. That is, he (the other graphic designer) was sitting next to me and we both were working on our motif in a way that allowed to find an agreement on the workflow...Workflow means: What effects do you use and which painterly principles are employed? Do we have more than one light source? Things like that...To me it was simply a matter of finding a common understanding: Can we agree on using the same stuff? And it worked great!"*

These remarks already suggest that technical circumstances play an important role in shaping the style and even the work design. When the graphic designer talks about the use of "stuff" that he and his colleague had to agree on, he is, inter alia, talking about Photoshop-tools, for example ready-made effect options or a selection of filters. These technical supplies are constitutive for the resulting style.

The graphic designer's remarks give an impression of how the development of a specific style, including a working style, takes place within situated practices in which the spatial proximity of the co-workers, their shared knowledge, common interests and skills are involved.[45] The result of this interaction between two individual graphic designers and the technology they use (both of them draw digitally using Photoshop) is a number of orienting/ordering visual artifacts, so called trial balloons or style explorations in which the collectively formulated main principles of a supra-individual guiding aesthetic style become manifested. Knorr Cetina (1999, p. 249) calls these kinds of visual artifacts viscourses: trial balloons,

---

[44] In some projects, the art directors make styleguides that formally express "what a specific design language is composed of" (quote by one of the graphic designers I interviewed). The guides serve as overarching schemes that entail the design vocabulary in a visible and traceable way.

[45] Of course, there are many more factors involved, but here I am mentioning only those emerging from the presented data.

sketches, tables and graphical representations on screens, boards and foils that serve within or instead of discourses. These viscourses duplicate technical objects by capturing them in a representation of reality along which the technical work proceeds (Knorr Cetina, 1999, p. 249).

> G.D.: "The style explorations are about narrowing the style more and more closely. First we make different varia-tions of a theme which are discussed in the team later on. Then we make a joint decision together by means of these first graphics."

Finally, the composition sketch gives the designer orientation and helps organizing the following work steps. One glance at the sketch, the designer explains, would reveal which card motifs are still left to design and how they have to be composed.

Therefore, viscourses can be seen as elements of "ethno-methods" that participate in processes of ordering, i.e., in the genesis and distribu-tion of knowledge (Knorr Cetina, 1999). This can also be seen within the context of my fieldwork: Interrupting his work for a while, the designer showed me a sketch and some trial balloons to make his work more trans-parent and comprehensible to someone who was not present in the con-cept-art phase of the project. Here, the viscourse helped fix a lack of knowledge on my side. Thus, it did not only structure the social relation between the two collaborating graphic designers but became part of the interaction between one of the graphic designers and myself. Finally, they influenced my own actions as a participant observer and even the design of this text. This illustrates another important aspect of viscourses: They are mobile and retrievable at any time. Moreover, they produce evidence (Knorr Cetina 1999, p. 249; cf. Latour's concept of "immutable mobiles", Latour, 1990). I suggest to see them as abbreviations of complex states of affairs, e.g., of a specific style which can hardly be verbalized. A picture, resp. a trial balloon, says more than a thousand words.

In the case described above, the viscourse serves the communication and coordination between individual graphic designers within the devel-opment team. More generally, diverse visual materials also carry and channel collective communication between different organizational units, such as developers and publishers. Hand drawn pencil sketches kept safe in sketchbooks that the 2D-artists carry with them in order to visualize an idea as soon as it comes to their mind, frequently show up at formal business meetings and informal working discussions. Here, the sketchbooks are handed around and the latest – more or less elaborated – pencil sketches (for example, of a new character) are reviewed, sometimes marvelled, sometimes criticized, and sometimes greenlighted by the participants (for example, developers, marketing staff and clients). It is not rare to see these analogue drawings end up on a scanner. After the image is digitalized, the idea can be modified and refined repeatedly by using an image editing program like Photoshop. By a mouse click it can be sent, i.e., communicated to the publisher who usually is not located at the same place as the developer. If the publisher authorizes the visualized idea, the image will reappear as reference in the background of the 3D-artist's modelling software (for instance, Maya) and serve as a foil for the translation of the 2D-image into a detailed 3D-model.[46] Once more, it becomes clear that viscourses circulate, how they pass and simultaneously bridge time, space and organizational boundaries. We get an idea how they interconnect, what different configurations they undergo, and how they slowly consolidate. Moreover, we can observe the involvement of different materials and technologies (e.g., paper, pencil, scanner, software programs) as well as the participation of humans.

Thus viscourses can be seen as socio-material practices that connect humans with humans, but also associate humans with non-humans, with materials, technology, work and organization. They are part of the social and define or design certain interactions. The graphic designers' considerations and agreements – manifested in the viscourses – will find their way into the final TC motif.

In order to add some more facets to my analysis, I will now focus on the process of realizing the TC motif, i.e., on the implementation of a so-called "realistic" style.

---

[46] With regard to the trading card game I'm using as main example in this chapter, it should be noted that this is a "flat" game, i.e., a game that undergoes a reverse developing process: Here, 3D-models posed and rendered in 3D-space serve as foil for the development of 2D-images which the finished game will primarily consist of. However, for example, in the development of 3D-realtime games it is 2D-images that serve as viscourses, i.e., vehicles for the communication of ideas and reference frames along which the final 3D-models are built.

3.2. Polygons for reality: low budget – low poly

The following ethnographic descriptions will tell a sub-story about the becoming of the design object, which is the TC motif. The sub-story I choose to tell is the implementation of a realistic style. Right from the outset, I want to make clear that the realistic style should not be understood as a rational plan preceding the design process. Rather, realism of the image emerges as an effect of a socio-material practice in a specific environment and under specific conditions, i.e., it emerges as "situated action" (Suchman, 2007). To take a closer look at this process, I will zoom into the design object and the design practice step by step. First, a wider focus will be set on the object to bring out the wider infrastructure of its environment and to bring in some of the wider ordering factors it is associated with.[47] I got to know about these factors from the designer's comments he made while working on the motif. I will then zoom closer in on the design object and emphasize observations instead of spoken comments. That will help to bring the concrete practices of digital image design to the fore. For this purpose, I will base my analysis on video data.

Let us start with a comment made by the graphic designer while he was working on one of the trading card motifs. We remember that a main element of the trading cards are 3D models bought from amateur tinkerers and professionals from the internet:

> G.D.: "So we have purchased these models, which can be easily done on the internet; we then rendered the stuff the way we had agreed on. And the last step now is actually to let these things look a little bit more real. Absolutely real is not what you want since you cannot achieve that kind of one hundred percent photo reality in low budget range anyway."

The targeted realistic style of the card design is a "hybrid style" (to borrow a term the graphic designer will use himself later on). This style,

---

[47] The use of the term "zooming in" is not meant to indicate that this perspective is taken from an external point of view, i.e., from a position outside of the network. ANT levels the distinction between inside and outside, micro and macro. Only the relations within a network are acknowledged. Either something is part of a network or it is not (cf. Law, 1992, p. 389; Law, 2007, p. 141; Latour, 1996).

which will make the later appearance of the card motifs look more realistic, is to be understood as a result or effect, not as a cause of heterogeneous components and factors involved in the design process. Among other
factors, it is economic conditions that help explain the shape and appearance of the motifs since they are developed in a low budget range. "It is a
task", so another comment by the designer, "to create photo-realistic images within a low budget framework". This economic factor becomes a
technical one when it comes to the purchasing of 3D models which – as in
this case – form the basis for the whole project, for example because they
are cheaper than photo motifs that you could also buy. Therefore, the developer must do with fewer monetary resources and correspondingly
cheaper 3D models which are characterized by a lower polygon count.
With regard to their form and surface structure, such "low poly models"
appear less realistic. The relationship between polygons and realistic appearance sounds almost trivial: If the polygon count is too low, forms that
are supposed to be round appear edged which challenges a certain idea of
reality. Watching the designer work on the TC motifs, I can see how he is
repeatedly challenged by what he calls "the classic problem of low poly
edges": Things that show up at the surface, borders and edges that he calls
"ugly", "square" or "edgy" need to be smoothed to make them appear
more realistic and fit into the overall picture. I will return to this observation below. Before that, I would like to briefly mention the role of the game
producers' expectations and assumptions concerning, for example, the
future development of technology and technological tools.

The example is taken from *The Art of Gothic 3*, a so-called "art book"
on the computer role-playing game *Gothic 3*. These kinds of art books
document the *making of* video games. My attention was drawn to this
specific book because it was among a list of books the graphic designer
explicitly recommended to me. With other words: When I was reading the
art book I followed the actor. As one can learn from the book, in the very
beginning of the project the concepters had to consider the usual question
how to realize the game within a limited budget, limited time, and the
limitations of current technology. In the case of *Gothic 3* the programmers
were quite optimistic. They expected that the capacities of the technological tools at hand would increase considerably within the next three years.
Therefore, they promised the graphic designers that they would not have
to worry about technical performance problems and should feel free to
work as detailed, small parted, and accurate as they wanted to. That
meant paradise for the graphic designers: Finally, they could use up as
many polygons as they deemed necessary to come up with a convincing

design. After two years, however, it became clear that computer technolo-gy would not develop as fast as expected. Thus, the high poly figures and landscapes had to be pruned to a much lower level of detail which must have hurt the graphic designers' souls (The Art of Gothic 3, 2006, p. 44).

This example shows that in the fast-paced fields of software based de-velopments the trust in a speedy improvement of technologies and tools is very high and therefore makes technological visions an important part of planning and organizing. In this example, the visions were inscribed into the graphical artifacts and shaped its design, at least temporarily. Without elaborating on this issue, here, we can just state that it is – inter alia – eco-nomic and related technical factors but also time and technological vi-sions that provide us with a partial explanation for the shape and appear-ance of a graphical artifact and the design of work.

4.3. A closer look – zooming in

Another aspect of "realizing" is that many of the rendered 3D models that are used for the TCG have evenly textured surfaces, poor of details. The models appear brand new, almost sterile, without a credible narrative that could help connect them to the real world. To create a "real-world effect" on the side of the viewer, the designer has to modify the textures by add-ing dirt, scratches, rust and other details. A clean and sterile image ele-ment prompts the designer repeatedly to change it and thus to create a semblance of realism. He points at a section within the motif in front of him and comments as follows:

> GD.: "In order to increase realism, all of this is still too clean. Here I should add some dirt. The way it looks now, it actually is too dull to seriously meet the demands of photore-alism."

The designer solves this problem by digitally drawing the modifica-tions into the image himself (using Photoshop) or by drawing upon pho-tographic elements that are transferred from the original source into the TC motif.

In the example I am giving, the designer is concerned with making the appearance of a military vehicle look more realistic:

>GD.: *"Now we need mud, mud and dirt. I can take that from other photographs."*

The designer turns to the right monitor and sifts through the files of the so-called image viewer, looking for materials that are relevant for the tuning of the card motifs. Besides the rendered 3D models, here is also a whole collection of different photos and photographic elements. Out of a vast variety of different designs that the image viewer offers him, he chooses a photo element reminiscent of an old green painted metal piece, drizzled with mud and similar to a metallic joint of an old heavy door. Using his mouse, he draws the graphic from the image viewer directly to the left computer screen where the image now appears in the foreground of the TC motif which he is working on in Photoshop (see Figure 2, next page):

>GD.: *"Again, the same principle: Actually, you cannot use the whole image for anything, but a certain color section, this one here, that is interesting; it is this rusty section and I can take it out along with all the other eroded sections and start to soil the vehicle."*

The designer selects only those elements that he considers "interesting": the brown, mud-like splashes and rusty looking elements. He strips them off the surface of the photo and then pulls them into his TC motif. He pushes them back and forth over the front tire and the ground-level of the rendered car-model's body (see Figure 3). After some back and forth movements in Photoshop the appropriate position is found. The densest area of the transferred texture is now on the front tire, isolated elements or mud splashes end up on the body of the car. Then the designer corrects the color of the transferred elements and adapts them to the ocher ground color of the motif. Part of the transferred elements still tower over the tires and the vehicle's body out into other areas of the picture. The designer "cleans" the image by removing the supernatant elements with the so called "eraser tool" offered by Photoshop.

Figure 2: Photoelement For Texturing. Stripping Splashes Off The Photograph

Figure 3: Transferred Splashes Being Positioned On The Rendered Car-Model

These descriptions of a certain practice show how a graphical artifact recovers shape. They show how human and non-human actors enter into a relationship and how heterogeneous entities interact while forming an association of photo elements and a rendered 3D model. Moreover, they illustrate the ability of the individual actors to initiate actions on the side of other actors or to delegate tasks within the network of actors. This all is about the question how all the actors are "associated in such a way, that they make others do things" (Latour, 2005, p. 107) and thereby help something new to arise, for example a digital picture.

Notice that initially the "photograph itself" is not of interest for the designer. The photograph and the designer are "disinterested" (Latour,

1987), they do not have a relation to each other. In order to produce interest, another actor is needed, in our case that is the 3D-model of the vehicle which is far too clean and thus initiates action by the designer who needs to soil the car in order to make it appear more realistic. It is the rendered model, so to speak, that awakes interest in the designer to search the files of the image viewer for suitable photographic material. Further, it is only a very specific area in the chosen photography which the designer is interested in, an area composed of colors that the rendered 3D model of the vehicle demands: rusty spots that remind of dirt and mud stains.[48] So the picture offered by the image viewer does not enter the TC motif as a whole; it is only a small section which is transferred to the card motif and which thereby is transformed to dirty and rusty spots on the tire and the body of a vehicle. In this process, the vehicle itself also changes, it becomes part of a new narration: now it is old and used, it drove through mush and mud, it was exposed to reality. In a certain way, all the splashes and spots become active[49] through their relation to the imaginations and mental activities of the recipient. Through this intermingling of non-materiality (imagination of the recipient) and visual materiality (the designed picture)[50] the spots become a constitutive part of a specific narration. At least we get an impression in how far a picture in its interaction with the gaze of the recipient can be considered more than a passive structure.

And what about G.D.'s role in this interaction? When G.D. draws and pushes the elements around in Photoshop, when he throws dirt onto the TC motif with specific tools provided by Photoshop, when he adapts colors and arranges shadows, etc., he becomes a graphic designer, an author,

---

[48] For a similar perspective, see Donald Schön (1983) who describes the design process as a "conversation with the materials of a situation" where „the situation 'talks back', and he [the designer] responds to the situation's back-talk." (Schön 1983, 78; cf. Schön 1991).

[49] See Kandinsky, Wassily (1947): Point and line to plane. Contribution to the analysis of the pictorial elements.

[50] I am aware of the ongoing discussion and differentiation of concepts like "image" and "picture" or the "material" and the "digital." However, here, I cannot present the details of these conceptual issues. For a meanwhile classic account of the differentiation between image and picture, see W. J. T. Mitchell (2005) What do Pictures want? The Lives and Loves of Images; for the debate on the digital and the material, see e.g. W. F. Haug (2002), Zur Frage der Im/Materialität digitaler Produkte. In Das Argument 44 (5/6). p. 619-636.

a tinkerer who narrates a story which began before he started telling it and which is not narrated by him alone. Seen under a certain perspective, all actors involved in this story (including me) are story-tellers, engaging in a process which is at the same time closely related to "translation", an endeavor "to connect, to displace, to move, to shift from one place, one modality, one form, to another while retaining something. Only something. Not everything. While therefore losing something" (Law, 2002, p. 95).

4. The association of disparate parts and trials of strength

Designers can be seen as system builders who like all "system builders seek to create a network of heterogeneous but mutually sustaining elements. They seek to dissociate hostile forces and to associate them with their enterprise by transforming them" (Law, 1989, p. 121).

I already mentioned how the high poly models of the figures and landscapes in *Gothic 3* lost the trial of strength against time and thus had to turn back to a "lower level of detail" to become part of the computer game. I also described how heterogeneous elements are not just brought together but need to be changed and adapted in order to enter into a relationship and help building a graphical artifact like a TC motif. The soil added to the rendered 3D model must first be detached from its original place, before it finds its way into the card motif as a texture element. This does not only serve a more realistic appearance of the rendered 3D model, but also the association of disparate elements that then can interact with each other in a stable compound. When the designer finally adapts the color of the transferred texture (dirt/mud splashes) to other image components, namely the colors of the ground, then a coherence of different image components (mud/soil/ground) is generated which shows in the (betraying) message to the viewer that the dirt and mud on the vehicle stems from the very same ground that can be seen on the card image. Here, we can see that associating the components in a way that brings about the graphical artifact is "contingent but not arbitrary" (Sørensen, 2009, p. 35). The meaning of digital pictorial motifs is dependent on a coherent appearance.

Another problem that needs to be dealt with is the already mentioned difficulty in working with low poly edges of comparatively inexpensive 3D models. G.D., the designer, calls this difficulty a "classic technical" and "render related" problem. When rendering the model, the low quota of polygons results in "unendearing sharp edges" that somehow show how the 3D model offers resistance against its transformation and transplantation. The trial of strength is not yet won and the opponent has not yet become a component of the digital image.

> GD.: *"Here are some more things that are very typical for render-elements. You always have such edge-effects and in most cases I render them away because this gets on my nerves, especially if I want to do something photorealistic [...]."*

Since the designer wants to build something that "feels homogenous" (see below), the "edge effects" need to be retouched. Otherwise the render elements would not merge with the other levels of the image but instead separate themselves from the rest of the picture. These edge effects "get on the nerves" of the designer who performs as a producer and recipient at the same time. They irritate and distract him, they threaten to destroy a photo-realistic impression and the "real world effects" he is aiming at. It seems that there is a dissociation impending, brought by the gaze of the viewer. Picture and gaze appear as opponents.

4.1. Internal conflict and the struggling gaze

The visual coherence and consistency of the whole technical image or visual artifact is an essential aspect in generating the TC motifs. They protect the image against dissociation, on the one hand (as I will show below) through the eye of the beholder – the gamer or user –, on the other hand through individual card designs within the entire TCG which will consist of more than 100 cards when completed. However, both trials of strength are related. Let us start the analysis with a short interview sequence where I start by asking the designer to comment on one of his earlier statements:

> S.P.: *"Why is it that one avoids too much reality?"*

> G.D.: *"It needs to be consistent. If you pursue utmost reality all the time and there are some motifs that are not convincing, they will tear down the whole project. That's not what you actually want; rather you try to find a hybrid style so that all the things feel homogenous."*

The card motifs – not seen as individual components but in their collective appearance and interplay in the TCG – have quite an impact on the success of the whole work project and on the survival of individual card motifs as well. Card motifs that could harm the whole project because they do not match the degree of reality in the other cards would bring inconsistency into the game. Therefore, they are sorted out. Interestingly, they threaten to dissociate the whole game, which means that the "hostile environment" (Law, 1989) the cards have to cope with is created by the cards themselves. The system builds its own environment. One strategy to protect the system against its own weaknesses and against self-destruction is the pursuit of a "hybrid style" that helps to keep the attack surface as small as possible.

The TC motif, however, is more than a network composed of inter- and intra-actions. It is not hermetic. Therefore, we must take the interactions with the external sphere which is part of the technical image into consideration and we must oscillate between image and viewer (cf. Akrich, 1992, p. 206). It is not only the developer of the TC motifs who interests us, it is also the viewer of the motifs, the user or the gamer, as well as the question how he is associated with the TC motif. The user's view can dissociate the card motif and simultaneously the whole game because the creation of realism and real world effects is always closely related to effects of reception. Although the use of a "hybrid style" aims at disarming the viewer's dissociating gaze, the card game stays vulnerable. How can you know if the graphics will please the user? Can you really argue about taste? How do you associate the user and the TC motif? Remember that the galley in Law's story had to master the way to Cape Bojador before it lost against the powers of the Atlantic Ocean (Law 1998).   ·

In game development, you will not throw your product into the waters of the market and watch if it will swim or drown. The risk to waste resources, human power and material and to lose money would be too high. In order to secure against such risks, there is an internal quality assurance (QA), composed of test gamers who simulate and configure (cf. Grint and Woolgar, 1997) the user by giving feedback regarding different aspects of the game, including aesthetics and functionality. In addition, there are softlaunches. In a softlaunch, for example, the game is put at the disposal of a selected group of users without advance marketing.

> *G.D.: "We have about 120 card motifs and for the soft-launch we would need about 75 to 80. Then we can see if the*

> *game has a chance to survive on the market and how the aes-*
> *thetics is evaluated. At that point the financial investment is*
> *not that high so that we could still say: "You know, our idea*
> *concerning the aesthetics does not really work. I think we*
> *should bring in more photorealism."*

Designers have ideas about various aspects of the world, "they make hypotheses about the entities that make up the world into which the object is to be inserted. Designers thus define actors with specific tastes, competences, motives, aspirations, political prejudices, and the rest" (Akrich, 1992, p. 208). Via "usability trials" (Grint and Woolgar, 1997, p. 78f.), they test the adequacy of their ideas and use the interaction with test gamers in order to update and generate knowledge about the users and their preferences. This knowledge is then translated into their work as well as into the TC motif, its design and appearance. Thus, they "inscribe" their "vision of (or prediction about) the world" into the visual artifact (Akrich, 1992, p. 208). The user's vision as well as his taste enter the design of work and the artifact which adds to the realism the designer is aiming at and helps to understand the TC motif as a heterogeneous, socio-material entanglement.

Conclusion

In this chapter I tried to employ a perspective on design practice borrowed from Actor-Network Theory, especially from its so-called material-semiotic methodology developed, among others, by Bruno Latour and John Law. Based on data gathered in the field of video game development and digital graphic design, I pursued three complementary goals:

First, decentralizing the subject by dislocating it from the center of its narrower and wider environment (for example, the workplace, the team, the organization, the market) and put it in the midst of things instead. Second, paying much more attention to the patterns of relation between humans and technology, including the relations between humans, things, time and space. Third, testing the fruitfulness of a method that starts with a focus on the design object – in the example I used this was virtual a trading card motif.

Although, some of the key assumptions of Actor-Network Theory, for example its analytical treatment of nonhuman elements as "actors" are quite controversial, its very specific approach of investigating the relations of things and concepts along the three goals mentioned above, can help to see these relations in a new light. Thus, the employment of a symmetrical perspective that does not draw upon the traditional view of the human as an entity *above* materials but sees the human *among* materials helped to identify the interrelatedness of various elements within the broader network of design practice.

My concrete empirical examples aimed to illustrate some of the key characteristics of socio-material assemblages and the decisive role that interactions between human and non-human actors play in their development. Thus, the attention was not on the classical assumption of stable ontologies but on patterns of relation. Following the designer who keeps the design object he is working on before his eyes, the researcher can try to pursue the gaze and the practice of the graphic designer in order to get an idea of how he needs not to be seen as a commando center, but rather as an effect of dynamic socio-material relationships that leave their traces on all actors and participants in the design network. For example, it was shown how characteristics of the graphic designers, the users, the tools, the technology, the workplace, the organization of work, aspects of time and space, interests, social and economic factors are inscribed in the design object. Moreover, it was shown that all of this can be identified as traces of dynamic interactions and as evidence for the reciprocity and complexity of design processes. Thus, the idea of design as a quality put into an object by a human creator is challenged. It seems to be more adequate to conceive of design as a process in which things and assemblages of things are shaped and shape their networks and environments (for example, the workplace, the team, the organization, the market, etc.) themselves. This representation certainly is more complex than the traditional accounts offered by Aristotelian and humanistic perspectives. It does certainly not facilitate the business of social scientists, but it challenges us to take things more seriously than some of us do.

References

Akrich, M. (1992), "The De-Scription of Technical Objects", in Bijker, W.E., Law, J. (eds.), *Shaping Technology / Building Society. Studies in Sociotechnical Change*. Cambridge: The MIT Press.

Callon, M., Law, J. (1997), "After the Individual in Society. Lessons on Collectivity from Science, Technology and Society", *Canadian Journal of Sociology*, 22 (2), pp. 165-182.

Callon, M. (1986), "Some Elements of a Sociology of Translation: Domestication of the Scallops and the Fishermen of St Brieuc Bay", in Law, J. (ed.), *Power, Action and Belief: A New Sociology of Knowledge?* London: Routledge, pp. 196-223.

Engeström, Y., Blackler, F. (2005), "On the Life of the Object", *Organization*, 12 (3), pp. 307-330.

Grint, K., Woolgar, S. (1997), *The Machine at Work. Technology, Work and Organization*. Cambridge: Polity Press.

Haug, W. F. (2002), "Zur Frage der Im/Materialität digitaler Produkte", *Das Argument*, 44 (5/6), pp. 619-636.

Haylicon Media (2006) (ed.), *The Art of Gothic 3*. Koch Media

Ingold, T. (2010), "Bringing Things to Life. Creative Entanglements in a World of Materials", Working Paper 15. (Original version (April 2008) presented at 'Vital Signs: Researching Real Life', 9th September 2008, University of Manchester. http://www.socialsciences.manchester.ac.uk/medialibrary/morgancenter/research/wps/15-2010-07-realities-bringing-things-to-life.pdf

Kandinsky, W. (1947), *Point and line to plane. Contribution to the analysis of the pictorial elements*. New York: Solomon R. Guggenheim Foundation.

Knorr Cetina, K. (1999), "Viskurse der Physik. Wie visuellen Darstellungen ein Wissenschaftsgebiet ordnen", in Huber, J., Heller, M. (eds.). *Konstruktionen Sichtbarkeiten*. Wien: Springer.

Latour, B. (1987), *Science in Action*. Cambridge, MA: Harvard University Press.

Latour, B. (1990), "Drawing Things Together", in Lynch, M., Woolgar, S. (eds.), *Representation in Scientific Practice*. Cambridge, MA: MIT Press.

Latour, B. (1996), "On Actor-Network Theory. A few Clarifications", *Soziale Welt*, 47 (4), pp. 369-382.

Latour, B. (1999), "A Collective of Humans and Nonhumans", in Latour B., *Pandora's Hope. Essays on the Reality of Science Studies*. Cambridge, MA: Harvard University Press, pp. 174-215.

Latour, B. (2004), "Why has Critique Run Out of Steam? From Matters of Fact to Matters of Concern", *Critical Inquiry - Special issue on the Future of Critique*, 30 (2), pp. 25-248.

Latour, B. (2005), *Reassembling the Social. An Introduction to Actor-Network-Theory*. New York: Oxford University Press.

Latour, B. (2008), "A Cautious Prometheus? A Few Steps Toward a Philosophy of Design (with Special Attention to Peter Sloterdijk)", in Hackney, F., Glynne, J., Minto, V. (eds.). *Networks of Design. Annual International Conference of the Design History Society*. 3rd September 2008, University College Falmouth, Cornwall, United Kingdom: Universal Publishers, pp. 2-10.

Latour, B. (2005), "From Realpolitik to Dingpolitik or How to Make Things Public", in Latour, B., Weibel, P. (eds.). *Making Things Public. Atmospheres of Democracy*. Cambridge, Massachusetts: The MIT Press, pp. 14-41.

Law, J. (1989), "Technology and Heterogeneous Engineering. The Case of Portuguese Expansion", in Bijker, W.E., Hughes, T.P., Pinch, T. (eds.). *The Social Construction of Technological Systems. New Directions in the Sociology and History of Technology*. Cambridge: The MIT Press.

Law, J. (1992), "Notes on the Theory of the Actor-Network: Ordering, Strategy and Heterogeneity", *Systems Practice*, 5 (4), pp. 379-393.

Law, J. (2002), *Aircraft Stories. Decentering the Object in Technoscience*. Durham: Duke University Press.

Law, J. (2009), "Actor Network Theory and Material Semiotics", in Turner, S.T. (ed.), *The New Blackwell Companion to Social Theory*. Oxford: Blackwell Publishing.

Mareis, C., Gesche, J., Kimpel, K. (eds.) (2010), *Entwerfen – Wissen – Produzieren. Designforschung im Anwendungskontext*. Bielefeld: transcript.

Mitchell, W. J. T. (2005), *What do Pictures want? The Lives and Loves of Images*. Chicago: University of Chicago Press.

Schön, D. (1992), "Designing as Reflective Conversation with the Materials of a Design Situation", *Research in Engineering Design*, 3 (3), pp. 131-147.

Schön, D. (1983), *The Reflective Practitioner: How Professionals Think in Action*. New York: Basic Books.

Sørensen, E. (2009), *The Materiality of Learning. Technology and Knowledge in Educational Practice*. New York: Cambridge University Press.

Suchman, L. (2007), *Human-Machine Reconfigurations: Plans and Situated Actions*. New York: Cambridge University Press.

Walker, J. A. (1989), *Design History and the History of Design*. London: Pluto Press.

Yaneva, A. (2009), "Making the Social Hold: Towards an Actor-Network Theory of Design", *Design and* Culture, 1 (3), pp. 273-288.

INDEX

3

3D models, 128, 253, 254, 260, 261, 262, 263, 267

A

activity oriented, 101, 107
agency, 6, 11, 33, 107, 134, 166, 174, 177, 193, 214, 215
America by Design, 195
appropriation, 4, 138, 139, 141, 166, 193, 194
Aristotle, 247
artifact, 2, 4, 5, 7, 8, 9, 10, 12, 22, 24, 43, 44, 45, 46, 50, 63, 64, 71, 72, 74, 77, 78, 79, 80, 81, 94, 106, 107, 108, 109, 110, 111, 112, 117, 119, 123, 131, 138, 141, 142, 168, 177, 184, 191, 192, 193, 194, 195, 210, 214, 217, 220, 244, 247, 248, 250, 251, 254, 255, 257, 262
ASML, 198, 203, 205, 207
AT&T, 199, 202
Australia, 10, 11, 165, 167, 168, 175, 176, 179, 184, 185, 186

B

basic research, 200
biotechnology, 209, 215
Black Saturday, 167, 175
bushfires, 167, 168, 169, 178, 179, 183, 186, 187
Busterspeed, 8, 22, 27, 28, 29, 30, 31, 32, 33, 34, 35, 36, 37, 38

C

Canon, 198, 203
CI (Cultural Infrastructures), 138, 140, 141, 142
climate change, 171, 186
communities of practice, 8, 21, 25, 32, 37
Community in Emergency Management, 165, 176
computer, 4, 14, 28, 32, 34, 47, 53, 54, 110, 135, 194, 197, 198, 200, 202, 213, 249, 251, 255, 261, 263, 267
concept art, 255
creativity, 11, 142, 157, 163, 165, 210, 237
crisis, 65
culture, 43, 75, 142, 166, 172, 175, 176, 184, 243

D

design trajectory, 12, 196, 197, 201, 204, 205
Dewey, John, 65, 110, 197, 212, 218, 219, 220, 221, 222, 223, 224, 225, 230, 240, 242, 243
diffusion, 5, 14, 138
distributed design, 7, 12, 192, 193, 194, 195, 196, 197, 198, 199, 200, 201, 202, 204, 205, 206, 207, 208, 209, 210, 211
division of labour, 217
duality of structure, 193

E

e-mail, 46, 52, 144, 254
emergence, 10, 12, 121, 131, 133,
    195, 210, 214
emergent phenomenon, 253

F

fabs, 200, 201
functions, 44, 47, 48, 61, 95, 105,
    154, 217, 226, 234, 239

G

Germany, 197
Gothic 3, 261, 267, 272

H

heterogeneous engineering, 3, 7,
    13, 16, 21, 24, 25, 194, 201, 213,
    249, 250, 252
Hewlett-Packard, 202
history, 43, 81, 85, 110, 171, 184,
    199, 202, 207, 209, 213
hybrid style, 260, 269
hypotheses, 270

I

IBM, 200, 201, 202
ICT (Information and
    Communication
    Technologies), 68, 164
infrastructuring, 137, 138, 139,
    140, 141, 143, 147, 154, 156,
    157, 158, 161, 164
innovation, 1, 11, 12, 21, 30, 43,
    109, 122, 138, 142, 161, 163,
    165, 192, 199, 201, 202, 215

innovators, 251
intellectual property, 209
internet, 12, 64, 253, 260
interoperability, 108
IT (Information Technology), 14,
    78, 80, 107, 108, 111, 158
Italy, 10, 26, 27, 72, 77, 125, 139,
    145
ITRS (International Technology
    Roadmap for
    Semiconductors), 205

K

knotworks, 166
know-how, 22, 44, 139, 148, 199

L

Latour, Bruno, 1, 2, 3, 15, 16, 25,
    33, 40, 45, 120, 126, 129, 130,
    134, 135, 138, 141, 161, 164,
    186, 219, 220, 221, 226, 242,
    243, 244, 247, 248, 249, 258,
    260, 265, 270, 272, 273
Law, John, 3, 5, 13, 14, 16, 17, 21,
    22, 24, 25, 36, 38, 39, 40, 117,
    119, 120, 134, 135, 194, 201,
    212, 213, 243, 244, 249, 250,
    251, 252, 253, 260, 267, 269,
    270, 272, 273
learning, 39, 41, 43, 112, 148,
    151, 169, 176, 177, 185, 215
legal reforms, 72, 73

M

mangled in practise, 211
material dimension, 194
materialism, 107

Mead, G.H., 196, 197, 214, 218, 219, 225, 226, 227, 228, 236, 237, 238, 240, 242, 243, 244, 245
memory devices, 9, 44, 46, 50, 51, 52, 54, 57, 58, 61
mobile phone, 47
monitoring systems, 27
Moore's Law, 201, 202, 205
MUSE (Museum of Science of Trento), 139, 141, 143, 144, 145
museum exhibitions, 140, 156, 157, 158

N

negotiation, 59, 204, 207, 208, 209, 210
Nikon, 198, 203
NR (nurse record), 73, 74, 76, 77, 78, 79, 81, 82, 84, 85, 86, 88, 89, 90, 91, 92, 94, 105, 106, 108

O

organizational design, 1, 38, 210, 247
OS (Organizational Studies), 3, 4, 5, 6

P

photographs, 50, 229, 254, 263
Photoshop, 254, 257, 259, 262, 263, 266
Playful Triggers, 165, 168, 169, 170, 184, 186
policy, 27, 112, 163, 175, 213
Portuguese, 40, 194, 250, 273
principle of free association, 249

R

R&D (research and development), 128, 131, 199, 202, 204, 206, 207, 208, 209, 215
resilience, 11, 166, 172, 174, 175, 176, 178, 179, 181, 182, 186
resistance, 49, 227, 237, 239, 248, 268

S

science, 3, 10, 11, 15, 65, 110, 112, 113, 134, 138, 143, 145, 149, 192, 193, 195, 200, 210, 212, 214, 220, 244, 247
SEMATECH (Semiconductor Manufacturing Technology Consortium), 202, 203, 206, 207, 208, 209, 212, 213
semiconductor industry, 12, 192, 197, 198, 199, 200, 201, 202, 204, 205, 209, 210, 212, 213
semiotics, 134, 219
shifters, 79, 82, 83, 85, 86, 87, 90, 91
silkscreen, 239
situated action, 6, 7, 195, 260
sketches, 12, 120, 128, 217, 219, 225, 228, 232, 235, 236, 237, 241, 253, 254, 258
Skype, 254
social capital, 11, 165, 170, 176, 182, 183
social constraints, 218, 240, 241
social networks, 165, 166, 167, 168, 170, 181, 184
spacious present, 196
Strauss, Anselm, 6, 7, 12, 17, 24, 26, 41, 195, 196, 197, 211, 213,

215, 218, 219, 223, 224, 225,
  230, 240, 242, 243, 245
STS (Science and Technology
  Studies), 3, 4, 5, 6, 13, 118, 138,
  164

T

tacit knowledge, 41, 94, 109, 163,
  165
technological breakthroughs,
  211
technological paradigm, 197
technological specifications, 204
technological systems, 2, 16,
  118, 134, 195, 212, 213, 254
technological tools, 9, 74, 250,
  261
technological visions, 262
TEE (Technologically Enhanced
  Environment), 139, 144, 158
TI (Technological
  Infrastructuring), 137, 154,
  155, 156, 157, 158

trust, 51, 168, 170, 173, 174, 175,
  176, 182, 199, 202, 209, 262

U

United States, 197, 199, 202, 208,
  212, 243
usability, 17, 28, 270

V

video game, 249, 250, 252, 254,
  270
viscourses, 13, 251, 253, 254,
  257, 258, 259
visualizations, 236
vulnerability, 172

W

working infrastructures, 9, 38

X

X-ray lithography, 201

www.ingramcontent.com/pod-product-compliance
Lightning Source LLC
Chambersburg PA
CBHW072057020426
42334CB00017B/1545